Clinical leadership made easy:
Integrating theory and practice

D1438248

Note

Health and social care practice and knowledge are constantly changing and developing as new research and treatments, changes in procedures, drugs and equipment become available.

The authors, editor and publishers have, as far as is possible, taken care to confirm that the information complies with the latest standards of practice and legislation.

Clinical leadership made easy: Integrating theory and practice

Edited by Judy McKimm and Helen O'Sullivan

QUAY
BOOKS

A division of MA Healthcare Ltd

Quay Books Division, MA Healthcare Ltd, St Jude's Church, Dulwich Road, London
SE24 0PB

British Library Cataloguing-in-Publication Data
A catalogue record is available for this book

© MA Healthcare Limited 2016

ISBN-13: 978 1 85642 431 8

Printed by Mimeo, Huntingdon, Cambridgeshire

Contents

About the editors

Professor Judy McKimm MBA MA(Ed) BA(Hons) CertEd DipHSW SFHEA FAcadMed is Professor of Medical Education and Director of Strategic Educational Development at Swansea University, UK. She works internationally in health professions' education and leadership development, leads the MSc in Leadership for the Health Professions at Swansea University and is Director of ASME's Educational Leadership international programme. From 2011–14, she was Dean of Medical Education at Swansea, worked in New Zealand from 2007–11, at the University of Auckland and as Pro-Dean, Health and Social Care, Unitec Institute of Technology. She initially trained as a nurse and worked in medical education from 1994–2004, latterly as Director of Undergraduate Medicine at Imperial College, London, leading the development and implementation of a new undergraduate medical programme. In 2004–5, as Higher Education Academy Senior Adviser, she was responsible for developing and implementing the accreditation of professional development programmes for teachers in HE. She has worked on over sixty international health workforce and education reform projects in Central Asia, Portugal, Greece, Bosnia & Herzegovina, Macedonia, Australia, the Pacific and the Middle East. She researches and publishes widely on medical education and leadership and has visiting professorships at Huazhong University of Science and Technology in China and Princess Norah bin Abdulrahman University, Kingdom of Saudi Arabia.

Professor Helen O'Sullivan PhD MBA BSc PFHEA is Professor of Medical Education and Associate Pro-Vice-Chancellor for Online Learning at University of Liverpool, UK. Helen is the Co-Convener of the Liverpool/Lancaster Emotions in Medicine Research Group and is interested in the role of emotional intelligence in developing medical professionalism and medical leadership. She has written widely on medical professionalism and medical leadership and was Director of Liverpool's Centre for Excellence in Developing Professionalism from 2006–11.

Contributors

Dr. Alex Till MBChB, Psychiatric Core Trainee, Health Education North West (Mersey)

Dr Jay Banerjee MBBS MSc(Ed Res) FRCS FRCEM, Consultant in Emergency Medicine & Associate Medical Director for Clinical Quality and Improvement, University Hospitals of Leicester NHS Trust

Dr Steven A Burr BSc(Hons) MSc PGDE(FAHE) MMedSci(ClinEd) PhD FIBMS FAcadMEd CBiol FSB SFHEA ERT, Associate Professor (Senior Lecturer) and Deputy Director of Assessment, Peninsula Schools of Medicine and Dentistry

Professor Arpan Guha MD DA FRCA FFICM FRCPE FCMI, Head, Postgraduate School of Medicine, University of Liverpool

Miss Yee L Leung BSc(Hons) MBChB FRCS(Tr&Orth), Consultant Spinal Surgeon, Musgrove Park Hospital NHS Trust

Hester Mannion, Medical Student, Swansea University College of Medicine

Dr Simon J Mercer MBChB MAcadMEd FHEA FCollT FRCA MMEd, Consultant Anaesthetist, Aintree Hospital and Director of the Centre for Simulation and Patient Safety, Liverpool

Dr Charlotte Messer MBChB MRCPsych, Consultant Psychiatrist, The Neville Centre, Leicester

Dr Michael Moneypenny BSc(Hons) MBChB(Hons) FRCA, Director, Scottish Centre for Simulation and Clinical Human Factors, Forth Valley Royal Hospital, Larbert

Professor Gillian Needham BSc (Hons) MBChB (Hons) FRCS(Edin) FRCP(Edin) FfacMedEd FHEA, Postgraduate Medical Dean, NHS Education for Scotland and University of Aberdeen

Dr Graeme Pettifer MBChB (Hons) BSc (Hons), GP Registrar, Health Education East Midlands

Denise Prescott MBA MA BA PGCE (HE) MCSP, Senior Lecturer & Academic Lead for Continuing Professional Development, Institute of Learning & Teaching, Faculty of Health & Life Sciences, The University of Liverpool

Dr Mike Rowe PhD, Lecturer, University of Liverpool Management School, Liverpool

Brigid Russell BA (Hons) Oxon, Masters in Business Administration (University of Manchester), Master Practitioner in Executive Coaching (Academy of Executive Coaching), Leadership Consultant, National Leadership Unit, NHS Education for Scotland, Edinburgh; Independent Coach & Consultant, Stirling

Professor Peter Spurgeon BSocSci PhD, Professor of Health Services Management, Institute of Clinical Leadership, Medical School, University of Warwick

Dr Junie Li Chun Wong MBChB MSc MRCP, Specialty Trainee in Dermatology, Royal Liverpool and Broadgreen University Hospitals NHS Trust

Dr Richard Wright MB ChB FRCS FRCS Ed A&E FRCEM PG Cert Med Ed, Consultant in Emergency Medicine, Honorary Senior Lecturer in Clinical Education, University Hospitals of Leicester NHS Trust

Acknowledgements

The editors want to acknowledge all the students, doctors in training and other colleagues who have contributed (directly and indirectly) to both the series and this book.

Particular thanks go to Dr Alex Till, who not only contributed chapters to the book but who helped selflessly in bringing the book to its final form.

Figure 2.1, 3.1, 8.1 is reproduced from NHS Institute for Innovation and Improvement and Academy of Royal Medical Colleges (2010a), by kind permission of the NHS Institute for Innovation and Improvement and Academy of Royal Medical Colleges; case scenario 2.3 is reproduced from Klaber and Lee (2011) by kind permission of Dr Bob Klaber; case scenario 2.4 is reproduced from NHS Health Education East Midlands (2014) by kind permission of Dr Adrian M Brooke and NHS Health Education East Midlands; Figure 3.2 is reproduced from National Leadership Council (2011b) by kind permission of the NHS Leadership Academy; Figure 3.3 is reproduced from NHS Leadership Academy (2013) courtesy of the NHS Leadership Academy; case scenario 10.2 is reproduced from NHS Institute for Innovation and Improvement and Academy of Royal Medical Colleges (2010a), by kind permission of the NHS Institute for Innovation and Improvement and Academy of Royal Medical Colleges; case scenario 12.2 is reproduced from Persaud (2004), by kind permission of Dr Raj Persaud; case scenario 14.1 is reproduced from Firth-Cozens et al (2002), by kind permission of Professor Jenny Firth-Cozens; case scenario 14.2 is reproduced from National Patient Safety Agency (2005), by kind permission of Dr Fiona Godlee; Figure 16.1 is reproduced from Scottish Government (2010a) by kind permission of the Scottish Government.

Foreword

Medical leadership, the norm in many countries, has been slow to take hold in the UK despite a number of national initiatives and a range of statutory roles. The tide finally appears to be turning and will inevitably gain momentum with the growing numbers of the newer generations taking a serious interest.

Engaging in medical leadership is challenging. Doctors embarking on a clinical career follow a well-trodden path with a highly developed bibliography and a training system which remains the envy of much of the world. For the doctor expressing an interest in leadership there are none of these although 'green shoots' are appearing. This book provides an invaluable compendium of most of what is known about medical leadership. Firmly rooted in evidence, the thorough referencing will be invaluable for all, refreshing to the medically-trained reader and helpful to the sceptics. Too much of leadership and leadership development has been based on mantra and fashion because it is easier so to do. This will not wash with a medical audience but this book will.

The structure is helpful with good summaries and key points. The stand-alone nature of the chapters easily allows one to dip in and out, while reading from cover to cover would impart an enviable knowledge of this complex but critical subject. There is something for everyone, be they an interested medical student, an established medical leader, a researcher or someone involved in leadership development – truly a magnum opus.

Peter Lees
Chief Executive and Medical Director,
Faculty of Medical Leadership and Management

CHAPTER I

Introduction

Judy McKimm, Helen O'Sullivan

Background and context

'Leadership is a journey, not a destination. It is a marathon, not a sprint. It is a process, not an outcome. (quoting John Donahoe)' (George et al, 2007)

This quote sums up both ongoing stories of the development of medical and clinical leadership (specifically from a UK context) and the development of this book. The writing of this book parallels an unprecedented time for UK health care and a radical reconsideration of the role of doctors in leading and managing health services. The book itself comprises chapters derived from a series of articles written for the *British Journal of Hospital Medicine* on various aspects of clinical leadership between May 2011 and June 2015. During those four years, huge changes have taken place – ranging from the policy backdrop; competency frameworks and models that provide direction for development and assessment; the concerns that exercise government and all those who work in the NHS; the organisations involved in medical leadership, and (most importantly in terms of this book) a huge shift in the way in which clinical and medical leadership are conceptualised. It should be noted that the terms 'medical' and 'clinical' leadership are used somewhat interchangeably throughout this book; while medical leadership refers specifically to that carried out by doctors, clinical leadership (that carried out in the clinical context and/or by clinicians, of any profession) is used in the literature and in day-to-day practice, so we have chosen to refer to both. The book title is slightly ironic, no leadership is 'easy', but we hope that the book helps people to understand why and how good and poor leadership exists and how they can improve their own practice.

Over the last four years, we have seen the rise (and fall) of competency frameworks; new funding models and reorganisations for the NHS; the devolved countries moving to new models of health care, and a fundamental rethink of the core values, culture and goals of the NHS in the wake of the Francis report (2013), the Keogh (2013) review of the 14 hospitals with the highest mortality rates in England, the Berwick (2013) report into patient safety and, in Wales, the Andrews report (Andrews and Butler, 2014). This series of damning reports into pockets of sub-standard, unacceptable care sent shock waves through the NHS and, in terms of medical leadership development, refocused attention on specifically how and what doctors should be leading and managing, other than direct clinical activities (such as ward rounds, clinical care, emergency situations). Again, while this book is primarily about leadership, our approach, reflecting the most current literature, is that doctors carry out both leadership and management tasks on an everyday basis. One is not simply a leader or a manager but, depending on one's position, interweaves these activities (hopefully relatively seamlessly) as part of one's role. Doctors therefore 'manage' care, they manage paperwork, they might manage budgets and they manage people. Leadership as seen from this perspective involves elements of setting goals and direction, motivating and inspiring colleagues and others, and taking responsibility for the actions of oneself and others. We explore this further in the book, particularly in Chapter 2.

Our approach

One of the ways in which we have sought to integrate theory with practice is by synthesising and distilling ideas from a wide variety of theoretical and practical perspectives – as Kurt Lewin says, 'there is nothing as practical as a good theory'. This integrative approach to leadership reflects the complexity and unpredictability inherent in large public sector organisations and systems such as hospitals or primary health care. We draw on a wide range of disciplines and approaches to shed light on and advance practice around medical leadership in contemporary health care. Readers of the book will come away with an understanding of the major theoretical perspectives and directions in contemporary leadership theory (from both the generic literature and

an emerging body of literature in clinical leadership) as applied to clinical and health-care settings. They will have had opportunity to consider theory as applied to different stages of medical leadership (senior leader (e.g. medical director, postgraduate dean), qualified doctor, doctor in training, medical student), in different contexts (the health-care system, organisation or culture, international examples) and at three different levels:

1. The intrapersonal – exploring theories and practice focussing 'on the personal qualities or personality of the leader as an individual'
2. The interpersonal – exploring theories and practice relating 'to the interaction of the leader with others' – as individuals or in groups or teams
3. The organisational or system level – theories and practice that consider 'leadership behaviours in relation to the environment or system'.

(Swanwick and McKimm, 2014, p55).

How to use this book

This book has been put together as a linked series of perspectives and commentaries on various aspects of medical and clinical leadership, typically triggered by a landmark report or publication or a shift in policy direction. The book therefore provides an account of the development of medical leadership as it has evolved in response to external and internal factors over the last nine years (*Table 1.1*). As such it should be of interest to anyone engaged in or interested in medical leadership.

However, this book is not a 'how to' of leadership activities or development and it certainly does not provide easy answers. Instead, we pose some key questions about leadership and provide some theoretical foundations for those who wish to develop a deeper understanding of key issues and challenges for medical leaders. What we aim to do is debunk some of the myths around leadership theory (i.e. that it is unrelated to practice and immaterial) and show that theories and concepts are helpful, there is evidence about what works and why, and most importantly theory gives us explanatory frameworks through which we can make sense of effective and poor leadership and develop understanding and self-insight about our own leadership behaviours.

Because the book has been written by individuals at all stages of leadership (including students and doctors in training), it also reflects the increasing

Table 1.1 Selected reports and frameworks influencing UK medical leadership development 2006–2015

Date	Influential report on health care (re leadership)	Influential publication on medical/clinical leadership	Competency framework/model
2006			NHS Leadership qualities framework (NHS Institute for Innovation and Improvement, 2006)
2008	High quality care for all: NHS next stage review final report (Darzi, 2008)	Engaging Doctors: can doctors influence organisational performance? (Hamilton et al, 2008) Engaging Doctors in Leadership: Review of the Literature (Dickinson and Ham, 2008) Aspiring to Excellence (Tooke, 2008)	Medical Leadership Competency Framework (NHS Institute for Innovation and Improvement/Academy of Medical Royal Colleges, 2010a) Medical leadership curriculum (NHS Institute for Innovation and Improvement/Academy of Medical Royal Colleges, 2008)
2009		Inspiring leaders: Leadership for quality (Department of Health, 2009a)	

2010	*Guidance for Undergraduate Medical Education* (NHS Institute for Innovation and Improvement/ Academy of Medical Royal Colleges, 2010b)
	Clinical Leadership Competency Framework Project NHSII/AMRC, 2011
2011	*The future of leadership and management in the NHS: No more heroes* (The King's Fund, 2011)
	Engaging Doctors: What can we learn from trusts with high levels of medical engagement? (Atkinson et al, 2011)
2012	*Leadership and management for all doctors* (General Medical Council, 2012a)
	Leadership and Engagement for Improvement in the NHS: Together we can (The King's Fund, 2012)
	Facilitators and Barriers to Leadership and Quality Improvement (Bagnall, 2012)

Table 1.1 Selected reports and frameworks influencing UK medical leadership development 2006–2015 continued

Date	Influential report on health care (re leadership)	Influential publication on medical/clinical leadership	Competency framework/model
2013	The Francis Report – into failings at Mid-Staffordshire Foundation Trust (Francis, 2013) Review into the quality of care and treatment at 14 hospital trusts in England with high mortality rates (Keogh, 2013) National Advisory Group Report on the Safety of Patients in England (Berwick, 2013)	Are We There Yet? Models of Medical Leadership and their effectiveness: An Exploratory Study (Dickinson et al, 2013)	Healthcare Leadership Model (NHS Leadership Academy, 2013)
2014	The Andrews' Report into sub-optimal care in ABMU Health Board (Andrews and Butler, 2014)	Dr who? Developing medical leadership talent. (Hay Group, 2014) Developing collective leadership for health care. (West et al, 2014)	
2014	Delivering high quality, effective, compassionate care (DH, 2014)		
2015		Leadership and leadership development in healthcare: the evidence base. (West et al, 2015)	Leadership and management standards for medical professionals (Faculty of Medical Leadership and Management, 2015)

emphasis placed on leadership development and quality improvement in education and training. This has been gathering momentum over the last few years and is slowly becoming embedded into training programmes for all doctors as well as being included in undergraduate medical education. So the book will also be of interest to doctors in training, medical students and those responsible for their education and training.

Finally, the book should also be of use to those interested in how leadership theory (particularly the generic leadership theory and approaches) can be applied to clinical practice. Sometimes, theory feels far removed from day-to-day clinical work. We hope that through the way it is explained and the case examples provided, that the links become clearer and the reasons why theory is important and useful become more apparent. If you are on an academic or leadership development programme or responsible for one, then the book should provide ideas for learning, teaching, further reading, workplace activities and projects, and assessment.

Finding your way through the book

Each chapter can be read as a standalone chapter because the book does not follow a chronological sequence. Instead we have grouped the chapters into four sections, with each section including chapters on different topics underpinned by relevant leadership theory:

- Leadership in context
- Leadership at all levels
- Leadership in practice
- Leadership development.

Mapping leadership theory through the book

The theoretical concepts and perspectives are woven through the book, with relevant theory explained in the context of the issues or topics discussed in each chapter (*Table 1.2*). In order to help the reader make sense of theories

Table 1.2 Key features, assumptions and mapping of predominant leadership approaches to chapters.
Adapted from McKimm and O'Sullivan (2015)

Leadership approach	Key features	Key assumptions	Chapter
Trait theories	Personality based, heroic leader, 'great man', resides in individual leaders' qualities; emotional intelligence	Leaders are born, not made Self-insight is important	7, 12, 13, 15
Task vs team, styles	Managing is a balance between task, team and individual	Leaders are also managers, others' behaviours can be modified	4, 5, 8, 12, 14
Contingency theories Situational leadership	Leaders' styles and behaviours are contingent on the situation	Leaders' behaviours can be modified	3, 9, 10, 12, 14
'New paradigms' – transformational, charismatic	Leaders' can transform people/ organisations through a mix of personality and 'people work'	The individual leader is essential to organisational success Leaders can 'learn leadership'	6, 7, 8, 9, 10, 12, 16, 17
Followership	Followers are as important as leaders	Followers and leaders together co-create what leadership entails	5, 9, 14, 15
Servant leadership	The leader wants to serve first and make a difference	Leaders' values are aligned with the organisation	9, 10, 12, 13

Table 1.2 Key features, assumptions and mapping of predominant leadership approaches to chapters.
Adapted from McKimm and O'Sullivan (2015)

Leadership approach	Key features	Key assumptions	Chapter
Authentic, value based, moral leadership	Followers value leaders who are consistent and authentic	Leaders own values are important	9, 10, 12, 13, 14
Adaptive leadership Leader as 'change agent'	Leaders need to adapt to and be comfortable working in complex situations in order to drive organisational change	Leaders work within complex, organic systems Those in the system have 'agency'	2, 4, 7, 9, 11, 14, 17, 18
Distributed or dispersed leadership	Leadership is at 'all levels' of an organisation	Leadership is a process, building social capital important, e.g. through development/ training	2, 4, 6, 7, 16, 18
Collaborative, collective, shared leadership	Leadership is about working together to achieve shared goals and outcomes, e.g. quality improvement	The more power we share, the more power we have All should be involved in improving health care	2, 5, 6, 7, 13, 17, 18

they might not have encountered before, each theory or concept is explained in the specific chapter. Below is an overview of the major theoretical perspectives and topics explored in the book, with an indication of the chapter(s) in which these can be found.

Chapter summary and overview

Section 1 – Leadership in context

Chapter 2 – Medical leadership: from policy to practice (p. 21)

Medical leadership is now becoming embedded at all stages of education and training. This chapter summarises key policy and practice drivers, highlights some of the debates around what constitutes medical leadership and provides examples of leadership development initiatives. It discusses:

- How clinical leadership is a key part of a whole system approach to improving health outcomes and patient safety
- The range of policy agendas that underpin the establishment of doctors' engagement in medical leadership
- How the Medical Leadership Competency Framework was widely embedded at all levels of education and training and that any collaborative initiatives exist providing opportunities for doctors at all levels to engage in leadership development activities
- The ways in which senior clinical leadership will be important in ensuring continuity and effective implementation of new initiatives. The NHS is poised for more structural change and differentiation between the four countries.

Chapter 3 – Leadership development in the UK: approaches in the four countries (p. 37)

Doctors at all levels, including those in senior positions, in health care and health-care education organisations are increasingly required to take wider leadership and management responsibilities. This chapter discusses:

- How doctors are being encouraged and supported to take on leadership and management positions, and how their engagement makes a valuable contribution to improving health-care management and delivery
- That although some consistency in approach to leadership development has been achieved through the use of the Medical Leadership Competencies Framework, deaneries/training boards, NHS trusts and the devolved countries have developed their own strategies for implementing leadership training
- That clinicians in (or aspiring to) senior leadership positions have a range of opportunities available, both UK-wide and in the four countries
- Development opportunities include local or regional training programmes, postgraduate qualifications, coaching and mentoring schemes, action learning and paired learning.

Chapter 4 – Medical leadership: an international perspective (p. 53)

Doctors are increasingly seen as key to embedding health service improvements and there has been much international debate over how best this can be achieved. This chapter takes an international perspective on medical leadership and leadership development through discussion of case study examples, research and initiatives from around the world. It considers:

- The international drive to manage resources efficiently and effectively as the costs of health care rise
- That leadership and management are seen as important to ensuring this occurs, although cultural differences exist in conceptualising medical leadership
- Leadership qualities and competencies have been defined with many common threads and it is useful to compare the UK with other countries.

Chapter 5 – Leadership in systems, organisations and cultures (p. 67)

This chapter reviews the complex nature of health systems, organisations and cultures, and suggests that a nuanced understanding of these is important when thinking about leadership and change. It discusses:

- How leadership in large, complex organisations needs to come from all levels and those working to make change need to be aware of structures, the system and cultures
- Culture often operates as a barrier to change, but crises can provide opportunities for meaningful change.

Chapter 6 – Leading and working in teams (p. 79)

This chapter considers the role of the clinical leader as a team member and leader and explores how an understanding of the structure and purpose of teams can help doctors work more effectively in the various teams with which they are involved. It describes:

- How teamworking is a key leadership skill, particularly in multidisciplinary teams which, when effective, contributes to improved health outcomes and patient care
- Teams need clear leadership, defined goals and review of performance, but leaders need to be aware of power, authority and control mechanisms that can undermine team working
- Many teams operate dysfunctionally, 'pseudoteams' have few of the characteristics of successful teams.

Section 2 – Leadership at all levels

Chapter 7 – Developing and harnessing the potential of doctors in training (p. 95)

This chapter considers existing leadership approaches operating within healthcare organisations and why and how these should be reviewed to harness the leadership potential of doctors in training through engaging in quality improvement activities. It suggests:

- That doctors in training are a valuable frontline leadership resource that need to be supported and developed into 'enlightened trainees'
- Transformational and collective leadership needs to replace outmoded command and control and hierarchical attitudes

- Engagement in quality improvement activities needs to be embedded routinely into systems and cultures, underpinned by improvement science training and should start to replace audit and quality assurance to develop a sustainable, system-wide approach to health-care improvement.

Chapter 8 – Medical leadership and the medical student (p. 107)

As leadership and management are increasingly seen as a vital part of the doctor's daily repertoire, medical schools are starting to implement leadership development programmes as a routine part of the curriculum with opportunities for some students to take extended study in leadership. This chapter discusses how:

- Medical students and doctors need to 'learn leadership' as part of their lifelong learning, this has been supported by competency frameworks and regulatory guidance
- Leadership development and assessment can be integrated into other parts of the undergraduate programme (such as professional development) although overcrowded curricula can make this challenging.

Chapter 9 – Towards a better understanding of clinical leadership (p. 121)

The effectiveness of leadership is important to everyone, yet it is frequently misunderstood and often represented as undesirable. Many theoretical models exist extolling the virtues which make a good leader, yet there is comparatively little practical advice. This chapter considers how well individuals understand their ability to influence others and how they could improve as leaders and specifically that:

- Staff-sensitive, patient-centred leadership can magnify values and improve outcomes for more people
- Leadership provides authority to make decisions, mobilise people towards a change but in turn requires being an advocate for the team and displaying a range of personal attributes and behaviours
- Leadership behaviours and skills can be learned.

Section 3 – Leadership in practice

*Chapter 10 – Doctor as professional, doctor as leader:
same attributes, attitudes and values? (p. 137)*

This chapter examines the links between medical professionalism and medical leadership and discusses how the values that are required to be a 'good doctor' are the same as those of a 'good leader'. The potential of this to inform the debate on developing and assessing both medical leadership and professionalism is evaluated. It explores how:

- A large body of work on defining professionalism exists and it is now an established part of undergraduate and postgraduate curricula
- Evidence is starting to emerge on the most effective ways to develop and assess professionalism and significant overlaps exist between professionalism frameworks and established leadership frameworks
- Studies of medical professionalism and medical leadership have much to offer one another in terms of identifying appropriate values and behaviours, teaching and assessment methods.

Chapter 11 – Clinical leadership effectiveness, change and complexity (p. 149)

This chapter explores how an understanding of approaches to leading and managing change and complexity science can help clinical leaders engage with and manage change in complex environments and systems more effectively. It discusses that:

- The ability to manage and be comfortable with change is a defining leadership characteristic
- All change involves some loss and grief, leaders need to be aware of the 'implementation dip' during which confidence and competence falls
- A range of models exist to help leaders manage and plan for change, linear models are useful for planned change but complexity theory and systems thinking provide us with different ways to facilitate emergent or transformational change, this needs adaptive leadership.

Chapter 12 – Personality, self-development and the compassionate leader (p. 163)

This chapter discusses how the publication of the Francis report aligned with contemporary thinking on leadership and professionalism and that development and demonstration of appropriate personal qualities is central to effective medical leadership. In particular it considers:

- The publication of the Francis report stimulated a reframing of medical leadership that incorporates care and compassion and that personal qualities are central to medical leadership and clinical engagement
- The qualities that underpin effective, value-led leadership are closely aligned with qualities that underpin professionalism
- A wide range of development programmes, resources and organisations support leadership and personal development and some evidence exists that personal qualities such as emotional intelligence can be improved through a development programme
- Assessment of behaviours based on demonstration of personal qualities should be embedded in workplace-based multisource feedback, appraisals and performance reviews for doctors in training and students.

Chapter 13 – The role of emotion in effective clinical leadership (p. 177)

This chapter explores the role of emotion in clinical leadership and medical practice and suggests that reports into poor health care and subsequent debate provide the opportunity for a reframing of how doctors and leaders might engage in 'emotion work'. It discusses how:

- The Francis report and subsequent publications and debates have stimulated a rethinking of how emotions are used as part of leadership, medical education and practice
- Emotion work and emotional labour have to be acknowledged as a routine part of doctors' work and doctors need to be trained and supported to use emotions effectively
- Clinical leaders need a high level of emotional intelligence, but emotional intelligence is only one component of 'emotion work' – a key leadership skill is being able to accurately judge the emotional and social 'temperature' and 'mood' of situations, teams and organisations

■ A key challenge for clinical leaders is to enable doctors to meet organisational demands while providing compassionate and safe clinical care in resource-constrained environments.

Chapter 14 – Don't follow your leader: challenging erroneous decisions (p. 191)

This chapter provides insight into how medical students and doctors at all levels can challenge decisions with a view to improving patient safety. It also discusses some of the difficulties and barriers in so doing, some of the underpinning reasons behind this and the important role of followership, namely:

■ A large body of work has identified the difficulties and barriers of challenging the decisions or behaviours of those in authority
■ A small scale, simulation-based study involving medical students produced similar findings to those involving senior doctors and in other settings relating to reluctance to challenge seniors
■ The concept of 'followership' provides an explanatory framework through which the relationship between students, doctors in training and senior doctors can be explained
■ Serious implications for patient safety arise if teams and cultures are based on hierarchies, over-reliance on positional power, and command and control leadership styles but more work needs to be done to determine the most effective ways of developing confidence and skills so that students and doctors in training can have clear, consistent and listened-to input into decision making.

Chapter 15 – Followership, clinical leadership and social identity (p. 201)

This chapter explores how the concepts of followership, social identity and social influence help clinical leaders and followers better understand how leadership processes function within and between individuals, teams and organisations, specifically:

■ Leadership cannot be understood or explained without consideration of followership

- Leaders need followers, but followers also need leaders, especially in times of crisis, rapid change or excitement – leadership-followership is relational
- The social identities of different professional groups provide powerful forces both for support and for resistance to leaders and leaders who do not meet followers' expectations or beliefs as to leadership attributes or actions (i.e. are not prototypical) may be collectively disapproved of by followers
- Maintaining clinical work contributes towards prototypicality, social identity and leadership acceptability.

Section 4 – Leadership development

Chapter 16 – Developing and assessing medical leadership (p. 217)

It is probably safe to say that the case for all doctors, not just those in formal leadership roles, to be trained in leadership and management competencies has now been made. The real issue, which this chapter discusses, is how to achieve demonstrable improvement in such behaviours, attributes, competencies and skills to improve patient safety, health outcomes and organisational performance. The chapter discusses how:

- Developing leadership and management skills and competencies is now an accepted part of training for all doctors
- The NHS Leadership Academy and other national bodies are providing development opportunities and assessment methods based around leadership models and frameworks
- The most robust approach to assessing leadership involves using a range of different tools including multisource feedback, self-assessment and objective measures.

Chapter 17 – Developing clinical leadership capacity among UK foundation doctors (p. 229)

This chapter provides a guide to how doctors in training can act as leaders within their workplace using various leadership and management tools and discusses one of the first academic foundation programmes in clinical leadership and management to be introduced in the UK. It describes how:

■ Foundation programmes provide relatively limited opportunities for trainees to develop leadership and management skills with a theoretical underpinning and these skills are not assessed fully
■ Academic foundation programmes provide those with an interest in clinical leadership and management with the opportunity to develop skills and gain an award
■ Foundation doctors can make effective contributions to health improvements if given the right support and resources but more work needs to be done to determine the most effective ways of developing leadership and management competencies in all foundation trainees.

Chapter 18 – Educating for improvement: supporting the engagement of doctors in training in health improvement and safety (p. 241)

This chapter discusses how doctors in training and medical students' routine, formal and meaningful engagement in quality improvement initiatives is a vital component of establishing a 'culture of care' and specifically how:

■ Many reports and case studies identify a need for a culture shift towards quality improvement and patient-centred care
■ Medical students and doctors in training are central to effecting widespread cultural change but are currently under-used, therefore organisational, cultural and system change at all levels is needed to fully integrate quality improvement
■ Embedding quality improvement into education and training curricula and supporting doctors to engage in quality improvement initiatives will help clinicians be more effective health-care leaders.

Section 1 – Leadership in context

CHAPTER 2

Medical leadership: from policy to practice

Judy McKimm, Helen O'Sullivan

This chapter considers the development of medical leadership in the UK over the last decade and, set in the wider policy, practice and professional context, at examples of leadership development initiatives at undergraduate and postgraduate stages and those for senior clinicians and medical managers. It is based on an original article by McKimm and O'Sullivan (2011). It particularly focusses on how the Medical Leadership Competency Framework (MLCF) (NHS Institute for Innovation and Improvement and Academy of Medical Royal Colleges, 2010a) impacted on leadership development at all levels. Later chapters explore some of the issues and strategies adopted by different organisations and specialities to develop and train existing and future leaders. Medical leadership is now embedded at all stages of medical education and training and it is therefore helpful to summarise key policy and practice drivers and highlight some of the debates around what constitutes medical leadership.

The policy and practice context

'Doctors must take lead responsibility for driving change in their organisations. Rather than blaming "management", all doctors must recognise their own managerial responsibilities' (Douglas, 2010).

Since its establishment in 1948, much attention has focused on how to manage the ever-growing NHS, with the primary rationale being that management was best done by 'managers' and clinicians should focus on caring for patients. The

Griffiths report (Department of Health and Social Security, 1983) led to specially trained managers being brought in from outside the NHS to engage in general management training schemes and this, coupled with the increased specialization of management, led to a separation between clinicians and managers with management often being viewed as 'the dark side' (Imison and Giordano, 2009).

As many writers have noted (Clark and Armit, 2010; Hadley et al, 2010; Swanwick and McKimm, 2011), a publicly funded NHS which employs nearly 1.5 million people inevitably results in debates and tensions around business and cost efficiency, patient expectations, the role of management, professional autonomy and responsibility and the provision of safe, high quality clinical care. Attempts to resolve such tensions and address the failure of the medical profession to monitor its own performance in high profile cases (such as the Bristol Inquiry, the Shipman Inquiry and the Royal Liverpool Children's Hospital [Alder Hey] Inquiry) led to a swathe of different policy and strategy initiatives at national and local levels. These initiatives attempted to identify a model of leadership and management which engaged doctors and other health professionals in taking clinical leadership and management roles while ensuring that the NHS 'business' runs efficiently to provide the right care, at the right place, at the right time – delivered by the right people.

Since 2008/9, clinical and medical leadership have become key watchwords for the NHS and for all those who work within it (see Chapter 1). In the foreword to *Inspiring leaders: Leadership for quality* (Department of Health, 2009a), David Nicholson, the then NHS Chief Executive, set out core tenets for all clinical leaders around the four principles of:

1. Co-production – all parts of the system working together on shaping and implementing change, engaging people across the system to work together to make change happen
2. Subsidiarity – ensuring that decisions are taken at the right level of the system, collaboratively with clinicians and patients, as close to the patient as possible
3. System alignment – quality as an organising principle to achieve complex cultural changes
4. Clinical ownership and leadership – in which the quality agenda will mobilise and empower clinicians: clinical leadership needs to be part of everything that we do.

Reflecting this policy shift, in 2012, the General Medical Council produced guidance for all doctors on leadership and management. This guidance aimed to provide information for doctors on what the General Medical Council and the public expect from all doctors, not just those with an organisational leadership position. For the first time, the General Medical Council clearly defined expectations, activities and behaviours concerned with leadership and management and set the policy and regulatory framework for doctors' engagement in leadership (General Medical Council, 2012a).

An increasing emphasis on quality improvement acknowledges the importance of health care being delivered within a whole complex system by clinicians and managers, in partnership with patients and communities. Over the last two decades, activities have increasingly focused on specifically engaging doctors in managing health systems at various levels, moving away from a focus on simply managing care at the level of the individual patient or population. Alongside this change in emphasis, a number of shifts have occurred which require doctors to take broader management and leadership roles. These include making structural changes within organisations (e.g. establishing clinical directorates, appointing medical managers), devolving budgets to local levels, setting up new commissioning and purchasing arrangements and embedding clinical governance throughout organisations (Hadley et al, 2010; Swanwick and McKimm, 2011). All clinicians, with doctors seen as having a particular leadership role, are considered instrumental to effecting widespread change in the NHS to improve patient safety, the patient experience and health-care outcomes. This sea-change has not been fully implemented and has not been without critics and problems, but, the direction of travel had begun to change. In 2013, however, despite the range of initiatives and policy shifts beginning to embed this new direction, a series of high-profile reports into poor care in the NHS (Francis, 2013; Keogh, 2013; Andrews and Butler, 2014) jolted the government and all health professions into reconsideration of the effectiveness of the initiatives and set the scene for another shift in direction on leadership development and clinician engagement.

Doctors as leaders

The story of how doctors in particular were encouraged and supported into health-care leadership through general reports and those from the profession itself reflects the policy background and health-care context described above. In 2005, the Royal College of Physicians produced an influential report – *Doctors in Society* – in which it concluded that medical leadership was seriously failing. The College recommended that 'the Royal Colleges and Faculties, medical schools, the British Medical Association, and other healthcare organisations take on the responsibility to develop a cadre of clinical leaders. These bodies need to define the skills of leadership that they seek, and implement education and training programmes to develop doctors with those skills' (Royal College of Physicians, 2005).

These views were further articulated in the Tooke report (Tooke, 2008) and by Lord Darzi (Darzi, 2008). Darzi specifically emphasised the key roles of all clinicians in working with patients and health systems as those of practitioner, partner and leader. The medical profession took hold of the ideas encapsulated in these reports in a very different way from other professions, particularly through the Enhancing Engagement in Medical Leadership project, a collaborative project involving the Academy of Medical Royal Colleges and the NHS Institute for Innovation and Improvement.

Emerging evidence indicates that widespread engagement with leadership of a high standard is related to good clinical outcomes. For example, Bloom et al (2010) noted that 'management quality – measured using a new survey tool – is strongly correlated with financial and clinical outcomes such as survival rates from emergency heart attack admissions'. Other research corroborates these findings and 'clearly indicates that medical engagement plays a crucial role in supporting organisational achievement and that leadership is essential in creating the appropriate culture for medical engagement to flourish' (Atkinson et al, 2011). However, for doctors at all levels to engage meaningfully in leadership and management, appropriate activities need to be defined and doctors trained to carry out these effectively.

Professionalism and leadership

The emergence of medical professionalism as a distinct discipline within medicine also brought many attempts to define professionalism and to articulate what it means for practising doctors and those in training (van Mook et al, 2009a). A widely regarded and concise definition was proposed by a working group of the Royal College of Physicians in 2005:

'Medical professionalism signifies a set of values, behaviours, and relationships that underpins the trust the public has in doctors.'

Further work on professionalism established a number of lists of skills and attributes of a 'good professional'. For example, Hilton and Slotnik (2005) suggest there are six domains where professionalism might be expected:

1. Ethical practice
2. Reflection and self-awareness
3. Responsibility for actions
4. Respect for patients
5. Teamwork
6. Social responsibility.

Much overlap exists between professionalism domains and the competencies required for medical leadership, in particular the areas of reflection and ethical practice, self-awareness and responsibility for actions (see Chapter 10). Emotional intelligence may also be a bridge between professionalism and leadership. Although there is evidence of a link between high emotional intelligence and leadership in general (Greenockle, 2010), the evidence linking emotional intelligence, professionalism and leadership is less well established (Fletcher et al, 2009). Interestingly, medical students recognize the need for leadership skills but are less convinced about the need for management skills, seeing them as separate entities (Levenson et al, 2010). However, all doctors need to understand resource management, the structure and function of various parts of the NHS, quality improvement and management performance as essential parts of the leadership–management overlap.

The Medical Leadership Competency Framework

The Medical Leadership Competency Framework (MLCF) was developed specifically in 2008 as an instrument weaving together management and leadership competencies, aligned with medical student, trainee and qualified doctors' day-to-day practice. The MLCF was one of the main outcomes from the Enhancing Engagement in Medical Leadership project and defines 'the leadership competencies doctors need to become more actively involved in the planning, delivery and transformation of health services as a normal part of their role as doctors' (NHS Institute for Innovation and Improvement and Academy of Medical Royal Colleges, 2010a). The framework has five domains: demon-

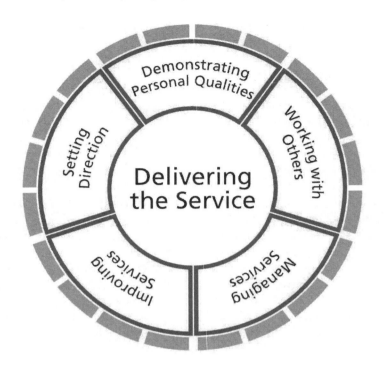

Figure 2.1 Medical Leadership Competency Framework.
From NHS Institute for Innovation and Improvement and Academy of Medical
Royal Colleges (2010a)

strating personal qualities, working with others, managing services, improving services and setting direction (*Figure 2.1*).

The unique aspect of the framework is that it is structured in three sections, covering the competencies that would be expected at medical school, during postgraduate training and post qualification. Supplementary updates on using the MLCF were produced for undergraduate programmes and for integrating the framework into postgraduate curricula (Clark and Armit, 2010). The MLCF was very influential in (a) providing a standardised framework for individuals and those responsible for training them and (b) focussing the medical profession on the importance of leadership and management skills and competencies.

Applying the Medical Leadership Competency Framework at undergraduate level

In 2009, the General Medical Council produced updated guidance for undergraduate curricula which set out specific standards and outcomes for medical schools, undergraduate medical programmes and medical graduates. *Tomorrow's Doctors* (General Medical Council, 2009) contains specific reference to leadership and teamworking within its three domains: the doctor as a scholar and scientist, the doctor as a practitioner and the doctor as a professional.

Tomorrow's Doctors notes clearly that graduates should be able to 'demonstrate ability to build team capacity and positive working relationships and undertake various team roles including leadership and the ability to accept leadership by others' (paragraph 22(d), General Medical Council, 2009). And paragraph 7 (outcomes for graduates) makes it clear that leadership is a central part of all doctors' working practice:

'In accordance with *Good Medical Practice*, graduates will make the care of patients their first concern, applying their knowledge and skills in a competent and ethical manner and using their ability to provide leadership and to analyse complex and uncertain situations' (General Medical Council, 2009).

Although *Tomorrow's Doctors* does not directly echo the MLCF, the Framework's competencies are represented in the outcomes of *Tomorrow's Doctors* and the document refers to the MLCF as a key source for further development. In order to ensure that all medical undergraduates are able to demonstrate these outcomes, medical schools need to provide structured learning opportunities. The MLCF provides many examples of the sorts of activities in which medical students can take part (see case scenario 2.1). Most of these are integrated into current curricula but medical programmes must make it clear to the students how they are developing these skills and clearly define them as 'leadership'. The Enhancing Engagement in Medical Leadership project team worked with a group of medical schools to develop guidance on how these competencies can be developed and assessed (Clark and Armit, 2010).

Applying the Medical Leadership Competency Framework at postgraduate level

'Teaching leadership is only a small part of the answer, trainees must experience leadership from their seniors and have real opportunities to demonstrate it themselves' (Douglas, 2010).

Empowerment, both as an attribute of leadership and as a tool in developing leadership, has been demonstrated to be effective (Gardner and Olson, 2010). Although medical students and doctors in training are working towards a career where responsibility, autonomy and authority are at the highest level, they often find themselves treated as the 'bottom of the ladder'. Students usually arrive in medical school having had an enormously successful school career and having had a range of leadership roles, such as head boy or girl, sport team captain, Duke of Edinburgh awards and many other impressive responsibilities. Most medical schools have a range of societies and other self-organising groups that provide an outlet for these attributes. Giving medical students and junior doctors responsibility for activities within the formal curriculum (for example becoming involved in committee work or taking leadership roles on problem-based learning

---

Case scenario 2.1 University of Liverpool

All undergraduate medical students at Liverpool are required to undertake an annual appraisal known as the Student Feedback Appraisal. Before this appraisal, students collect feedback on their professional behaviour from tutors, clinicians and their peers and undertake a series of tasks relating to their career management and professional development. One of the activities required from year 2 onwards concerns leadership tasks. In year 2 students are introduced to leadership styles and asked to analyse and compare the leadership styles of two clinicians who they have come across in a workplace setting and who they have identified as 'good leaders'. In years 3 and 4 the students document their progress towards meeting specified outcomes from the Medical Leadership Competency Framework so that they can make a direct link between the work that they are doing and the leadership and management competencies expressed in the Medical Leadership Competency Framework.

activities) allows them to develop their leadership skills and can improve the outcomes for the programme (see Chapter 8 for more details of undergraduate developments).

At postgraduate level, all foundation trainees are required to participate in an audit project which enables engagement with clinical governance, quality improvement and management activities at local level and enables trainees to take a leadership role (see case scenario 2.2). In the foundation programme, a range of generic competencies has been described that relate to teamworking, leadership and collaborative working. For a few academic foundation trainees, the opportunity exists for specific training in clinical leadership and management. Here, the academic competencies were mapped onto the MLCF to produce a framework for clinical leadership and management that combines foundation competencies with those of the MLCF. (See Chapter 17 for how this was put into practice in an academic foundation programme.)

In 2015, the General Medical Council embarked on a wide-ranging consultation on the next iteration of its standards and guidance for undergradu-

---

Case scenario 2.2 First year foundation trainees at Leighton Hospital

Dr Salman Zalman, the Postgraduate Clinical Tutor and Foundation Programme Director at Leighton Hospital (Mid Cheshire Hospitals NHS Foundation Trust), has led a project for first year foundation trainees. In this project, first year foundation doctors were divided into teams and asked to identify a problem with the Trust and to design and implement a solution. The trainees have a short series of introductory lectures on the structure and organisation of the NHS, the concept of clinical leadership and the role of doctors in management. Each group had a mentor from within the management of the Trust and senior Trust managers were present at the final presentations by the groups and awarded prizes for the best projects. One of the projects, to redesign the foundation teaching timetable, was implemented and is now in operation for the subsequent foundation year one trainees.

Evaluation of this project demonstrates an increase in knowledge and understanding of management and leadership by the trainees who took part in the project as well as an improvement in attendance at the following year's foundation programme. This indicates a desired outcome for the trainees (improved leadership and management skills) and an improved outcome for the programme (better attendance from subsequent years).

ate and postgraduate education which is planned to be introduced in 2016 (General Medical Council, 2015). This will undoubtedly include more specific guidance on leadership and management.

Senior clinical leaders

As each country has developed its distinct approach to health service design and delivery so the workforce development needs around delivery require some bespoke arrangements around the leadership and management development of trained staff. Such policy and strategic developments represent major advances in the preparation of clinicians in management and leadership and put the UK at the forefront internationally. Senior medical leaders will increasingly be required to demonstrate strategic and high level leadership and management skills, many of which cannot be acquired by experience alone. With the introduction of leadership frameworks and approaches across the UK, more structured and targeted leadership and management development programmes for clinicians in senior roles are being provided, supported by national standards including those from the General Medical Council (2012a) and Faculty of Medical Leadership and Management (2015) and by leadership frameworks or models. As leadership and management elements are being introduced on a reasonably consistent UK basis in undergraduate programmes, and foundation and speciality (including GP) training programmes, so it is at the 'trained doctor' stage that the four UK countries vary most in their approaches to leadership development. Such development tends to be delivered either by local organisations as part of staff or organisational development or via national programmes. At local level, leadership development should be aligned with service improvement strategies and at national level, with wider policy agendas.

Each of the successive leadership frameworks and models has provided specific guidance which supports and acknowledges clinicians' greater involvement in leading and managing their organisations in the longer term. These frameworks are part of facilitating long-term cultural changes which should ultimately see all clinicians acquire competencies in management and leadership as a routine part of their training (Spurgeon et al, 2011). Because the requirement for doctors' leadership and management development has only really been in place for a small number of years, there is a training lag and a 'lost generation' of trained doctors and other health professionals with development needs. This poses major challenges for those responsible for medical education and training and for the clinicians themselves:

1. How to provide the right, 'just in time' development opportunities for large numbers of doctors in training
2. How to provide development for senior, qualified doctors, some of whom wish to go 'into management', but the vast majority of whom do not.

At the most senior level of clinical staff it has always been recognized that specific training and development opportunities are needed to tackle the demands and challenges of managing and leading health systems. A range of development opportunities exist at organisational, national and UK levels for such leaders. National strategies must ensure that staff at every level who need leadership development have a route to achieve it. Leadership development activities, accessed through whatever routes are available, must be affordable and aligned to the planned needs of health services. The common domains and approaches of all the frameworks, echoed in the latest publications from West and colleagues (2014, 2015) are based on shared, distributed ('leadership at all levels') and collective leadership. In this sense it seeks to emphasise that each individual is able to make a contribution to the leadership process as and when his/her particular set of skills and qualities are appropriate. In this way the approaches to leadership development are universal and inclusive rather than focussing on the rare and largely unrealistic notion of charismatic or hero leaders (The King's Fund, 2011).

Nonetheless, it is acknowledged that a relatively small group of senior leaders are in designated, positional leadership roles where authority and influence are vested in the role, usually through hierarchy, positional power and status. Clinicians in such roles are often asked to accept roles in leading major innovations or change programmes, for example in England leading the Quality, Innovation and Productivity and Prevention programmes aimed at securing very significant reduction in overall costs while maintaining or indeed improving service quality. Although clinicians have usually achieved success and recognition in their own field, many have had very little training in the change management and leadership skills required. Aside from taught programmes, workshops and organisational support, some development activities are very relevant to senior leaders as they focus on broadening experience and providing external support over the long term: paired learning, coaching and mentoring, and action learning sets.

Paired learning

This activity links up individuals from different health professions or managers with one another to learn about one another's work and the challenges that face one another. It has been rolled out across London into many NHS Trusts by the London Leadership Academy (see www.londonleadingforhealth.nhs.uk/programmes/paired-learning and case scenario 2.3, from Klaber and Lee, 2011) and is also enabled in Scotland.

Coaching and mentoring

Coaching and mentoring are becoming essential skills for all doctors (General Medical Council, 2013) and a number of medical Royal Colleges (e.g. Royal College of Psychiatrists, Royal College of Physicians) offer mentoring to doctors. Coaching and mentoring are also extremely helpful in developing senior leaders' leadership skills. A mentoring scheme for medical leaders is provided by the Faculty of Medical Leadership and Management (see www.fmlm.ac.uk/professional-development/coaching-and-mentoring/mentoring-scheme), launched in 2014. Schemes for executive coaching are offered by a number of organisations on a UK-wide, national, regional and organisational basis. The Faculty of Medical Leadership and Management also offers support via the

---

Case scenario 2.3 Paired learning

'At Imperial College Healthcare NHS Trust we have established an innovative "paired learning" scheme which has paired SpR level clinicians and Band 7 and 8a managers together in a leadership development scheme. This work-based programme uses a combination of informal conversation, work-shadowing, workshops and improvement project work to enable participants to better understand each other's perspectives and to drive learning. Evaluation of the programme showed demonstrable outcomes related to improved quality of patient care and greater efficiency. In addition participants reflected on their personal learning and the potential for future culture change in terms of stronger partnerships and collaborative working.' (Klaber and Lee, 2011)

Coaching Network to help doctors find a coach that suits their needs. A report by Dr Penny Newman in 2011 which considered the barriers to women doctors achieving senior leadership positions suggested that 'coaching and mentoring for women doctors in isolated senior leadership roles should be routinely offered where women doctors are a significant minority' (NHS Leadership Academy and NHS Midlands and East, 2011, p. 8). In Wales, attention is also being paid to developing and retaining women in leadership posts and coaching, role-modelling and mentoring are seen as critical to making change. As in the other countries, across NHS Scotland, coaching and mentoring is widely used as a means of supporting and enabling the development of leadership capability. The National Leadership Unit in NHS Education for Scotland manages a national register of external executive coaches whose services are accessed either as part of a formal programme of leadership development (e.g. a brief intervention programme for those who are relatively new to executive leadership roles) or as a stand-alone package of development. Several of the Scottish Health Boards have developed in-house coaching capacity and are able to offer staff at all levels and across all disciplines access to high quality coaching.

Action learning sets

A number of different group activities exist to support leadership development, particularly involving learning from or supporting peers around issues and challenges. These include action learning sets, step-back groups and problem-based learning. Case scenario 2.4 describes action learning sets in action.

Faculty for Medical Leadership and Management

The Faculty for Medical Leadership and Management was established in 2011 to promote the advancement of medical leadership, management and quality improvement at all stages of medical careers. It aims to ensure that doctors in management and leadership roles have received high quality, appropriate training. Peter Lees, the founding faculty director, noted the 'diverse range of medical leadership positions in the UK which are essential to the delivery of better health and health care. These roles are increasingly complex and challenging and it is, therefore, very timely to establish the Faculty' (Lees, 2011). In 2015, the Faculty of Medical Leadership and Management launched its professional standards in medical leadership and management and this heralds the way forward for doctors to become accredited in these skills. Such moves also reflect the processes of international organisations such as the Royal Australian College of Management and Administration which enables doctors with key management roles to belong to a college which supports the 'speciality' of management and administration (McKimm et al, 2009). (See also Chapter 4.)

Case scenario 2.4 Action learning sets

Health Education England, working across the East Midlands, ran a series of action learning sets for post-foundation trainees aiming to develop their leadership skills.

'Action learning sets are a method by which groups of people meet to explore solutions and decide upon suitable action to take to solve a particular problem. By working collaboratively with other health professionals, questions are raised which may not ordinarily be thought of by the individual, leading to an increased number of potential solutions. It also allows participants to understand how professionals from other areas respond to problems, and therefore adapt their own ways of working accordingly.

The aims of the course are to produce transformational leaders, as once the group arrive at an appropriate solution, the participant can confidently take the solution back to their team, enhancing their leadership abilities as well as implementing effective solutions.

Action learning is an accelerated learning tool which can be applied to any number of different workplace (and personal) issues and challenges. In action learning, groups or 'sets' participants meet regularly in order to explore solutions to real problems and decide on the action they wish to take. When doing this in the set, the stages include:

- Describing the problem as we see it
- Receiving contributions from others in the form of questions
- Reflecting on our discussion and deciding what action to take
- Reporting back on what happened when we took action
- Reflecting on the problem-solving process and how well it is working.'

The project was well evaluated by participants who said that they felt their leadership understanding and skills had been improved. (NHS Health Education East Midlands, 2014)

Conclusions

At the time of writing, the impact of recent health (and social care) leadership development arrangements have not yet been fully felt, but in England it is likely that the MLCF will be replaced by the Healthcare Leadership Model (NHS Leadership Academy, 2013), with its focus being on developing and improving the leadership and management behaviours of all health workers, not just doctors. It is also unclear how further devolution of medical leadership and management activities in the four UK countries will have an impact, but what is very evident is that much effort and activity exists around 'professionalising', recognising and developing leadership and management capability and increasing capacity, among medical students, doctors in training and qualified doctors, whether they are in formal leadership roles or not.

Against the backdrop of likely further structural changes in the NHS and with the legacy of reports into sub-standard care being felt across the NHS, it remains clear that the expectation of doctors to take leadership and management roles at all levels and engage in leading change, quality improvement and innovation is now fully embedded in policy and practice agendas. The role of the doctor as health-care leader and manager is one which all practitioners, health-care delivery and education and training organisations need to both implement and support.

Key points

- Clinical leadership is a key part of a whole system approach to improving health outcomes and patient safety
- A range of policy agendas underpin the establishment of doctors' engagement in medical leadership
- The Medical Leadership Competency Framework was widely embedded at all levels of education and training
- Many collaborative initiatives exist that provide opportunities for doctors at all levels to engage in leadership development activities
- The NHS is poised for more structural change and differentiation between the four countries. Senior clinical leadership will be important in ensuring continuity and effective implementation of new initiatives.

CHAPTER 3

Leadership development in the UK: approaches in the four countries

Judy McKimm, Peter Spurgeon, Gillian Needham, Helen O'Sullivan, Christine McGowan, Jackie Parsons, Brigid Russell, Diane Taylor

Introduction

Doctors in all positions in health care and health-care education organisations are increasingly required to take wider management and leadership responsibilities, including those at senior level. A range of development programmes is available to support these existing and aspiring leaders at local, regional, national and UK levels. This chapter is based on the article by McKimm et al (2011a).

Most developed health systems across the world have in the past few years advocated the increasing engagement and participation of clinicians in the management and leadership of their organisations. Although the challenges are slightly different for each country common themes emerge which are underpinned by:

1. The recognition that service improvements sought by governments can be blocked or frustrated by powerful clinical groups unless clinicians feel directly involved in the design and planning of these changes
2. The financial pressures facing most governments require innovation and radical change that will need to be driven by committed and positively engaged clinicians

3. Strong evidence that effective leadership of true teams, and collective leadership approaches, are linked to improved quality of patient care (West and Dawson, 2012; West et al, 2015).

Such involvement represents a cultural shift requiring all clinicians to recognize their wider role in supporting the goals of the organisation. In the UK, one approach to achieving this objective was the establishment of the Enhancing Engagement in Medical Leadership Project, run jointly by the NHS Institute for Innovation and Improvement and the Academy of Medical Royal Colleges. This project, which ran for six years in total, developed key products:

1. The Medical Engagement Scale – a measure of how involved doctors are in the wider performance goals of their organisation (Spurgeon et al, 2011)
2. The Medical Leadership Competency Framework (MLCF) (NHS Institute for Innovation and Improvement and Academy of Medical Royal Colleges, 2010a)
3. The Clinical Leadership Competency Framework (NHS Institute for Innovation and Improvement and Academy of Medical Royal Colleges, 2011).

Since this work was completed, spin-off work, building on the Enhancing Engagement in Medical Leadership Project has progressed somewhat separately in all four UK countries. The general health context and policy background and early work around the Medical Leadership Competency Framework is discussed in more detail in Chapters 1 and 2 respectively, as well as throughout the book. In this chapter, we particularly focus on more recent developments in the UK: in England (via the Leadership Academy), in Scotland (the Professionalism and Excellence in Scottish Medicine Group; Scottish Government, 2009, 2014), in Wales (through Academi Wales) and in Northern Ireland (through the Health and Social Care (HSC) Leadership Centre NI, in consultation with HSC Trusts and DHSSPSNI).

Leadership frameworks: a mixed approach

In the UK, medical training is regulated by the General Medical Council, and UK devolved countries and regions have taken their own approaches to leadership development. The situation with the use of 'leadership frameworks' across the four countries is also mixed:

- The MLCF still prevails for the medical profession UK-wide
- The (NHS England) Healthcare Leadership Model – referred to later in the chapter – applies for all other staff in NHS England
- Wales (and possibly Northern Ireland) is piloting the Healthcare Leadership Model. Both countries are taking a more interprofessional, cross-sector approach reflecting their integrated health and social care policy agendas
- Different arrangements are emerging across NHS Scotland. There are discussions about a 'health and social care' (in the light of health and social care integration) or a cross-public services 'leadership framework'. Several territorial Health Boards have adopted their own local arrangements.

The Medical Leadership Competency Framework

The MLCF, demonstrated in *Figure 3.1*, was specifically designed for doctors and has now been incorporated into the education and training of all doctors in the UK through inclusion in professional standards and outcomes statements. Referred to within the MLCF are 'undergraduate', 'postgraduate' and 'continuing practice' which are used as a spectrum to guide users as to what competencies are expected in relation to their current role in clinical practice.

At undergraduate level, this is through its inclusion in *Tomorrow's Doctors* (General Medical Council, 2009), which specifies the outcomes of undergraduate curricula (see Chapter 8). See also the General Medical Council's 2015 consultation document on combined standards for undergraduate and postgraduate education and training (General Medical Council, 2015). Although the MLCF is a formal requirement, the coverage across different medical schools is uneven but slowly developing as the schools become more familiar with its content.

At postgraduate levels, the MLCF was integrated into the Foundation Programme Curriculum (General Medical Council, 2010; UK Foundation Programme Office, 2013) and the 2010 and forward specialty training curricula of each medical Royal College/Faculty (see Chapter 17 for a more detailed discussion). While the MLCF does not prescribe how the competencies are delivered, it is understood that the 'medical model' of postgraduate training is workplace based and implementation of this curricular component is thus mostly purposively experiential through learning on the job linked to work-place-based assessments, especially supervised learning events. Again, at postgraduate level the main obstacle to implementation is the knowledge and confidence of clinical and educational supervisors who may not themselves have been exposed to training in this topic area. A support guide for supervisors and trainees at postgraduate level has been developed (Spurgeon and Klaber, 2011) to provide practical guidance for use in work-based settings. See Chapters 2, 8 and 17 for more examples and information.

Figure 3.1 Medical Leadership Competency Framework. From NHS Institute for Innovation and Improvement and Academy of Medical Royal Colleges (2010a)

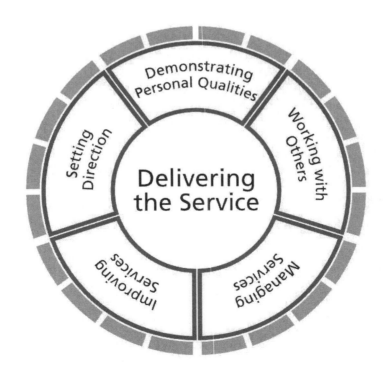

The Clinical Leadership Competency Framework

The MLCF formed the basis of the Clinical Leadership Competency Framework (NHS Institute for Innovation and Improvement and Academy of Medical Royal Colleges, 2011) which held the same five domains but focussed on all frontline clinical professions rather than just doctors. Referred to within the Clinical Leadership Competency Framework are 'student', 'practitioner' and 'experienced practitioner' which are used as a spectrum to guide users as to what competencies are expected in relation to their current role in clinical practice.

The Leadership Framework

The Leadership Framework, demonstrated in *Figure 3.2*, was developed through the National Leadership Council (of NHS England). It built upon the MLCF and Clinical Leadership Competency Framework by incorporating as its basis the five core domains of these frameworks but added two further sections ('Delivering the strategy' and 'Creating the vision', see below) aimed specifically at senior leaders in hierarchical or positional roles. This therefore highlights the training and development needs of all types of staff, both clinical and non-clinical.

Figure 3.2 Leadership Framework. From NHS Leadership Academy (2011)

For example, 'Delivering the strategy' involves positional leaders in a range of tasks such as:

- Engaging with key individuals and groups to formulate strategic plans to meet the vision
- Striving to understand others' agendas, motivations and drivers in order to develop strategy which is sustainable
- Creating strategic plans which are challenging yet realistic and achievable
- Identifying and mitigating uncertainties and risks associated with strategic choices.

Each of the skills associated with the two extra domains is described in more detail in the Leadership Framework (NHS Leadership Academy, 2011). This provided the basis for developing senior clinicians who have moved into these senior, positional roles and included a 360° development tool designed to support individuals in identifying their relative strengths and weaknesses and specifying training needed (National Leadership Council, 2011).

The Healthcare Leadership Model

Following the NHS Health and Social Care Act 2010 reforms, a new Leadership Academy was established in England. The Academy decided that a revised leadership model was required, perhaps feeling a need to be seen to be responding to the much publicised failings at Mid-Staffordshire NHS Foundation Trust. The rationale for the development of another Framework seems somewhat questionable since a) the existing Leadership Framework charged with not preventing the events of Mid-Staffordshire was not implemented until 2010 – well after the problems at Mid-Staffordshire happened and b) the pervasive command and control management style may have contributed to the NHS' problems. If that was the case then the MLCF, Clinical Leadership Competency Framework and Leadership Framework with their emphasis upon shared leadership would seem to have been an appropriate response.

Nonetheless the NHS Healthcare Leadership Model was developed consisting of nine leadership dimensions, each rated on a four-part scale (NHS Leadership Academy, 2013). The nine dimensions, demonstrated in *Figure 3.3*, being: inspiring shared purpose, leading with care, evaluating information, connecting our service, sharing the vision, engaging the team, holding to account, developing capability and influencing for results. A series of subsidised leadership development programmes have also been developed for various levels of staff in England (see later). The model is not seen as mandatory and the MLCF and Clinical Leadership Competency Framework remain the models endorsed by the medical and clinical professions. It builds again on the two previous frameworks but with a focus on behaviours rather than competencies, it is for all NHS staff and includes a 360° appraisal tool. As noted, Wales is piloting the use of the model and Northern Ireland is considering it.

Leadership development across the UK

A number of activities are UK-wide, including the work of the Faculty of Medical Leadership and Management, established by the Academy of Medical Royal Colleges. The Faculty of Medical Leadership and Management is a now well-embedded, UK-wide organisation that aims to promote the advancement of medical leadership, management and quality improvement at all stages of

Figure 3.3 NHS Healthcare Leadership Model. From NHS Leadership Academy (2013)

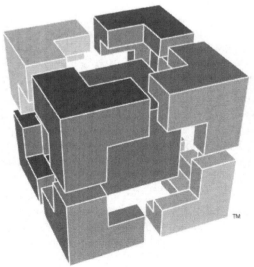

1. Inspiring shared purpose
2. Leading with care
3. Evaluating information
4. Connecting our service
5. Sharing the vision
6. Engaging the team
7. Holding to account
8. Developing capability
9. Influencing the results

the medical career for the benefit of patients. The launch of the Faculty of Medical Leadership and Management's leadership standards in 2015 aims to provide a national framework against which senior leaders can be measured and which they can aspire to (www.fmlm.ac.uk).

For many years, a range of postgraduate qualifications (e.g. Postgraduate Certificate, Diploma, Masters and other relevant higher education courses) have been available to medical leaders, as well as short courses (commercial and in-house designed and delivered) that do not lead to a formal qualification but allow individuals to support their own development as leaders. Despite the high quality of many of these programmes (e.g. MBAs at Cranfield, London Business School) there has been a view that the content has not always been appropriately oriented to the needs of the NHS or its clinicians.

Many programmes have sought therefore to provide more specifically for the increasing number of clinicians taking up leadership roles. The NHS Leadership Academy provides a range of development opportunities for NHS clinicians and managers, including those for senior managers, women, BME (black and minority ethnic), executives and aspiring senior managers and leaders (see www.leadershipacademy.nhs.uk/programmes). The King's Fund in London provides a range of development opportunities for clinicians with varying length and focus, e.g. programmes for clinical directors and leads, senior medical and nursing directors and a top management programme. Other examples include the Royal College of Physicians of London's medical leadership Masters programme for medical directors and aspiring chief executives (Royal College of Physicians, 2011).

Trusts and Health Boards also work with universities or other organisations to deliver leadership development, both in-house (e.g. for clinical directors or Board members) and in university settings. Other initiatives in which senior clinical leaders can engage include the Health Foundation's leadership fellowships for health professionals, including the prestigious Harkness Scholarships (see www.health.org.uk/areas-of-work/topics/leadership). NHS London offers a range of 'Leading for Health' programmes at all levels including fellowships in clinical leadership (Darzi fellowships) for aspiring clinical leaders, mentoring, talent, coaching and development programmes for senior leaders (see www.londonleadingforhealth.nhs.uk/programmes).

It can be seen that all doctors at all levels need leadership and management skills in order to carry out their professional duties effectively and that a range of initiatives exist to support this development. But what about those professionals who aspire to leadership positions within organisations as well as those who develop into academic leaders or leaders in medical education? Those who may be interested in these career routes need a structured and supportive continuing professional development framework in leadership and management. In addition, doctors benefit from being able to take on secondments and to undergo coaching and benefit from a mentor (Ham et al, 2010). For 'senior leaders' a range of development opportunities exist at local, specialty, national and international levels. Within organisations, many doctors have already taken advantage of leadership and management programmes, but the view that 'medical leadership' requires the establishment of tailored programmes has led to the development of a variety of programmes specifically for doctors. As with many postgraduate training activities, programmes are often offered as collaborations between postgraduate medical education bodies, medical Royal Colleges, universities and national leadership development agencies.

Towards differentiation and integration

As the four countries of the UK have become more mature in exerting their devolved powers, so activities in leadership education and training have also become distinct and differentiated. This has led to a range of programmes being offered, led by the NHS Leadership Academy (in England), NHS Education for Scotland (in Scotland), Academi Wales (in Wales) and the Health and Social Care (HSC) Leadership Centre (in Northern Ireland). See Chapter 2 for examples of development activities for senior leaders.

Regional initiatives also exist, with most postgraduate local education and training boards in England and the deaneries in Scotland, Wales and Northern Ireland offering leadership development for most levels of postgraduate trainees and some for qualified doctors. Finally, most NHS trusts and health boards also offer leadership development, often as part of an overall organisational development and capacity building strategy, this is usually for consultants, medical directors, staff grade doctors and clinical directors. Reflecting national developments for a more integrated approach to leadership development, a number of interprofessional initiatives has also been established such as the NHS East of England senior clinical leaders' programme and a range of Masters' programmes at universities throughout the UK. That leadership development often occurs for specific professional groups (e.g. doctors, nurses) may need to be kept under review as this is somewhat against the spirit of collaborative practice in health care and may run counter to other interprofessional development activities (World Health Organization, 2010; McKimm et al, 2011a).

While senior clinicians can undertake individual activities based on their needs and interests, such as postgraduate qualifications, it is examples of activities established by the relevant bodies in the four UK countries that focus on capacity building which are included here. Such initiatives form part of a strategic approach to leadership development that is somewhat easier to roll out in the smaller countries than in England, where the scale is larger and impact less easy to measure. We discuss examples of these national initiatives next.

Leadership development in Scotland

The Scottish Government sets the strategic direction for leadership and management development for NHS (and now with statutory integration of services, health and social care staff) and oversees implementation through a Leadership Advisory Board. Implementation of leadership development is through a combination of local (Health Board and Integrated Joint Board) action, and national action through the National Leadership Unit in NHS Education for Scotland. A national strategy for leadership development has existed since 2005 (Scottish Executive, 2005; Scottish Government, 2010a). Since 2010, the key policy focus has been on the implementation of the strategy for healthcare quality (Scottish Government, 2010b) and on the 2020 vision for health and social care (Scottish Government, 2011a; 2013b). The shape and focus of leadership development, at a national level, has been closely aligned with this strategic direction to assure intended outcomes. In 2013, the national approach to leadership and management development across Scotland was incorporated within the national workforce strategy, *Everyone Matters* (Scottish Government, 2013a). The Leadership Framework was used within NHS Scotland in 2012–13, but the National Leadership Unit and a number of the health boards have now reverted to using the NHS Scotland Leadership Qualities Framework pending the work on an integrated (health and social care) framework.

For doctors working in NHS Scotland, the Chief Medical Officer and Scottish Academy of Medical Royal Colleges have led an initiative titled Professionalism and Excellence in Scottish Medicine (Scottish Government, 2009; 2014) aiming to inspire medical engagement and leadership development in an aligned, inclusive and integrated way. The development of a Scottish Clinical Leadership Fellowship (since 2013) (see case scenario 3.1) and the local adoption of paired learning across a number of Health Boards, drawing on the experiences in NHS London and elsewhere (Klaber et al, 2012), are at the heart of this approach. In addition, the Scottish Patient Safety Programme (www.scottishpatientsafetyprogramme.scot.nhs.uk/) and its fellowships have provided the opportunity for clinicians to become more integrally involved in the implementation of strategy for health-care quality and quality improvement Scotland-wide.

In Scotland, doctors at consultant level and in lead clinician roles have access to multidisciplinary leadership development opportunities provided at national level (through NHS Education for Scotland) (e.g. the two national programmes, 'Delivering the Future' and 'Leading for the Future'). There is an increasing focus at local (Health Board) level on providing leadership and management development for those in lead clinician roles, e.g. a programme for consultants across NHS Highland, NHS Grampian and NHS Tayside.

Increasingly, leadership development in Scotland, Wales and Northern Ireland is being developed and delivered on a cross-public service basis, in the spirit of public service reform (e.g. Scottish Government, 2011b) and in

---

Case scenario 3.1 Scottish Clinical Leadership Fellows

Scottish Clinical Leadership Fellows are doctors in training who are selected through a highly competitive process to spend a year out of their clinical training in full-time leadership development. A number of host organisations are involved, in which the Fellow will be based and develop project work that will be supervised. The development of the Fellowship is a key component – these doctors meet together regularly and co-create their experience through action learning. They each have an executive sponsor who is a senior leader/manager in their host organisation (e.g. in Scottish Government it is the Deputy Director General; in NHS Education for Scotland it is the Chief Executive Officer), a project supervisor from the host, who guides and directs project work, and regular access to mentorship from trained colleagues in the National Leadership Unit who can be used by the group to draw on a range of psychometric and analytic tools, e.g. Myers-Briggs Type Indicator. Project outputs have been highly relevant to policy and strategy, and we await longitudinal tracking of graduate Fellows to understand the impact on their career direction and future choices. These Scottish Fellows have some elements of their experience aligned to similar Fellows under the Faculty of Medical Leadership and Management scheme in England, and in Wales. From 2015 all four UK countries will be operating clinical leadership fellow schemes.

support of the structural and policy reform around health and social care integration. Most leadership development is offered on a multidisciplinary basis, reflecting the complex and multidisciplinary nature of the workplace. How-

---

Medical leadership development in Wales

Academi Wales (funded by Welsh Government) leads clinical leadership development in Wales.

Context

There are seven Welsh Health Boards and three All Wales Trusts. There is strong support from the Chief Medical Officer for clinical leadership engagement and development. A prudent health-care agenda drives integrated health and social care provision (Hussey, 2013; Aylward et al, 2014a).

Scoping identified a high level of local multi-professional management and leadership provision. Wales Deanery offers four Clinical Leadership Training Fellows per year and supports F2 doctors to undertake a postgraduate certificate. Public Health Wales – Improving Quality Together and 1000 Lives programme underpin the prudent health-care agenda.

Example activities

Clinical leadership conference, learning event and summer school
Training for medical directors, mental health strategic leads, leadership fellows, senior leaders

Successes and challenges

Successes:
- Development and delivery of a specific medical leadership offering (*Figure 1*)
- Engagement of medics at all levels on the Medical Leadership Programme
- Positive evaluations to date
- Provision of an accredited development programme for Clinical Leadership Training Fellows: Postgraduate Certificate in Clinical Leadership.

Challenges:
- Ensuring content is aligned to the needs of all group members
- Engagement and development of primary care doctors to support the primary care agenda
- Developing a critical mass of medical leaders.

---

ever, some initiatives are targeted for specific professional groups (see www. nes.scot.nhs.uk/education-and-training/by-theme-initiative/leadership-and-management.aspx and below relating to Wales and Northern Ireland).

Conclusions

The last ten years have seen considerable effort to ensure that health-care professionals gain competence in management and leadership. The MLCF has been embedded in undergraduate and postgraduate medical education and

Medical leadership development in Wales (continued)

Looking to the future
Formal evaluation of the impact of the Medical Leadership Programme 12 months post programme. Continuing in partnership with Chief Medical Officer to progress engagement work. Focus on development for GP cluster leads. Continue the discussion/research on women in medical leadership.

Figure 1. Academi Wales: Medical Leadership Programme

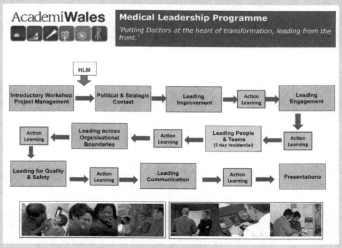

Medical leadership development in Northern Ireland

Context

There are five Health and Social Care Trusts and Ambulance Trusts which employ 3900 medical staff including consultants, staff and associate specialist doctors and doctors in training. Each trust organises their own internal development programmes. The HSC Leadership Centre provides a range of regional leadership development programmes. Northern Ireland Deanery provides management training for doctors in training and continuing professional development for GPs.

Example activities

Within organisations:
- 'Living Leadership' – a seven-module, multi-professional programme – for medical directors/associate medical directors and their senior clinical and managerial colleagues
- 'Excellence in clinical leadership' – two one-day events for consultants and those in formal leadership roles
- 'Making it happen' – specific modules for staff and associate specialist doctors
- 'STEP programme' for doctors in training

Regional
- HSCLC 'Acumen' – a six-month programme for medical directors with other executive directors
- HSCLC 'Leading the Way' for assistant Medical Directors
- Regional Succession Planning for Tier 3 and 4 posts

Successes and challenges

Successes:
- Expansion of leadership development provision for doctors in past three years
- Doctors are leading the development of medical leadership
- Blended approach
- Integrating medical leadership development with other clinical and managerial colleagues
- Bespoke development for doctors where appropriate

Challenges:
- Ensuring development is not synonymous with development programmes.

training across the UK and should ensure a level of competence is achieved by all doctors at UK specialist or GP registration. Thereafter, as is evident in the different devolved countries' approaches to onward and top team leadership development, strategies are now much more closely aligned to nations' health-care policies and strategies through capacity building and engagement of a range of health workers. Ambitious potential leaders of health care will continue to pursue high quality, relevant leadership development that best suits their learning styles and other needs. Postgraduate qualifications (to Masters' level and beyond) and embedded leadership programmes for all doctors in training will sit alongside other development routes such as paired learning, action learning sets, mentoring programmes and coaching provision to meet the needs of senior clinicians moving into leadership roles.

Medical leadership development in Northern Ireland (continued)
The following describe a range of initiatives in Northern Ireland to support medical leadership development:

- Providing support for service improvement led by doctors
- Revising medical leadership structures and appointing doctors to new roles leading directorates
- Undertaking medical engagement surveys and developing improvement plans
- Developing mentoring and coaching, so that senior doctors develop and support junior colleagues
- Developing medical leadership framework to describe the role, focus, behaviours, performance measures and key connections for doctors at all levels

Looking to the future
Start earlier
Core/specialist training; introduction of clinical leadership fellows; accredited management skills training for each year of training; undergraduate training – intercalated medical leadership degree

Spread wider
Quality Attributes Framework to describe doctors' involvement in quality improvement at three levels

---

Key points

- Doctors are being encouraged and supported to take on leadership and management positions, and their engagement at all levels makes a valuable contribution to improving health-care management and delivery
- Although some consistency in approach to leadership development has been achieved through the use of the Medical Leadership Competency Framework, postgraduate medical systems, NHS trusts and the devolved countries have developed their own strategies for implementing leadership training
- Clinicians in (or aspiring to) leadership positions have a range of opportunities available, both UK-wide and in the four countries
- Development opportunities include local or regional training programmes, postgraduate qualifications, coaching and mentoring schemes, action learning and paired learning.

CHAPTER 4

International perspectives on medical leadership

Helen O'Sullivan, Judy McKimm

Introduction

Significant proportions of both high income and low and middle income countries' economic activity are devoted to delivering health care and many concerns have been expressed about how to improve the quality of health care within a climate of financial constraints and rising expectations. As the costs of health care have risen, so have pressures to manage these costs and improve performance, with increased financial and clinical accountability at organisational, department or unit and individual levels. Doctors are increasingly seen as key to embedding health service improvements and much international debate has occurred over how best this can be achieved. This chapter takes an international perspective on medical leadership and leadership development through discussion of examples and initiatives from around the world. It is based on an original article by O'Sullivan and McKimm (2011c).

Ham and other authors argue that the combination of heightened expectations and lagging improvements in performance can be attributed to the fact that health-care systems behave as a professional bureaucracy (Ham, 2008; Baker and Denis, 2011). In professional bureaucracies, positional power resides in highly qualified and well-educated professionals who deliver the front-line service (Mintzberg, 1983). This type of organisation is highly resistant to change, especially change resulting from policy or managerial directives (Baker and Denis, 2011).

To gain improvements through change in this type of organisation it is crucial to engage professionals in the leadership and management of that change. This engagement has been fundamental to approaches in the UK stemming from the engaging medical leadership project (NHS Institute for Innovation and Improvement and Academy of Medical Royal Colleges, 2010a), in the call for 'collective leadership' (West et al, 2014) and is echoed around the world in a range of initiatives aimed at engaging and developing doctors as health-care leaders.

Case studies

A scan of recent publications and commentaries highlights a number of systems of medical leadership development that are frequently held up as exemplars of excellence. We discuss the drivers for engaging doctors and other health professionals in leadership and management in the UK in other chapters (e.g. Chapters 2 and 3) but similar drivers exist across the world and governments and organisations are seeking ways of delivering high quality care within economic constraints.

Learning from international evidence and practice – Wales

Aylward et al (2014a, 2014b) provide commentaries on the Welsh Government's drive towards 'prudent health care' advised by the Bevan Commission 'the NHS in Wales, like other health-care systems around the world, is facing the twin challenges of rising costs and increasing demand, whilst continuing to improve the quality of care' (Aylward et al, 2014b, p1). The Commission has drawn on international evidence and examples of research, practice and evidence from Brazil, Canada, Holland, New Zealand, Sweden and the US to inform its system-wide, holistic strategy which will be implemented throughout Wales (Aylward et al, 2014b). While the focus is on co-production of better health in partnership with the public, professionals and wider communities, engaging doctors in planning and delivering these new services will be key. In 2013, the Chief Medical Officer for Wales invited Dr Jack Silversin, an international authority in the relationship between doctors and organisations, to give a series of webinars. The webinar themes and recommendations for the clinician engagement strategy in Wales were subsequently summarised in a paper which identified four barriers to engagement and four foundations for engaging doctors (Hussey, 2013), see *Table 4.1.*

'In Wales, the task of clinical engagement has been explicitly identified as including all clinical professions and although there are undoubtedly issues that impact particularly on doctors, this must always be seen within the context of a multidisciplinary team. Four specific areas where Dr Silversin's analysis suggests it will be important to focus efforts are:

Building alignment and common cause around the goals of quality improvement.
Supporting the development of doctors and other clinical staff who are undertaking leadership roles.
Supporting the education and development of clinical staff in training.
Exploring the potential for a 'compact' to build common cause and engagement with primary care'. (Hussey, 2013).

Next we consider three international examples of engagement of doctors in leadership and management: the Danish and Italian systems and a private health-care company in the USA – Kaiser Permanente.

Table 4.1 Barriers and foundations for engaging doctors in leadership

Barriers to engagement	Foundations for engaging doctors
Ambiguity	Be clear what you mean by the term 'engagement'
Disagreements over business decisions and costs	Respond to basic, legitimate needs doctors express
Attitudes to leadership, especially medical leadership	Clear the air and build trust – share perspectives and value differences
The difficulty of adaptive change	Make a case for change that is clear, compelling and urgent

Denmark

The Danish system stands out in comparison studies as having made excellent progress towards engaging doctors with leadership and management (Ham, 2008; Kirkpatrick et al, 2009). Historically, Denmark has required a doctor to be present on the management board of each hospital and to be involved in decisions about general management. At clinic level, only doctors and nurses are involved in management.

Within this structure, clinicians dominate the leadership and management positions and these roles are seen to be valuable and valued by the medical profession. In addition, it is argued that the more consensual style of politics in Denmark has led to less resentment and confrontation between medical professionals and government-imposed changes and reorganisations (Kirkpatrick et al, 2009). Indeed Kirkpatrick et al (2009) argue that Danish doctors have developed a 'continental' style of professionalism with an emphasis of pursuing power and status through the organisations of the state. In contrast, UK medicine has remained a 'liberal profession' with the emphasis on independence and autonomy which leads to a culture dominated by ideas of self-employment and a detachment from administration.

In addition to the advantageous structural and cultural environment, Denmark has also set up a comprehensive leadership development framework in undergraduate and particularly in postgraduate education (Ham, 2008). This is based on the CanMEDs framework established in Canada (Royal College of Physicians and Surgeons of Canada, 2005) and includes 'The physician as a leader and administrator' as one of the key standards (Ham, 2008). Postgraduate medical education includes a compulsory 10-day leadership development programme with doctors being offered further training once they are appointed as specialists.

Italy

Aardvold et al (2011) describe an educational visit made by five orthopaedic trainees and their consultants from the UK to the Rizzoli Orthopaedic Institute in Bologna, Italy. The purpose of the visit was to compare leadership styles and values in Italy with the systems that they were used to in the NHS. Although the trainees reported many areas in common between the NHS and the Rizzoli Orthopaedic Institute such as team working and multidisciplinary working, there is a striking note of envy in the trainees' report at the working conditions that they were part of in Italy.

The differences that the trainees highlighted seem to be related to two main issues. First that the surgeons in Italy were perceived to be more valued than their counterparts in the NHS. This manifested as respect from staff and tangible evidence such as professional quality offices and other facilities. The other issue was autonomy and a culture of trust. The Italian surgeons were able to choose interesting cases to show the trainees during their visit whereas this would have been more difficult in the UK where surgeons have little control over their lists. There was deemed to be more trust between the health-care professionals and the hospital managers. The report concluded with some recommendations for NHS leadership and particularly the need for doctor leaders in the NHS to be fully engaged.

Kaiser Permanente

The largest American not-for-profit insurance organisation, Kaiser Permanente, has been highlighted as a successful model of integrated, cost-effective care (Light and Dixon, 2004; Ham, 2008). It focusses on providing high quality, evidence-based medicine and embedding quality improvement across the whole organisation which has resulted in improved care for its members (Schilling et al, 2010; Institute for Health Policy, 2013). This organisation has many areas of interesting practise that have contributed to its success but in terms of leadership, three areas are highlighted by its chief executive as the most fundamental: joint leadership, alignment and management training for physicians (Crosson, 2003).

- Joint leadership – a model of joint leadership is practised, where partnership working is modelled at the highest levels of the organisation. This compares with the model of shared leadership that is the basis of many competency frameworks
- Alignment – the mission, strategy and operational goals of the organisation are aligned and the values are shared by everyone working for the organisation. They have worked hard to remove the conflicting incentives that occur when physicians focus solely on patient care and administrators focus on resources and productivity
- Management training – all physicians undergo management training through a series of in-house staff development programmes as they believe

that understanding how a complex organisation works is as important as clinical skills. They also develop what they believe to be critical skills of collaboration and cooperation, negotiation and persuasion as well as delegation and teamwork.

This combination of shared values and goals, as well as a systematic approach to management through evidence-based care and leadership training, ensures that Kaiser Permanente remains an exemplar of medical leadership (Ham, 2008).

Medical leadership development: international examples

While it is clear that there are moves in many different countries towards engaging doctors with health-care leadership and management, the impact of these changes on health improvements and quality has yet to be fully understood or investigated. This section selects three examples of countries which have taken a structured approach to leadership development through definition of competencies and provision of opportunities to develop as a 'doctor-leader'.

Canada

Chadi (2009) provides a comprehensive analysis of the Canadian system. Although the term 'medical leadership' has only recently come into regular use, it has been used in medical education since 2005 through the CanMEDS standards (Royal College of Physicians and Surgeons of Canada, 2005). The framework was overhauled with a new draft version published in 2015 (Frank et al, 2015). The 'leader' role is new (it replaces the former 'manager' role), holds expected leadership competencies outline in Table 4.2, and is described as follows:

> 'The CanMEDS Leader Role describes the engagement of all physicians in shared decision-making for the operation and ongoing evolution of the healthcare system. As a societal expectation, physicians

demonstrate collaborative leadership and management within the healthcare system. At a system level, physicians contribute to the development and delivery of continuously improving healthcare and engage with others in working toward this goal. Physicians integrate their personal lives with their clinical, administrative, scholarly, and teaching responsibilities. They function as individual care providers, as members of teams, and as participants and leaders in the healthcare system locally, regionally, nationally, and globally' (Dath et al, 2015).

Table 4.2 CanMEDS 2015 role competencies for the 'Leader' role (Frank et al, 2015)

Key competencies	Enabling competencies
Physicians are able to	Physicians are able to
1 Contribute to the improvement of health-care delivery in teams, organizations, and systems	1.1 Apply the science of quality improvement to contribute to improving systems of patient care 1.2 Contribute to a culture that promotes patient safety 1.3 Analyse patient safety incidents to enhance systems of care 1.4 Use health informatics to improve the quality of patient care and optimise patient safety
2 Engage in the stewardship of health-care resources	2.1 Allocate health-care resources for optimal patient care 2.2 Apply evidence and management processes to achieve cost-appropriate care
3 Demonstrate leadership in professional practice	3.1 Demonstrate leadership skills to enhance health care 3.2 Facilitate change in health care to enhance services and outcomes
4 Manage career planning, finances, and health human resources in a practice	4.1 Set priorities and manage time to integrate practice and personal life 4.2 Manage a career and a practice 4.3 Implement processes to ensure personal practice improvement

The CanMEDS framework, widely referenced and respected, holds regulatory powers in all speciality education programmes which, alongside mandatory accredited professional development schemes, run through the Physician Manager Institute (Royal College of Physicians and Surgeons of Canada, 2005), recognises the need for more formal development of clinical leadership.

Academic institutions also offer programmes that prepare physicians for leadership, for example, McGill University offers a joint MD MBA programme that aims to prepare fully competent physicians who have also been fully trained in health-care management (www.mcgill.ca/desautels/mdmba) and the University of Toronto provides a 'Leadership Scholars' programme which is interprofessional, involving doctors as well as other health professionals.

Chadi (2009) describes several structural issues in the Canadian health-care systems that act as barriers to engagement by doctors in leadership which could be addressed through increasing recognition of leadership in the career structures of doctors and giving priority in leadership appointments to leaders with a strong clinical background. In addition, he notes a key positive element of Canadian health-care management is that health ministers in the government have recently been practising physicians, which gives a level of understanding of health-care provision that is beneficial to effective health-care delivery (Chadi, 2009). The article also comments on the selection of medical students and suggests that Canada finds ways to select students who have the potential to become great leaders.

Australia and New Zealand

The cultural backdrop in Australia and New Zealand is that of a need to engage doctors more fully at all levels in health-care leadership and management with a view to improving health-care outcomes (including those of indigenous peoples) and patient safety. The Royal Australasian College of Medical Administrators was established in Australia in 1976 and in New Zealand in the late 1990s. It provides opportunities for registered medical practitioners to gain vocational registration in medical administration (as a branch of medicine) through at least 3 years of supervised medical administrative experience and/ or completion of a relevant approved masters' degree. Royal Australasian College of Medical Administrators has defined a Medical Leadership Curriculum which includes a competency framework (*Table 4.3*) setting out seven roles of the medical leader, based on the roles in the CanMEDS framework, divided into sub-themes and aligned with key goals.

Table 4.3 Royal Australasian College of Medical Administrators (2011) Medical Leadership and Management Curriculum Framework (*continued overleaf*)

Medical leader	**Key goals:** • demonstrate intelligent leadership • achieve high levels of self-awareness • manage self in relation to others • serve in and lead from management roles	
Sub roles	**Role competency themes**	**Key goals**
Medical expert	Systems and organizations Governance Strategy and design Medical perspectives	• bring medical input to organisational decision-making and influence others • analyse complex problems to discern risks and benefits of actions and plan appropriately • design and implement appropriate governance systems • work within a team consulting with other health professionals to achieve organisational goals
Communicator	Effective communication Align competing interests Convey information Synthesize information Develop rapport	• engage with stakeholders to communicate within and outside the organisation • analyse complex information and evidence to formulate policy and make decisions • convey relevant information and explanations to diverse groups • develop shared understandings and align competing interests • understand effective communication methodologies and pathways

Table 4.3 Royal Australasian College of Medical Administrators (2011) Medical Leadership and Management Curriculum Framework (continued)

Sub roles	Role competency themes	Key goals
Advocate	Promote health Social determinants of health Identify community needs Respond to health issues	• respond to the health needs of patients and populations • respond to the health needs of communities and systems • identify the determinants of health for populations • influence policy and practice to optimise health outcomes
Scholar	Application of new knowledge Facilitate learning Evidence-based decision making Continuing professional development	• maintain and enhance professional activities through ongoing learning • critically evaluate information for decision making • facilitate learning for all stakeholders • demonstrate the ability to apply research skills to management tasks
Professional	Reflective practice Value systems Patient first behaviour Ethical practice	• demonstrate awareness of ethical issues in managerial and clinical decision making • demonstrate 'patient first' behaviour • demonstrate behaviour that is always within the value systems of the College • demonstrate a commitment to doctor health and sustainable practice

Table 4.3 Royal Australasian College of Medical Administrators (2011) Medical Leadership and Management Curriculum Framework (continued)

Sub roles	Role competency themes	Key goals
Collaborator	Facilitate consultation Build relationships Prevent and resolve conflict Lead teams	• participate effectively and appropriately in an inter-professional health-care team • work effectively with other health professionals to prevent, negotiate and resolve inter-professional conflict • build effective relationships with all stakeholders • engage and facilitate appropriate consultation around key issues through a variety of mechanisms
Manager	People and performance Prioritize resources Systems at work Effective organizations	• think on your feet while analysing, determining options and acting within real-world timelines • adopt a systems approach to all management tasks • be familiar with methods used to prioritise resources and allocate these to appropriately achieve organisational priorities • implement appropriate human resource management

In both Australia and New Zealand, increasing emphasis on the role of doctors as leaders and shapers of health care and clinical governance has been placed plus a recognition that medical leadership needs to be distributed at all levels, include the highest levels of government and in health boards. Management and leadership competencies are also enshrined in the Australian Medical Council (2009) Standards for undergraduate education thus supporting the early development of doctors as leaders. Attention is also starting to be paid to leadership development opportunities aimed at improving health and opportunities for under-represented groups. One example is the collaboration between Medical Deans Australia and New Zealand and the Australian Indigenous Doctors Association Capacity Building for Indigenous Medical Academic Leadership Project. Although Health Workforce Australia and Health Workforce New Zealand are each beginning to take a broader view of workforce needs, competencies, outcomes and training in their own countries, leadership development still tends to be siloed (in organisations, professional groupings and professional bodies) and unsystematic, rather than system-wide and interprofessional (McKimm et al, 2009). Examples of prudent approaches to health care which have transformed services, evidencing high level strategic leadership, can be found, e.g. in Canterbury District Health Board in New Zealand (Timmins and Ham, 2013).

Korea

Lee et al (2010) investigated the leadership competencies defined as important to the medical faculty through interviews with a large number of medical professionals. A wide range of specialities was represented with varying levels of seniority. Factor analysis identified the following competencies:

- Professional ability, ethics/morality, self-management, self-development and passion
- Public interest, networking, social participation and active service
- Motivating, caring, promoting teamwork, nurturing, conflict management, directing, performance management and systems thinking
- Organizational orientation, collaboration, voluntary participation and cost-benefit orientation (Lee at al, 2010).

The authors concluded that these competencies should provide a framework for leadership development which could help plan educational activities, and inform career development plans and appointment to senior roles. Although these competencies emanate from a cultural perspective that is quite different from Anglo-Saxon cultures, there are significant areas of overlap with other frameworks, but with a greater emphasis on public service and commitment to the organisation than is found in other frameworks. In Chapter 10, we discuss the strong alignment between leadership competencies and behaviours and those expected of professionals and this is an international phenomenon. Differences between western and eastern models can therefore also be found in frameworks of professional practice in other parts of Asia (see for example Ho et al's (2014) study in China).

Conclusions

Over the last few years, there has been a shift in focus towards a more active engagement of doctors at all levels in both leading and managing health-care improvements, clearer definitions of the expectations of doctors and specific support for doctors in the form of leadership development opportunities. In many countries, professional standards in undergraduate and postgraduate education and training include clinical leadership and management and increasingly specific medical leadership competency frameworks are being used. Development programmes typically include in-house training courses, masters' level programmes, coaching and mentoring schemes, workplace-based learning and participation in health innovation projects. Many of these are now led by the relevant professional bodies, such as medical colleges, and there are examples of specific colleges or faculties being established in clinical leadership, management or administration which acknowledge the importance of this as a 'speciality' in its own right.

Although leadership must be learned and applied in context, we can gain insight into our own cultures by exploring and understanding how medical leadership is perceived and understood elsewhere. Many international studies comment that involving doctors in leadership cannot be achieved simply by providing training and development, but that system-wide approaches to enabling and expecting doctors and other clinicians to take responsibility for the improvement of health-care outcomes for communities and populations are required (Ham, 2008; Brook, 2010; Baker and Denis, 2011; Hussey, 2013). This system-wide approach is now starting to be embedded in health-care strategy and policy initiatives (see Chapters 2 and 3).

Taking an international perspective highlights a growing acknowledgement that developing doctors as leaders and managers needs to be considered within broader systemic and structural changes, through active engagement of students and practising professionals with quality and safety improvement initiatives. The challenges for all countries include how to effect such transformational change within relatively entrenched health systems, cultures and structures; how to facilitate interprofessional and collaborative learning; how to change ways of working and acknowledge the importance of followership, emotional labour and team working and provide effective leadership development opportunities for all those who need them.

Key points

- As the costs of health care rise, there is increased pressure internationally to manage health-care resources more effectively and efficiently
- Many countries have defined the leadership qualities that they want in their doctors through competency-based frameworks
- Historical and cultural factors are important in explaining the differences between approaches to medical leadership internationally
- International comparisons are useful in improving medical leadership engagement and development in the UK.

CHAPTER 5

Leadership in systems, organisations and cultures

Denise Prescott, Mike Rowe

Introduction

This chapter reviews some of the principal debates surrounding the ideas of organisational culture, leadership and change as they relate to the NHS, to make explicit the complex and contested nature of these ideas. It is based on the article by Prescott and Rowe (2015). As austerity impacts upon the NHS, the variations between devolved authorities and between clinical commissioning groups and other bodies make it increasingly difficult to talk about a single and uniform NHS (Klein, 2007, 2013; National Audit Office, 2012), let alone prescribe a model of change or of leadership appropriate to the whole organisation. Instead, all health-care practitioners have a responsibility for the future of the NHS and, through individual and group actions and inactions, the institutions in which people work are shaped and reshaped. Recognizing the importance of individual agency and responsibilities is as much about innovation and leadership as it is a response to the Francis report (2013).

The chapter first reviews the complex environment in which health-care practitioners work and considers the idea of top-down understandings of policy and organisational change. Studies of implementation problems in other public services emphasize the unintended consequences of change. Austerity adds a further level of complexity in the different responses to the financial pressures that are to be found in public service agencies. In this context, of increasing variation and complexity, the impact of the Francis Inquiry and other reports is explored and suggests that a greater emphasis on thinking about change and leadership should be placed upon the individual and his/her scope to influence and to act. Far from there being an implementation science, health-care practitioners all need to take responsibility for shaping the NHS of the future (West et al, 2015).

On complexity in systems

Changes in the NHS over the past thirty years can be interpreted from a number of different perspectives. There are arguments about efficiency and about improving quality, but there is also a clear succession of efforts to change the ways in which professionals make decisions. Griffiths sought to constrain discretion by introducing management to hospitals (Department of Health and Social Security, 1983). The 1989 reforms (Department of Health, 1989) sought to strengthen management and, at the same time, extend the influence of primary care in decision making. Many of the reforms of the New Labour era may be understood in a similar light, with the idea of commissioning emerging as its clearest expression (Klein, 2006). The days of the hospital administrator, as caricatured in the British television programme *Yes Minister*, are long gone. However, with freedoms and managerial autonomy have come central concerns with quality and standards.

In one sense, the lingering presence of bureaucratic thinking can be felt in Performance Assessment Frameworks and other forms of monitoring and audit (Power, 1994; Department of Health, 2000). This tendency, to speak of freedom to make decisions, of choice and, more recently, of personalized medicine, is overlaid with a level of scrutiny and evaluation that, in practice, can stifle precisely these ideas. Policy innovations have begun to emerge in the devolved administrations. Variations in long-term care, in priorities and in the role of the private sector offer the potential for policy learning and transfer. In practice, variation has become politicised, perhaps particularly in Wales, as any variation in standards that arise as a consequence are scrutinized (National Audit Office, 2012; Hardman, 2014).

Differences in outcomes and systems find echoes in the wide variety of responses made to austerity and changing pressures and priorities in regions and localities across England, as well as in the devolved countries. The NHS is now not a single national service but rather, it is a complex web of institutions and relationships, shaped by local forces and people responding to external policy stimuli in very different ways (Klein, 2006; National Audit Office,

2012). In this confused context, *Equity and Excellence: Liberating the NHS* (Department of Health, 2010) established clinical commissioning groups with responsibility for the health care of communities and 80% of the NHS England budget (Barr, 2014). This is in marked contrast to Northern Ireland, Wales and Scotland, where care is provided through regional health boards and where primary and secondary care is integrated at a local level (National Audit Office, 2012). Although political and operational responsibility for health care lies with four national executives, regulatory bodies such as the General Medical Council and the Nursing and Midwifery Council remain organised on a UK-wide basis, as are the professional bodies, aggravating the complexities of structures and systems within which health professionals work.

On unintended consequences

However, throughout the past thirty years, and in contrast to the first thirty years of the NHS, one consistent thread is that of change. Organisational forms and boundaries have changed at a bewildering rate and scarcely has one change been launched than the next is announced. For all the language of evidence, of evaluation and of learning, one obvious message all too often escapes those in positions of power – policy rarely, if ever, achieves the intended outcome. In studies of policy implementation, this is well understood (Hogwood and Gunn, 1984; Hill and Hupe, 2012). Indeed, the problem is well expressed in the extended title of Pressman and Wildavsky's (1973) classic text on the subject:

'Implementation: How Great Expectations in Washington Are Dashed in Oakland; Or, Why It's Amazing that Federal Programs Work at All, This Being a Saga of the Economic Development Administration as told by two sympathetic observers who seek to build morals on a Foundation of ruined hopes'.

Beyond the sense of disappointment this title expresses, it misses the unintended consequences of change and, in particular, of changes overlaid upon changes. Indeed, one might see the NHS not so much as a system but as the outcome of a concatenation of unintended consequences (Klein, 2006; Timmins, 2012).

And austerity

These complexities are compounded by external drivers, especially economic ones. In an effort to address health inequalities, real term spending on the NHS increased significantly during the Blair government (Barr, 2014). For many managers in the NHS, as in all other public services, this experience of growing budgets and investment is all they have known. This growth concealed some of the pressures that were emerging, pressures associated with an ageing population and rising demand (Grant et al, 2012). But two key questions that austerity is asking of managers and leaders in the NHS today are:

- How to manage these pressures with a declining budget?
- How to maintain services and innovate with less?

Organisations are responding in various ways to the crisis that straitened financial times provokes. These responses echo those observed during the 1970s, particularly in American cities, and research into those experiences provides insight into the situation in different NHS institutions (Behn, 1980). Aside from the obvious pressures on organisations, cuts produced unanticipated consequences across organisational and service boundaries as withdrawal of one service exerted pressure elsewhere. Flexibility and the ability to cope with these pressures were constrained just as they were most needed, always affecting the poorest most severely. Just as innovation becomes essential to meet these challenges, the ideas that emerged were starved of resources in overcommitted organisations (Biller, 1980).

As well as innovation, it became fashionable to talk of leadership at this time. Glassberg (1978) identified three types. The first, the 'cut the fat, tough guy', will be familiar to many today. He/she is focused on the financial demands, changing services and reaching decisions using accounting technologies, treating individuals, whether staff or patients, as numbers to be balanced. The second leader, the 'receiver in bankruptcy', seeks to scale down the organisation smoothly, upsetting nobody and avoiding difficult choices, a balancing act that can feel like aimless drifting with the only hope being an external change, whether economic or political. It is the third, the 'revitalising entrepreneur', that government ministers and senior officials visualise as they talk of developing leaders in the NHS. These are the leaders who exploit the situation to drive through ideas that, in easier times, seemed unnecessary or ones that could be introduced over time. Case scenario 5.1 describes such a project.

Case scenario 5.1 The Angel Centre – 'revitalising entrepreneurship'
Background
The community served by the Angel Centre in Salford has a long history of poorer than average health and higher rates of smoking, drinking and drug abuse. Life expectancy was lower than the national average and yet there was a lower than average take-up of health services in relation to the level of need together with late diagnosis of cancers and other life-threatening conditions.

The Angel Centre was established in the late 1990s through Health Action Zone funding, and became part of a national network of 360 healthy living centres. It was hosted by the NHS in Salford and, in 2011, the centre 'span out' of the NHS to create one of the country's first public service mutuals. The new organisation is called Social adVentures and is a co-owned social enterprise where service users and staff have equal ownership of the organisation.

What was done?
The Centre was established in order to 'inspire local people to lead healthier and happier lives'. Social adVentures defines happiness as 'enjoyment of a full meaningful life and health as a state of complete physical, mental and social wellbeing'. Its approach regards patients as people who bring capacity and resource with them which they can contribute to improving their own state of wellbeing.

The Centre makes health care more accessible by placing a GP surgery in a friendly community building and café. Medical staff have social prescribing options, including healthy eating programmes, personal development, physical activities, creative expression, accessing information technology, gardening, music, culture and social and economic opportunities. This last provides support for the development of social enterprises. The approach taken throughout places emphasis on the individual's role in his/her own health and wellbeing and strives to support them to release that capacity sustainably (for further information, see www.socialadventures.org.uk/).

The Centre also works in partnership with health services providers bringing them together with patients and their families and carers so that together they can design more effective services. The emphasis is that health professionals are working with and not for the community with all partners having resources to contribute.

Continued overleaf

Boyne (2004, 2006) has drawn lessons on organisational turnarounds from the private sector and identifies three strategies:

- Retrenchment: withdrawal from some markets or contraction by reducing activity or selling assets
- Repositioning: becoming more dominant in existing markets or by diversifying into new ones
- Reorganisation: planning, (de)centralisation, human resource or cultural change initiatives.

After thirty years of public service reform that has emphasized competition, these responses will be familiar to many in the NHS. But, despite leadership frameworks and the like, no single direction or sense of purpose has been set out, but rather, divergence and confusion.

Case scenario 5.1 The Angel Centre – 'revitalising entrepreneurship' (continued)

Outcomes

The work of Social adVentures is valued and achieves against the Five Ways to Well-being (New Economics Foundation, 2008): connect; give; take notice; be active; and keep learning as well as against evidence of sustainable changes in healthy behaviours. A recent Social Return on Investment evaluation valued at £10.21 the impact of every £1 invested in Social adVentures.

Tips

- Work with the most important people – those whose health you are trying to improve – using their knowledge, ideas and assets and creating the space for them to co-produce their own health and wellbeing
- Environments matter – the spaces you create must feel homely to the people you are seeking to serve
- Partnership working must mean something – if you do not feel that there is equal respect between those involved then this must be addressed, otherwise the solutions which come out of these processes will not be sustainable
- You need to deal with the whole person the whole time
- Health is ultimately very connected to happiness.

And on cultures

The Francis Inquiry report (Francis, 2013) (and subsequent reviews) threw some of these tensions and dilemmas into sharp focus. The management of a health-care trust had become much like the management of other organisations. Decisions were made remotely, on the basis of reports and of numerical data. Presenting these data to external audiences in the best light, partly in order to achieve foundation trust status, was a central concern for the senior team. In theory, their ambition to develop the trust was built upon an organisation that was performing well, with an emphasis on process as opposed to patient outcomes (Barr, 2014). But, beneath the abstract data, standards of care were not what they should have been. Pressures and priorities that were abstract at a senior level were very real on wards and in specialist teams. Indeed, one might interpret aspects of the report as indicating that, because the internal language of decision-making was largely about data and information, the patient had long since ceased to be a focus of concern, but was a unit to be processed in a way that could be presented numerically to external audiences. That is to say, a culture developed that is alien to most people's understandings of the NHS. And while it is atypical, it is not a unique case. Indeed, Boyne (2004, 2006) would recognize the familiar strategies he observed in private organisations.

Culture is sometimes spoken about as if it is homogenous. Francis illustrates very clearly that there is no one NHS culture. Indeed, the report also illustrates, along with the work of others (e.g. Schein, 1996), that there are different cultures within hospitals and other organisations (see Chapters 11 and 18). Practitioners will recognize these differences in their encounters with staff as they go about their daily duties. Some units and teams are open and helpful where others, performing similar duties, are obstructive. Different professions tend to exhibit different behaviours, developing professional silos and tribes (McKimm, 2011a; Francis, 2013). If we add into the mix the impact that austerity is having, it becomes clearer that to speak of culture is to miss the many cultures and micro-climates to be found in large organisations, such as hospitals.

On agency

However, this places the emphasis on structure. Yes, the professions are different, performance targets do affect behaviours and we are constrained by institutional systems and processes. But we need also to recognize the scope for our own agency, together with others around us. Research consistently demonstrates the degree to which individuals talk of their lack of choice and of the constraints they experience while exercising discretion routinely (Lipsky, 1980; Schön, 1983). The emphasis on structure tends to suggest that individuals are powerless to affect the nature and the quality of the service they provide however observations in public service and other institutions demonstrate the degree to which they actually define the service received in the way they exercise their discretion (Maynard-Moody and Musheno, 2000; Lea, 2008; Watkins-Hayes, 2009; Dubois, 2010; Evans, 2010). Some programmes appear officially bound by rules and structures which, on closer inspection, are the product of local custom and practice rather than any externally imposed requirements (Rowe, 2002). Case scenario 5.2 demonstrates an initiative which brings together many aspects of the themes being discussed, in particular how revitalising entrepreneurship can help energise and improve service delivery.

Not only do individuals make decisions and exercise discretion but their actions also make structures. Organisational structures are not embodied in buildings but in the behaviours of people. The Francis report (2013) criticises health professionals' failure to deliver appropriate care and called for the re-establishment of professional behaviours, values and attitudes conducive to a caring environment. Likewise, the report calls for a culture in which the public and patients both expect and receive transparency and candour. Higher education institutions are now being directed towards the integration of core values including care and compassion within undergraduate health professions' curricula.

On the science of improvement

It is in this environment of opacity and confusion that government reform efforts seek to impose order. Indeed, government policy assumes there is an order in the first instance and that it can be altered. Manifestations of this sense that change from above can be engineered are to be found in some of the ideas emerging from the Behavioural Insights Team at the Cabinet Office (see, for example, Behavioural Insights Team, 2012) and, in health, in the work around the ideas of improvement science (e.g. Shojania and Grimshaw, 2005; Berwick, 2008; Lobb and Colditz, 2013; Nilsen et al, 2013). These differing

---

Case scenario 5.2 'Pass on the Memories'

Background

With a progressively elderly population there is increasing incidence of dementia, affecting an estimated 800 000 people in the UK. The cost of caring for dementia sufferers is approximately £26.3 billion a year with £4.3 billion of this attributed to direct health-care interventions (Alzheimers' Society, 2014). Such is the impact of the condition that David Cameron has set this as one of his priority areas (see "Prime Minister's challenge on Dementia 2020) with emphasis on services designed around the patient and their carers (Department of Health, 2015).

Traditionally, health-care provision for dementia patients has been delivered through a 'day hospital' model whereby patients are transported into the health-care setting for nursing care and rehabilitation. A major limitation of this is the time spent by patients being transported to a setting which is unfamiliar and potentially disorientating to them. Additionally, the costs of maintaining and staffing the physical environment have proved economically challenging for many hospital trusts. As such there has been a need for clinical leaders to use an entrepreneurial approach and rethink models of care delivery in response to both patient and economic need (Boyne, 2004, 2006).

What was done?

One such example of thinking differently and repositioning care delivery is an innovative programme to support people with dementia, established in the 'heart' of Liverpool in 2012. The 'Pass on the Memories programme' was funded by Mersey Care NHS Trust working in strategic partnership with Everton in the Community (a charity founded through Everton Football Club). Service users and carers meet weekly at Goodison Park and undertake an interactive and personalised programme including reminiscence workshops and visits to local places of interest. The programme is supported by health-care professionals with an overarching aim of stimulating memory and promoting the wellbeing of people with dementia.

Continued overleaf

approaches to understanding and seeking to influence change share a common strand: the sense that, if only the right mechanisms, incentives or combination of pressures could be discovered, then we might hope to see improvements. At the heart of their frustration are the professionals and public servants who, despite the evidence, stubbornly continue to do the wrong things. If only they could be changed.

Conclusions

The idea of the 'revitalising entrepreneur' as a leader in the current climate appears to have the attributes required for innovation and change in times of austerity, rather than a technocratic vision of change or more conventional styles of leadership. The Francis Inquiry report, Keogh review (2013) and other investigations underline the need for leadership at all levels and in all professions throughout the complex worlds of NHS institutions. This echoes the conclusions of Lord Darzi (Darzi, 2008) who advocated for a model of distributed leadership, based on inclusivity and with the patient at the centre of decision-making processes.

Case scenario 5.2 'Pass on the Memories' (continued)

Outcome
Care delivery is being evaluated through Mersey Care NHS Trust's Service User and Evaluation Group. However, a significant additional benefit to this new model of care delivery has been the development of a carers group, where members have benefitted from mutual support and engagement.

Tips
- Effective partnerships with non-NHS organisations can make a meaningful difference to patients and carers
- A holistic care approach is required, considering both the service user and his/her carer
- Environments matter – the spaces you create must feel like home to the people you are seeking to serve.

The dilemma for a large scale bureaucratic organisation like the NHS is the culture shift required at every level of the organisation. Whether challenging poor practice, responding to emerging policy agendas or commissioning in new and more imaginative ways, the actions of many thousands will constitute the NHS that emerges in the coming years. Making those actions conscious and reflective and making choices to act in particular ways, will be an innovation in itself, and one from which change will undoubtedly emerge. The need here is for leaders, throughout the many organisations and cultures that constitute the NHS, who will actively engage in the process and be prepared to give their 'emotional labour' (see Chapter 12). It also requires an expansive structure in which leadership is encouraged within the many complex and adaptive systems in which health-care professionals work (Fraser and Greenhalgh, 2001).

Key points

- Leadership in large and complex systems, such as the NHS, needs to come from the top, bottom and middle
- Health-care practitioners need to be alive to the enablers, opportunities, points of resistance, structures and cultures in which they operate
- Culture often operates as a barrier to change
- In every crisis, opportunities also arise to review current practices and to make changes that, in easier times, would not be considered.

CHAPTER 6

Leading and working in teams

Helen O'Sullivan, Michael J Moneypenny, Judy McKimm

Introduction

This chapter considers the role of the clinical leader as a team member and leader and explores how an understanding of the purpose and functions of teams can help doctors work more effectively in the various teams with which they are involved. It is based on an article by O'Sullivan et al (2015). Health care is primarily delivered by a range of health workers and managers working in a number of interlinked teams. Effective teamwork is increasingly important as a result of the complexity and specialisation of care, ageing populations with comorbidities and rise of long term-conditions, global workforce shortages, changes in skills mix of health workers, safe working hours' initiatives and shifts towards more integrated health and public services. 'Our challenge is not whether we will deliver in teams, but rather how well we deliver in teams' (Schyve, 2005).

Team types

Given the importance of teams to the delivery of effective health care, clinical leaders need to be able to lead, work within and between teams as seamlessly as possible. Understanding what makes teams function well and less effectively can help leaders overcome some of these teamworking challenges.

The teamSTEPPS programme identifies different, inter-related team types that support and deliver health care:

1. Core teams – involved in direct patient care, usually (but not always) based where the patient receives care
2. Coordinating teams – responsible for operational and resource management and allocation
3. Contingency teams – emergent, crisis, time-limited, formed from various core team members
4. Ancillary and support services – service delivery, e.g. cleaners, porters, catering, medical records
5. Administration – executive leadership, define culture, policies, staff expectations (Agency for Healthcare Research and Quality, 2008).

Drivers for improved team working and leadership in health care

Whether as components of clinical competence and communication skills, commitment to professional competence, or working in partnership, effective leadership and teamwork are increasingly recognised as essential skills in clinical care (e.g. Francis, 2013). In the UK, the National Confidential Enquiry into Maternal Deaths stated that poor teamwork was a leading cause of sub-standard obstetric care (for example see Cooper and McClure, 2005). In the US, the Institute of Medicine's report 'Crossing the Quality Chasm' (Institute of Medicine, 2001) emphasised the need for improved leadership and teamwork in clinical practice (as discussed by Chakraborti et al, 2008). Hjortdahl et al (2009) suggested that effective leadership improves team performance and goal achievement and other research has shown that good teamwork reduces errors, reduces mortality and morbidity rates and improves patient safety (Neily et al, 2010). From a social perspective, as the population ages, more patients will present with multiple health problems, requiring effective interdisciplinary teamwork and leadership (Xyrichis and Ream, 2008).

Since 2009, a number of high-profile inquiries into poor health care have made clear links between leadership, multidisciplinary teamwork, high quality health care and good health outcomes. The Francis (2013) report detailed the failings in care at the Mid-Staffordshire NHS trust. Poor leadership by nursing, medical and boardroom staff was highlighted as a particular area of concern. It also called for 'effective teamwork between all the different disciplines and services' (p.110) and emphasised the importance of good leadership: 'The common culture and values of the NHS must be applied at all levels of the organization, but of particular importance is the example set by leaders' (p.78). The Keogh mortality review (Keogh, 2013) subsequently reported on 14 hospitals with high standardised mortality ratios. Poor leadership was again identified as a cause of patient harm. The Prime Minister then asked Don Berwick, former president of the US Institute for Healthcare Improvement, to report on patient safety. His report – 'A promise to learn – a commitment to act: Improving the Safety of Patients in England' (Berwick, 2013) – recommended that: 'All NHS leaders and managers should actively address poor teamwork' (p.16) and gave guidance on the shift in leadership behaviours required.

Leading and building a health-care team

Ezziane et al (2012) suggested that the key areas for consideration when leading or building a health-care team are communication, decision-making, patient safety, conflict resolution and identifying appropriate roles for individual team members.

Communication

As noted above, adverse events resulting from error happen at unacceptably high rates in the inpatient setting, with ineffective or insufficient communication among team members being a contributing factor. Electronic communication has increased in the last ten years and has removed several important aspects of human interaction, potentially fragmenting, isolating and de-skilling health-care workers, who like many face situations such as that discussed in case scenario 6.1. Clinical leaders must therefore look for appropriate methods of communication to better direct their teams. Regular meetings that create an environment that welcomes independent expression of a team member's views are particularly important (Ezziane et al, 2012).

Tools that help team members communicate include:

- SBAR (Situation, Background, Assessment, Recommendation)

- Callout
- Check-back
- Handover or Handoff (e.g. 'I pass the baton' – Introduction, Patient, Assessment, Situation, Safety concerns, Background, Actions, Timing, Ownership, Next) (World Health Organisation, 2011). See case scenario 6.1.

Decision making

In a group or team setting, a leader has to be aware of the tendency for 'group think' where members of the team go along with decisions for fear of being ostracised for challenging a decision. This is linked to the issues of leadership and hierarchy discussed in the section on 'power distance' below. Leaders of a health-care team need to find a leadership style that encourages challenge and nurtures independent thought.

Case scenario 6.1 handover

Paul found himself increasingly worried as he came to the end of his F1 training. He felt he had never really been taught to do a handover properly and everywhere he had worked did it slightly differently. He couldn't understand why nurses seemed to be so well prepared for their shift – was it because they had such a long handover ('report')? He didn't know as he wasn't allowed in the room. As an F2, he was going to be more responsible for more sick patients especially at night.

He talked with the deputy medical director about this as he'd started to read about structured medical handovers. She asked him to find out more and see what they could do, particularly as a new electronic record and prescribing system was being introduced in the autumn, perhaps there was a way of improving handover alongside this and learn from other professional groups? Could there be a way of having reports like the nurses? Might 7-day working provide opportunities for this?

Patient safety

Patient safety is a key focus for improving health care in the UK (Institute for Healthcare Improvement, 2015). Health-care teams have learned from other sectors such as the aviation industry in procedural and mechanised ways of cutting down on errors. Setting clear goals around patient safety and quality improvement help to focus team members' activities towards a patient-centred approach to care.

Conflict resolution

One of the downsides of precluding 'groupthink' from a team is a potential increase in conflict. Following disagreement, confrontation and escalation may occur and can create long-term disharmony in teams. It is therefore important that a clinical leader is able to foster negotiation and compromise in such situations, more specifically aiming towards group-trust, shared commitments and mutual respect of opposing views (Ezziane et al, 2012).

The World Health Organization patient safety guide (World Health Organization, 2011) describes three useful tools to help empower team members:
1. The 'two-challenge rule' (voicing and restating concerns at least twice)
2. CUS (I am Concerned, I am Uncomfortable, this is a Safety issue), a three-step process for assisting people in stopping an activity
3. DESC Script for resolving conflict (Describe the specific situation/behaviour/issue; Express how the situation makes you feel; Suggest other alternatives; state the Consequence).

Identifying appropriate roles

Porter-O'Grady (2010) suggests that failure of role-assignment to team members is one of the most significant causes of stress in the workplace. Several methods and types of analysis can be used to ensure that there is clarity of role and purpose in the team.

The above points are reinforced by West et al (2015) in their review of the evidence base for leadership in health care. Specifically referring to team working and leadership, they note that:

- Effective team working is essential for organisational success
- 'Leadership clarity is associated with clear team objectives, high levels of participation, commitment to excellence and support for innovation' (p12)
- Conflict within teams leads to poor outcomes and processes
- Shared leadership is a predictor of team effectiveness.

Specifically we should ask: What are we trying to accomplish? How will we know that a change is an improvement? What changes can we make that will result in improvement? (Institute for Healthcare Improvement, 2015).

West and Lyubovnikova (2013) suggest that teams which have low levels of interdependence, shared objectives and reflectivity are known as 'pseudo-teams' – while they may appear team-like, they have few of the characteristics of effective, high performing teams. The detrimental impact of such pseudo-teams is compounded in that most health professionals work in many teams, in different contexts, and over time (O'Leary et al, 2011). Being able to work in multiple teams therefore requires an adaptive mix of flexibility, credibility and authenticity, and leaders need also to be able to effect communication and manage activities between teams.

Another way of thinking about 'when good teams go bad' (e.g. as described in the Francis Report, 2013) is the 'Nut Island effect' (Levy, 2001). The 'effect' describes a team that became both physically and psychologically distanced from senior management and started operating against its own rules. Levy suggests that this can be very dangerous for organisations and disasters (such as the one in Nut Island when sewage outflow into Boston Harbour reached crisis levels) can occur. The Nut Island effect can be seen to some extent throughout the NHS, both across its component parts and within organisations. Levy suggests that management need to keep in touch with people on the 'shop floor' through a variety of means and listen when they say there are problems, not just leave them to carry on and find their own solutions. Enabling the voicing of concerns is a key component of risk management.

Multi-professional teams

As services become more integrated and person-centred, health workers increasingly work in multi-professional teams. Multi-professional teamworking can be defined as:

'A dynamic process involving two or more health professionals with complementary backgrounds and skills, sharing common health goals and exercising concerted physical and mental effort in assessing, planning, or evaluating patient care. This is accomplished through interdependent collaboration, open communication and shared decision-making. This in turn generates value-added patient, organisational and staff outcomes.' (Xyrichis and Ream, 2008)

Whatever the makeup of the team, research has shown that the quality of leadership is crucial to improved outcomes for patients and that an engaging, authentic and shared leadership approach is the most effective (West et al, 2015). While leading or working within uni-professional teams can be very challenging, additional and specific challenges exist when working in multi-professional teams.

First, multi-professional teams tend to have complex structures. While uni-professional teams usually have a single reporting line, multi-professional teams often have more complex structures – perhaps reporting to different senior managers, and having separate supervisory and, often, funding arrangements. Second, multi-professional teams include a range of different professionals. The leader typically comes from a background in one profession and they will have to gain the respect of the full range of professions within the team. Acknowledging and working with potential issues of authority, power and control and resolving conflicts are essential skills for team leaders (Barrow et al, 2014). Leaders who can work adaptively within such complexity are likely to be more successful.

It is vital that leaders establish and maintain credibility but this can be difficult when they are responsible for other professionals, clinical practice or activities that did not form part of their education or training. Working with, motivating, leading and supervising people with a range of values and skills bases raises issues about professional identity (Anning et al, 2010). Professional identity (the values and scope of practice that defines a profession) can be very positive – it binds people together and helps them feel that they belong to a community of practice. However, because each professional identity requires people to see members of professions different from theirs as 'the other', this can lead to 'in groups', 'out groups', misunderstandings and miscommunications. Leaders who understand this and can negotiate and agree common values, goals and approaches to care will help bring team members together around a shared purpose and way of working, despite their professional backgrounds.

Leaders of multi-professional teams also need to be 'boundary crossers' (Mathur and Skelcher, 2007), that is, have the ability to work with a range of professional groups in a way that engenders confidence. They will need to take a 'translational' role, learn to speak the 'language' of different professional groups (including health managers) and demonstrate respect for all team members' perspectives. A distributed or shared leadership style will be a good fit in most contexts and the leader will need to strike a balance between maintaining an authoritative and confidence-inspiring leadership style and being able to admit when they do not have sufficient knowledge about a profession to make a decision.

Team working and power relations

Barriers to effective teamworking include changing roles; changing settings; medical hierarchies; the individualistic nature of medicine and instability of teams (World Health Organization, 2011). In medicine, physicians have traditionally been at the top of the power structure and, consequently, have the greatest potential to impact those around them, including patients and other members of the health-care team. This phenomenon is commonly referred to as 'power distance'. Power distance occurs when individuals in positions of less power are reluctant to challenge those with greater authority and can lead to detrimental outcomes for patients and unhelpful ways of working such as sabotage, working around and passive aggression or rebellion (Barrow et al, 2014). In some environments, such as the battlefield or emergency situations, strict adherence to the established power structures is vital but in other contexts, power distance may actually result in harm. The power distance index was part of Hofstede's cultural dimensions theory which gives insight into the impact of cultural difference and leadership in global business (Hofstede et al, 2010). Using a low power distance management or negotiation approach (i.e.

engaging or nearby leadership) with someone accustomed to a high power distance culture may be counter-productive and vice versa. Power distance may also describe the leadership relationship between doctors and other health-care professionals, especially nurses.

Leader–follower relations

While leader–follower relationships involve dominance and some deference, this can be catastrophic in consequence when people feel they cannot speak out. The airline industry has many examples of where the hierarchical nature of the leadership among the crew resulted in catastrophe. The crash of Korean Air Flight 801 in 1997, for example, was attributed primarily to the rigidly hierarchical power structure in the cockpit, which prevented the crew from speaking up until it was too late. In medicine, lack of clarity in the leadership structure and inability to challenge the leadership decisions of others can be equally catastrophic, see for example case scenario 6.2.

In a study (see Chapter 14), medical students were placed in a simulated acute situation as part of their course on leadership and professionalism. As sample of the students were placed in situation where a senior colleague made

---

Case scenario 6.2

In March 2005, Elaine Bromiley, a 37-year-old mother of two, was scheduled to undergo a routine sinus operation under general anaesthesia. Unfortunately there were complications with managing her airway after she had been anaesthetised. Two consultant anaesthetists and a consultant ear, nose and throat surgeon were unable to obtain a definitive airway and she suffered hypoxic brain damage. Her life support was switched off some days later. An independent report into her death criticised the lack of communication within the team (Harmer, 2007). Her husband, Martin Bromiley, an airline pilot and expert in human factors training in aviation, stated:

'The lead anaesthetist... in his own words "lost control". There was a question mark, in the inquest, about who people felt was in charge at different points... There was certainly a breakdown in the decision-making processes and it would appear that the communication processes dried up amongst the consultants.' (Clinical Human Factors Group, 2008)

---

a deliberate and potentially life-threatening error. Where students didn't challenge the senior colleague, the most common reason for not speaking up was 'assumed hierarchy', i.e. the senior is not questioned simply because they are more senior, rather than perceived to be more experienced (the second most common reason for not speaking up) (Moneypenny et al, 2013). In a similar simulator-based study, St Pierre et al (2012) looked at the willingness of residents and nursing staff to challenge deliberate errors committed by attending physicians. They found that the attending was only challenged in 28% of situations. When they did challenge they used crisp advocacy-inquiry (40%), an oblique statement (35%) or addressed the problem without pursuing it further (25%). When asked why they did not challenge, 37% had no answer, 35% admitted to there being a discrepancy between what they knew and what they did, 12% explained that the authority gradient prevented them from speaking up, while 8% stated that attendings routinely violated standard operating procedures without being challenged.

Collaborative, shared, collective leadership

Responses to adverse events and reports on teamworking routinely emphasise the need to move away from a hierarchical, 'command and control' leadership style to one of distributed, shared, collaborative or collective leadership. The evidence that this type of team and organisational leadership impacts positively on health outcomes, the patient experience and staff morale is growing (West et al, 2015). The strong focus on quality improvement and patient safety philosophies drawn largely from non-health-care, safety-critical industries (such as aviation and nuclear power) underpins health professionals' leadership and teamwork, all of which aligns with a change in culture that promotes patient-centredness and high quality, safe, compassionate care (Francis, 2013). A key challenge that remains for leaders is to facilitate, support and empower individuals and groups to speak out and act when they see poor or unsafe health care.

Teaching and assessing teamwork

Professional standards, frameworks and guidance exist to help practising doctors, educators and learners to work out what knowledge, skills and behaviours are required to work in and lead teams effectively. In 2012, the General Medical Council published *Leadership and management for all doctors* outlining standards expected of doctors (General Medical Council, 2012a). These documents make it clear that effective teamworking and leadership is a professional obligation, expected of all doctors. In England, the Healthcare Leadership Model has been introduced which aims to help professionalise leadership at all levels of health care through defining expected leadership behaviours (NHS Leadership Academy, 2013). Such frameworks and standards help educators and learners to define what is expected from them.

The Faculty of Medical Leadership and Management was established in 2011 to 'promote the advancement of medical leadership, management and quality improvement at all stages of the medical career' (Faculty of Medical Leadership and Management, 2014). Membership provides access to events, expertise, coaching and mentoring support and a range of resources on leadership and management. In 2015, the Faculty of Medical Leadership and Management *Leadership and Management Standards for Medical Professionals* were launched, again to assist medical leaders and managers to benchmark themselves against best practice.

Worldwide, there has been an increase in defined leadership curricula and the provision of training in non-technical skills, professionalism, teamwork and leadership at all levels (see Chapter 4). Teamwork and leadership have most commonly been subsumed under the banner of professionalism or non-technical skills in both undergraduate and postgraduate training. A number of teaching, learning and assessment methods have been developed to assist with these challenging educational aspects and evidence is emerging as to their effectiveness. In classroom-based situations, facilitating learners to work in multiple teams with directed reflection and to engage in team-building exercises can be beneficial, even before they are working clinically.

Structured observation of clinical and other teams can also help provide insight into how teams work in practice, supported by presentations around teamworking, who works in teams and by consideration of patient safety issues when teams go wrong. For example, the objective structured teaching exercise (OSTE) has been developed to help faculty teach professionalism in clinical settings (Lu et al, 2014). Acquiring, practising and obtaining feedback on teamworking and leadership skills in a longitudinal developmental way is best undertaken through workplace-based learning and assessment, including multi-source feedback, e.g. the team assessment of behaviour (TAB) assessment in the Foundation Programme. Structured portfolios, which combine practical assessment with reflection, can help support long-term teamworking and leadership development.

Written tests include prioritisation tests and situational judgement tests and while these can be helpful to provide a point in time assessment, unless they form part of a programmatic assessment, they do not aid long-term practice development. Simulation provides many opportunities for practising skills and obtaining feedback on teamworking: through simple role play to engagement in high fidelity scenarios. For example, the University of Dundee has developed a postgraduate ward simulation exercise which assesses teamwork and leadership skills such as the 'ability to prioritise competing demands, make safe informed decisions, prescribe safely and manage the care of three patients' (Stirling et al, 2012).

Khan et al (2011) argue that the realistic simulated environment improves memory recall and application of this information. This supports the use of simulation-based assessment in terms of its catalytic effect on promoting positive behavioural change (Norcini et al, 2011). In addition, the simulated environment may provide the opportunity for learning in action, which appears to be a more effective learning method (O'Sullivan et al, 2012). In their study with medical undergraduates, Paskins and Peile (2010) found that students thought that the use of mannequin-based simulation allowed them to develop teamwork skills not only as a more efficient team member but also as a leader. This finding supports the use of simulation to assess teamwork and leadership. The authors also found that students exposed to simulation were more confident in their clinical attachments and that they valued both repeated exposure and the feedback on their performance. Khan et al (2011) also argue for the use of simulation in the longitudinal assessment of performance, helping to 'bridge the gap between the classrooms and the clinical environments'.

Conclusions

Being able to work effectively in and lead teams as required is a vital skill for any health professional because effective teams form the cornerstone of high quality health care and contribute to health improvement and patient safety. Much research evidence tells us that high performing teams have clear shared goals, clarity of leadership that is authentic and distributed throughout the team, creative (not destructive) conflict and effective communication. Team leaders and members treat one another with respect and mutual trust, they know their strengths and roles, and power, authority and control are not allowed to become issues. Team members are empowered to challenge if they feel patient safety or care is at risk. The challenge for leaders is to create and maintain this culture across and between multiple teams in what are often very complex and rapidly changing contexts.

Key points

- The ability to work within and between teams is a core leadership skill
- Effective multidisciplinary teamwork contributes to improved health outcomes and a higher quality of care
- Effective teams need clear goals, shared leadership and ongoing review of performance
- Leaders need to be aware of power–distance, authority and control mechanisms which can undermine effective teamworking
- Many teams operate dysfunctionally – 'pseudoteams' have few of the characteristics of successful teams, i.e. interdependency, reflexivity and shared objectives.

Section 2 – Leadership at all levels

CHAPTER 7

Developing and harnessing the leadership potential of doctors in training

Alex Till, Graeme Pettifer, Judy McKimm, Helen O'Sullivan

Introduction

This chapter considers existing leadership approaches operating within health-care organisations and suggests why and how these should be reviewed to harness the leadership potential of doctors in training through engaging in quality improvement. It is based on the article by Till et al (2014).

One of the key guiding principles of the NHS is its aspiration to provide the highest standards of excellence and professionalism, putting patients at the heart of all it does (Department of Health, 2009b). In recent years this guiding principle has sometimes been compromised and led to catastrophic lapses in the care provided to (often very vulnerable) patients who must be protected and who must be able to trust doctors with their lives and health. A key challenge the medical profession faces is how to overcome lapses in care and develop institutional cultures in which all those involved in delivering the service put the patient first by prioritising the delivery of high quality care and patient safety (Berwick, 2013; Francis, 2013). Doctors' ability to do this is one of the most striking features yet one of the defining weaknesses of the NHS. Often the service fails to engage many doctors in leadership and management roles to an extent that it disempowers and alienates them – one of the common themes running through landmark inquiries and reports (The King's Fund, 2011; Francis, 2013; Keogh, 2013).

Leadership approaches

The Francis report (2013) identifies doctors in training as the 'valuable eyes and ears' on the frontline. Keogh (2013) goes further and suggests that they must be harnessed as an extraordinary leadership resource and that their energy, creativity and ideas must be used so they can act as powerful agents for change. A fundamental shift away from existing leadership styles is needed to successfully unlock and focus doctors in training's inherent enthusiasm for promoting excellence in health care and their ability to act as the strong, influential clinical leaders needed within our health services. Many writers have emphasized this, including Bohmer (2010) who highlights the ways in which doctors in training can adopt active followership and 'little l' leadership to influence quality improvement.

Authoritarian leadership and clinical autonomy

Leaders must welcome and respond to safety concerns directly, rapidly and, most importantly, openly to enable 'followers' to raise concerns when they believe that a lack of skills, knowledge or resources is placing patients at risk of harm (Berwick, 2013). For some years, however, it is has been noted that western health care has enshrined (and rewarded) a culture in which leadership is hierarchical and primarily functions through dominant 'command and control', 'heroic' and authoritarian leadership styles (Swanwick and McKimm, 2010; The King's Fund, 2011). Combined with an historical expectation that the delivery of quality care is a personal responsibility, this leadership style typically results in a fierce attachment to individualized clinical autonomy. Such autonomy is in direct conflict with a systems approach to quality and safety, the notion of collective leadership, and the need for attention to be paid to the non-technical aspects of clinical medicine (e.g. teamwork, communication) which account for the overwhelming majority of adverse events (Reinertsen, 2003).

In contrast, within the business world, where authoritarian leaders have a very positive effect on productivity (e.g. Goleman et al, 2002), research has shown that highly authoritarian leaders have a damaging effect on health workers and their patients (Alimo-Metcalfe and Alban-Metcalfe, 2005). In particular, their controlling, closed-minded and power-orientated approach creates a repressive and dictatorial regime whereby a culture of fear among staff is fostered, they are demoralized, and feel robbed of the authority to make decisions (Bass, 2008; Commission on Dignity in Care for Older People, 2012). Ultimately, this can lead to teams being afraid to report errors, being less inclined to admit mistakes and under-performing in their leader's absence, resulting in higher levels of unsafe practice and poor quality care (Giltinane, 2013). Keogh (2009) identified that if doctors in training are led in an authoritarian manner and not given the opportunity to discuss and report on quality of care by challenging the status quo, then threats to patient safety will remain unrecognized.

Moving away from a traditional 'command and control', hierarchical leadership style to collaborative, shared, distributed leadership or collective leadership (West et al, 2014) has been identified as one of the enablers for doctors in training to take responsibility for compassionate and effective patient care alongside colleagues from other professions. Integral to this ideological shift is a simultaneous investment in patient safety and quality improvement science training to equip medical students and doctors in training with the skills and knowledge to improve safe patient care and the quality of health services. These coordinated actions will help doctors stay true to their core professional values of delivering excellent high quality health care and support the development of the leadership potential required to enable the NHS to survive, thrive and become not only one of the leading, but one of the safest health-care institutions in the world (Berwick, 2013).

Transformational leadership

While a shift towards collective leadership is being promulgated, many of the concepts that underpin transformational leadership are still highly relevant. As leadership theory develops, each approach or concept supplements others: effective leaders and successful organisations must draw from a range of approaches to fit the situation or context.

In terms of a transformational leadership style, leaders should execute the 'Four I's' – Idealised influence, Inspirational motivation, Individualised consideration and Intellectual stimulation (Bass, 2008) – and consider adopting a coaching and mentoring relationship with their followers. Consultants' investment in time, energy and personal know-how through supervision will be pivotal in facilitating the growth and development of the knowledge, skills and behaviours embedded within our doctors in training. Used effectively, this will create a generation able to lead in the highly complex, rapidly changing environment that characterizes the NHS and to deliver tangible improvements through innovation, creation and approaching old situations in creative new ways (Avolio and Bass, 2002; The Health Foundation, 2011b; Warren and Carnall, 2011).

Leaders vs leadership

As leaders and leadership capacity is developed, it is important to remember that within complex health-care systems and organisations this operates at three distinct levels: the intrapersonal, the interpersonal and the system or organisational (Dickinson and Ham, 2008, see also Chapter 12). Leaders require intrapersonal abilities to use their authenticity, congruence and 'charisma' to be seen as a role model whom followers want to emulate. They need the interpersonal skills and emotional intelligence to stimulate and engage followers to explore new approaches and finally, the understanding of the organisation or system so that they can translate the organisation's vision, strategies and activities to followers who then take ownership and responsibility for service delivery and improvement. Here, leaders also need to acknowledge the complexity of systems and take a complex adaptive leadership approach (Plsek and Wilson, 2001).

Effectively delivered, this leadership disperses personal attention to the extent whereby leadership becomes a fluid and emergent property of the group with 'little l leaders' and 'active followers' dispersed throughout (Bohmer, 2010). Ideally, cultural and professional barriers become dissolved with all members of the health-care team contributing to patient care at the appropriate time, in the appropriate context and in an appropriate fashion (Avolio and Bass, 2002; Bass, 2008). Within case scenario 7.1 we see one such mechanism to try and achieve this and reduce the 'power gap' frequently existing between front-line health-care professionals and their leaders.

Leadership for the future – shared, distributed and collective?

Over the last two decades in the UK, a shift in the theoretical concepts under-pinning health-care leadership and culture has been occurring. As noted above, previously dominant cultural norms are becoming outdated and the negative effects of authoritarian leadership on safety culture increasingly recognized (Alimo-Metcalfe, 1998; Alimo-Metcalfe and Alban-Metcalfe, 2005). The con-cepts of transformational leadership (Bass, 2008) and emotional intelligence (Goleman et al, 2002) are increasingly enshrined in policy rhetoric and leader-ship quality frameworks as embodying the essence of clinical leadership (e.g. NHS Confederation and The Nuffield Trust, 1999; NHS Institute for Innova-tion and Improvement and Academy of Medical Royal Colleges, 2010a).

While transformational leadership and emotional intelligence emphasize the qualities and influence of individual leaders (and have been critiqued for the focus on developing individual leaders' qualities) such concepts also exhort leaders to place value and attention on the development of followers who previously were almost seen as passive recipients of their leaders' actions. Transformational leaders recognize the need to engage and develop their fol-lowers by inspiring, motivating and empowering them to not only expand

---

Case scenario 7.1 Being the 'eyes and ears'

The Chief Executive of a large hospital takes two hours a month to meet with groups of doctors in training from different departments over a pizza lunch. He says that although he 'walks round' the hospital on a daily basis, through these meetings he hears about a wide range of practices which could be improved. He notes how refreshing it is to hear from the doctors who genuinely want to improve patient care and uses the meetings as a 'barometer' to test out how some of the patient safety and care initiatives (such as 'say your name'; 'provide a drink') are going. By hearing directly from the doctors in training, he learns about some of the barriers and helpful activities going on around the hospital and feels it helps them to keep in touch and come to him if they wish to raise something that is worrying them. The doctors in training think this is a good idea, they feel valued and listened to, and they have already seen some changes based on the meetings.

---

their potential, by broadening their horizons and satisfying their higher order developmental needs, but also by contributing to maintaining high standards of care, achieving better health outcomes and the shared vision of, in this case, high quality care (Avolio and Bass, 2002; Bass, 2008).

The King's Fund (2012) describes the most effective transformational leaders as working through their followers and achieving objectives by sharing and distributing leadership throughout the team so that leadership becomes a collective property. The notion of transformational leadership is shifting to incorporate shared, distributed and collaborative leadership, in which social capital and capacity is being built. Such capacity building includes fostering a sustainable leadership resource through the development of followers and, as identified by the NHS Constitution, by motivating and empowering followers to put forward new ways to design, manage and deliver more effective and safer services for patients and their families to achieve higher levels of excellence and a consistent focus on the needs of the patients being served. This brings in notions of 'servant leadership' (Greenleaf, 2002) in which leaders and followers understand that leadership is not about them as an individual but rather their ability to establish leadership broadly across the organisation as a whole (Bass, 2008; Darzi, 2008; Department of Health, 2009b; The King's Fund, 2012).

The trend for transformational leadership has been supplemented by calls to adopt a strategy for collective leadership (Eckert et al, 2014; West et al, 2014). By applying this strategy, 'the leadership culture must be understood as the product of collective actions of formal and informal leaders acting together to influence organisational success' (Eckert et al, 2014). This cultural shift requires coordinated activities, drawing on a range of leadership approaches, to empower all members of the health-care team to harness the leadership capabilities of doctors in training.

Harnessing capability

Doctors in training want to give more than is currently expected of them and make a significant contribution beyond clinical care by leading improvements that improve the quality of care for patients (Bagnall, 2012), but harnessing their capability is challenging. Simply understanding the requirement for a cultural shift in leadership towards a transformational or collective approach will not in itself foster a nurturing environment for trainees. Opportunities must be developed to enable doctors in training to implement change and deliver results. For example, Keogh (2013) suggests that doctors in training can gain penetrating insights into potential patient safety threats, see the whole spectrum of care and gain awareness of the patient perspective by working over the whole 24-hour period, 7 days a week.

Quality improvement

One such cultural shift is from clinicians' focus on quality assurance (audit) to quality improvement: 'achieving better patient experience and outcomes through changing provider behaviour and organisation through systematic change methods and strategies' (Øvretveit, 2009). Developed appropriately and in the right circumstances, the capability of doctors in training can be harnessed through quality improvement, using a large but undervalued (in leadership terms) part of the medical workforce (The King's Fund, 2012; Keogh, 2013). Central to this is using methods from quality improvement science which challenge a traditional philosophy that delivery of high-quality care is an individual's autonomous decision and responsibility, to one that takes full account of the overall systems in which care is delivered. This moves further away from a 'blame culture' and makes the delivery of high-quality care and the duty to identify and reduce the risks to the safety of patients everyone's responsibility (Berwick, 2013). One of the strengths of engaging doctors in training (through education and training initiatives) as central to NHS organisations' innovation and improvement strategies is that they can use their energy, creativity and ideas to reduce errors, improve safety and transform health care by identifying areas for improvement that more experienced clinicians may take for granted.

Doctors in training therefore need to be equipped with the skills to understand and implement quality improvement science and be given the opportunities to lead and participate in quality improvement projects within their clinical environment (Boonyasai et al, 2007; The Health Foundation, 2011b; Berwick, 2013). Vital to this combination of theoretical and experiential learning is collaboration between medical educators and health-care leaders to embed this approach early within undergraduate education and postgraduate training (Ogrinc et al, 2003). Despite an already crowded curriculum, investment in and formal incorporation of quality improvement education is essential if we are to realise the widespread improvements needed within the NHS. To successfully achieve this, we must leverage regulatory requirements, such as the General Medical Council's mandate for quality improvement activity to be incorporated in doctors' appraisal and revalidation, and the growing requirements within postgraduate curricula for trainees to have undertaken quality improvement projects.

Alongside these initiatives, the doctor in training's position within formal and/or informal organisational networks should be considered. While formal authority is an important source of influence and power, change can be successfully orchestrated from those centrally positioned within informal networks through accessing stakeholders, information, opportunities and personal support (Battilana and Casciaro, 2012). One of the key roles of a clinical leader is to support doctors in training in their efforts to establish a position within these networks, especially when they are new to an organisation or team.

Benefits of engaging doctors in training

The benefits of harnessing capability are clear, with many, as outlined in case scenarios 7.2 and 7.3, beginning to realise this. The potential for the NHS to be a learning organisation through providing opportunities for collaboration and engagement in quality improvement is a powerful impetus for improving patient safety (Berwick, 2013). Through direct observation of the benefits of their actions, doctors in training can enhance their leadership skills and their engagement in constructive conversations about improving safety and prioritising future quality improvements (Diaz et al, 2010; The Health Foundation, 2011b). Harnessed and developed from the outset, doctors in training can help establish a culture firmly rooted in continuous quality improvement, deliver the highest possible quality of care to patients and provide the best possible deal for the taxpayer (Dickinson and Ham, 2008; The King's Fund, 2011; Berwick, 2013). Furthermore, employing organisations will see direct benefits from their investment in doctors in training. Trainees' job satisfaction, wellbeing and productivity will increase as they feel more valued. In turn, this is likely to increase their loyalty to the investing health-care organisation and aid staff retention; this is particularly important as trainees frequently change jobs nationally and organisations can lose their investment.

The 'enlightened doctor in training'

While the development of current medical leaders might incorporate new approaches, cultural shifts towards collective leadership and the responsibility for system changes to facilitate engagement of doctors in training are important. Attention needs to be paid to how individual doctors are developed and the development of the 'enlightened doctor in training' is imperative. This is a doctor who recognises him-/herself as a powerful agent for change (more so than his/her seniors) able to influence the quality of care that a patient receives. Other agents for change could be other members of health professions such as nurses and health-care assistants.

Rather than being disillusioned by the barriers and challenges that exist within the NHS, the enlightened doctor in training looks beyond this to what can potentially be achieved. The enlightened doctor in training takes heed of the strength, courage and determination shown by inspiring patients who fight

---

Case scenario 7.2 'Beyond audit'

The London Deanery's 'Beyond audit' initiative aimed to recognise, encourage and support doctors in training to participate and lead quality improvement initiatives (Dharamshi and Hillman, 2011). The Deanery provides a wide range of online resources, such as templates for planning and evaluating projects supervised by 'Darzi fellows' (senior trainees appointed to undertake longer term projects, typically with a year out of training). This type of scheme is now widespread in the UK with many deaneries and local education training boards offering similar schemes where doctors in training at various levels (from FIs through to near-consultants) learn from their peers and share experiences and knowledge. Some schemes are underpinned by opportunities to gain postgraduate qualifications in clinical leadership or quality improvement. Embedding the scheme at local level is vital in order for the trusts, health boards or organisations to engage the doctors in valued quality improvement projects and to develop a sustainable culture of quality improvement. If organisations can identify projects in which the trainees can engage, provide supervisors or mentors who can break down barriers and help them network and provide a forum for dissemination, the trainees' capability is harnessed and their energy is aligned with organisational goals.

life-threatening or debilitating disease on a daily basis to develop the internal motivation to fight and challenge expectations. The doctor in training is proactive, relishing the opportunity to seize frustrations and, rather than waiting for change to happen, like their patients, overcomes this.

Exerting an inherent passion for high quality health care and desire to 'do no harm' (which health-care professionals exhibit as they enter their professions) the enlightened doctor in training shares concerns, frustrations and ideas with followers and uses this as a powerful tool to effect change and uphold patient safety though quality improvement. While such internal values and motivators are not endemic throughout the workforce, without large scale cultural change the enlightened doctor in training will remain a minority and their propensity for change, to deliver high quality health care throughout the NHS, will not be realised.

Case scenario 7.3 'Passing the baton'

In 2013, the University Hospitals of Leicester NHS Trust identified five critical safety actions as part of its strategy to address patient safety issues by improving clinical practice:

- Acting on results
- Improving clinical handover
- Relentless action to early warning scores
- Senior clinical review/ward rounds
- Implement and embed mortality and morbidity standards.

A large number of people and teams are involved in the actions, with each area broken down into different smaller projects. As part of their Academic Foundation Programme in Clinical Leadership and Management, three of the F2s were matched to different projects for a year. While the F2s themselves did not necessarily complete their parts of the projects, because the programme is embedded in the Trust's activities, the following year, another group of F2s picked up these projects and took them forward. Passing the baton enables the Trust to maintain momentum for longer-term projects, senior managers know they will have a new group prepared to take projects on and can earmark these for the doctors in training. The F2s are reassured that they don't have to finish a project if its duration needs to be longer and they are encouraged to take a longer-term view of sustainable change, rather than fall foul of 'projectitis'.

Conclusions

Doctors are frequently seen at the head of health-care teams and their leadership role is increasingly important (Tooke, 2008). Enabling doctors in training to work at an 'enlightened level' will help drive impetus and momentum for change and the cultural transformation necessary for leadership of high quality health care. Without transformation in action, harnessing capability and collective leadership, the complexities and unanticipated challenges of clinical medicine are likely to leave many doctors in training frustrated and disillusioned. To develop the motivation for improvement at scale, their willingness to be 'agents for change' must be encouraged and leadership skills must be recognized alongside research and academic skills (Bagnall, 2012). Leadership education and training should no longer remain a minority interest but core to any discipline related to the modern NHS.

In keeping with this shift towards full integration, the focus must not only be on immediate service provision but also on a transformation of the clinical environment into an active training opportunity with time provided within rotas for regular supervision and reflection. Supporting this, mentorship and a transformational and collective leadership style needs to be adopted by senior clinicians to encourage doctors in training to overcome the ingrained attitudes and 'ways of doing things' to undertake activities beyond clinical practice, such as quality improvement (The Health Foundation, 2011b). The challenge ahead is to ensure that leadership is present at all levels, reaches every individual and is exercised across shifts 24/7. Doctors should be encouraged to think of themselves as leaders, not because they are personally exceptional, senior or inspirational to others, but because they can see where improvements are needed and actively engage with quality improvements (Turnbull, 2011).

The combination of investment and formal incorporation of quality improvement science training into the mandatory teaching requirements for all specialties, alongside offering doctors in training the opportunity to actively participate in practical improvements to systems of care, will harness their enthusiasm and dedication to lead and will help develop this substantial, but undervalued part of the medical workforce. Drawing on an informed, appropriate range of leadership theories and concepts to underpin clinical practice will help leaders and followers alike to effect sustainable, meaningful health-care improvements.

Key points

- Embracing and developing doctors in training into enlightened trainees as a frontline NHS leadership resource must be incorporated as a matter of routine
- Transformational and collective leadership must replace authoritarian, hierarchical attitudes to unlock the potential of doctors in training to harness their capability to act as powerful agents for change
- Proactive systems of quality improvement must replace traditional cultures of audit and quality assurance to improve patient safety and challenge the status quo
- Mandatory quality improvement science training must begin early in medical education, supported by dedicated time to apply this in clinical settings.

CHAPTER 8

Medical leadership and the medical student

Helen O'Sullivan, Judy McKimm

Introduction

As leadership and management are increasingly seen as a vital part of the doctor's daily repertoire, medical schools are starting to implement leadership development programmes as a routine part of the curriculum with opportunities for some students to take extended study in leadership. This chapter is based on an article by O'Sullivan and McKimm (2011a).

'Our clear view is that doctors have for 25 years, perhaps longer, been failing to give the leadership of which they are eminently capable, and which society rightly expects of them' (Royal College of Physicians, 2010).

This quote sums up the consensus that doctors need to take on and develop leadership and management. A logical consequence of this requirement is the need to make leadership and management development much more explicit in the undergraduate curriculum. This is endorsed by the General Medical Council in the 2009 version of *Tomorrow's Doctors*:

'Medical students are tomorrow's doctors. In accordance with *Good Medical Practice*, graduates will make the care of their patients their first concern, applying their knowledge and skills in a competent and ethical manner and using their ability to provide leadership and analyse complex and uncertain situations' (General Medical Council, 2009).

What's the research evidence?

Although policy agendas and professional standards demonstrate a clear need for doctors to develop leadership and management skills, the benefits of introducing development initiatives in the undergraduate years are unclear. Reflecting the relatively recent focus on targeted leadership curriculum developments, no clear empirical evidence exists to suggest that leadership development in undergraduate programmes has an impact on doctors' subsequent leadership qualities and abilities.

Three studies carried out in the USA describe examples of leadership development in undergraduate programmes. A survey of medical school curricula suggested that leadership and team working skills can be successfully introduced into curricula. However, the authors concluded that many of the exercises designed to develop leadership and team working were conducted in the clinical setting, learning outcomes for leadership development were implicit rather than explicit and that leadership development was rarely the main purpose of the activity (O'Connell and Pascoe, 2004). An optional retreat to develop leadership and teaching in medical undergraduates took place at Mount Sinai School of Medicine (Smith et al, 2007) and in self-reported pre- and post-test evaluations, participants reported significant improvements in their leadership skills. This was maintained in a follow-up post-test, 11 months after the programme. The participants indicated a strong preference for experiential learning and for working with an experienced mentor. Varkey et al (2009) surveyed the views of medical students and faculty members on what leadership and management skills need to be developed in the undergraduate years, asking medical students in which of these areas they felt that they had made sufficient progress. They concluded that the best place to start the lifelong learning required is in undergraduate programmes. Emotional intelligence, confidence, humility and creativity are considered the most important personal qualities required in a medical leader. Teamwork, communication, resource management and quality improvement are the most important knowledge and skills to be taught in undergraduate programmes. Students felt least competent in areas of resource management, business practice and knowledge of leadership theory. They identified simulation, role play, faculty-led study groups and case studies as the most effective teaching methods.

A study of 22 medical chief executives in the NHS reported highly variable experiences of training and development for their posts (Ham et al, 2011). The report concludes that these self-styled 'keen amateurs' needed a more structured and formal approach to their development and that this should start much earlier in their career. This is consistent with a study of UK senior health professions' educators which notes variable (or no) experience of leadership development, a need for formalised structured programmes and lack of succession planning by organisations (McKimm, 2004).

A number of writers suggest that leadership development should start in the undergraduate programme (e.g. Clark and Armit, 2008). In 2009 and 2010 a series of recorded consultation events in medical professionalism '21st century doctor: your future, your choices' involved 492 medical students in detailed discussions. Students were asked their views on medical leadership and management. The report summarising the findings recommends more leadership and management development in the undergraduate curriculum and further discussion and consultation on how to best achieve this (Levenson et al, 2010). Finally, a study investigating differing perceptions of male and female leaders in medicine concluded that all doctors would benefit from more understanding of what leadership and management entailed at undergraduate level (Crolla and Bamforth, 2011).

It is more difficult to establish an empirical link between undergraduate leadership training and patient outcomes, but two studies demonstrate the potential. As part of a quality improvement project at Ohio State University Medical Centre, first and second year medical students were required to complete a self-paced online program that provided preliminary education in quality improvement, patient safety, leadership, teamwork, and patient-centred care. They then completed a face-to-face session that comprised multimedia simulation in the use of a preoperative surgical safety checklist and role play in the use of the checklist. Results of the study included an increased knowledge of quality improvement methodology, an improved understanding of the evidence supporting the need for quality improvement projects within health systems, and a greater awareness of available quality improvement projects. In addition, students' attitudes towards quality improvement changes with an increased belief that quality improvement is the responsibility of all health professionals. This study concluded that leadership education with a focus on quality improvement can be effective in early medical education and can result in students' actions that have the potential to support improvements in patient outcomes (Gonsenhauser et al, 2012). Before that, Hunziker et al (2010) demonstrated an improvement in patient outcomes in a randomised controlled trial where medical students were given leadership training before completing a high-fidelity simulation exercise in cardiopulmonary resuscitation.

Leadership and management skills

'Obviously, leadership is an important part of management but every doctor is a leader... even the junior doctors are leaders in respect to the medical students, a fourth year (student) is a leader in respect to a third year, ...managers are leaders in an organisational sense whereas all doctors are leaders' (Levenson et al, 2010).

This quote from a medical student acknowledges that undergraduates need to have leadership skills in order to be successful medical students (let alone successful doctors) but highlights the potential reluctance in medical students to recognise the need for specific management skills. At medical school it can be argued that leadership and management development has two aims. First, to provide all students with the leadership and management skills that they will need to be a doctor and the understanding to work with in the health service that employs them (Chantler, 1999). Second, the curriculum must also offer inspiration and development opportunities for those who show potential for senior leadership at this early stage.

What is the difference between leadership and management?

Leadership and management are often used interchangeably and there is a lot of overlap between the two activities and some debate over precise definitions of each. Both leaders and managers may have involvement in setting direction, allocating resources and motivating people. Over the last decade, there has been a shift from the NHS being managed by 'professional' managers, the majority of whom did not have clinical backgrounds, to a mixed model where non-clinical managers work alongside clinical managers to deliver the service. This partly came about to address the widening divide between managers and clinicians. Managers were typically seen as target driven, budget focused and not appreciative of the complexities of delivering high quality patient care whereas doctors were seen as subverting management decisions and failing to understand the need to work towards targets and keep to budgets (McKimm, 2011b). Management was seen as 'the dark side' (Spurgeon et al, 2011).

Such stereotypes were not only unhelpful, but also did not reflect the reality of many experienced clinicians and managers who worked together in harmony. However, increasing calls have been made to address these issues and engage doctors more actively in leadership (e.g. Imison and Giordano, 2009). While it is now widely accepted that all doctors need leadership skills as part of being a professional, there is still some ingrained reluctance to see management as being a key role. Some doctors see management as a diversion from patient care and a compromise to their commitment to put the patient first (Levenson et al, 2010). A medical student expressed the following reservations:

'These words "leaders" and "managers" are bandied about a lot and I have trouble actually seeing what that would really mean for a doctor. I can see what NHS managers do but I am not sure if that means a doctor taking the role of an NHS manager or just managing a medical team' (Levenson et al, 2010).

Part of the role of medical educators should be to help medical students understand the differences and appreciate the importance of both of these activities.

What styles of leadership could be introduced at undergraduate level?

Leaders are often characterised as all powerful, charismatic and heroic individuals who personally take their organisation forward against great odds. In the current economic climate it is argued that we are in a 'post-heroic' leadership phase where a more inclusive and engaging style of leadership is appropriate (Alimo-Metcalfe and Alban-Metcalfe, 2006). Indeed, a longitudinal study of effective leadership in public sector organisations has shown that one personal quality – the ability to engage with others – is a significant predictor of organisational effectiveness (Alimo-Metcalfe et al, 2008).

It is not always easy for medical students and junior doctors to see where they might fit into the large bureaucracy of the NHS, and more difficult still to see what sort of leadership or management role might be appropriate. Followership and the ability to take leadership from another is an important part of the undergraduate experience to prepare students for working effectively in multidisciplinary teams (see Chapter 15). In a study of newly graduated doctors and nurses, '70% of nurses thought nurses should make decisions on behalf of an interprofessional team, but 80% of doctors disagreed' (Barrow et al, 2011). Although this work was done in New Zealand, similar views would probably be expressed in other contexts. For example, the Royal College of Physicians (2010) suggested that doctors must accept that they will no longer automatically be leaders of the multidisciplinary team, even though patients may continue to assume that the doctor is in charge. Many medical schools already have extensive programmes of interprofessional and multidisciplinary training and some aspects of team working and leadership may fit into this context.

Raising awareness of leadership development in undergraduates can have a significant impact on the way that they perceive their potential role in future leadership. For example, after a three-day leadership development programme delivered for undergraduate medical students at Hull-York Medical School, students showed a significant increase in their acceptance of the need for leadership training and the idea that everyone is a leader (Dobson et al, 2008).

Curriculum frameworks

In response to the need for doctors' more active involvement in the review, planning, delivery and transformation of health services, the Academy of Medical Royal Colleges and the NHS Institute for Innovation and Improvement with a wide range of stakeholders established a UK-wide project: Enhancing Engagement in Medical Leadership.

One outcome was the Medical Leadership Competency Framework (MLCF) (*Figure 8.1*) (NHS Institute for Innovation and Improvement and Academy of Medical Royal Colleges, 2010a), which described the skills and competencies that medical students and doctors need in order to contribute to

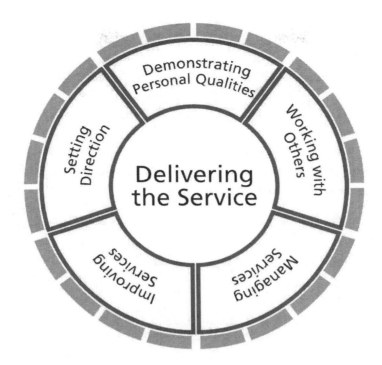

Figure 8.1 Medical Leadership Competency Framework. From NHS Institute for Innovation and Improvement and Academy of Medical Royal Colleges (2010a)

running successful services. The framework has five domains: demonstrating personal qualities, working with others, managing services, improving services and setting direction, but rightly recognises that not all of these will be as important to medical students so developed a separate section for undergraduate medical education.

In *Guidance for Undergraduate Medical Education: Integrating the Medical Leadership Competency Framework* (NHS Institute for Innovation and Improvement and the Academy of Medical Royal Colleges, 2010b) the Framework was mapped to *Tomorrow's Doctors* (General Medical Council, 2009) to ensure consistency between it and the General Medical Council's outcomes for medical education. In 2012, Powell et al used an online questionnaire to investigate the extent to which the MLCF was being used to structure leadership development in undergraduate medical education. Sixty-nine course leads were invited to participate in the questionnaire study and were asked whether they teach each MLCF competency, which teaching methods they use, and how long they spend teaching each competency. A map of current leadership teaching was produced showing that all MLCF competences are taught to varying degrees across the curriculum. The study did not explore the quality of teaching provided or what the students actually learn.

Developing leadership and management skills in undergraduates

Opportunities exist in the curriculum to practice and demonstrate leadership skills, many of which are set out as specific outcomes in the 'Doctor as a professional' section of *Tomorrow's Doctors*. This outlines some of the types of activities that can be incorporated to enable students to demonstrate each aspect of the MLCF. Some of the suggestions (labelled 'a possible scenario for...') are taken from the guidance for integrating the MLCF into undergraduate medical education (NHS Institute for Innovation and Improvement and the Academy of Medical Royal Colleges, 2010b) which includes resources already in use in a number of UK medical schools and is supplemented with detailed guidance giving specific outcomes for each stage of the Framework.

Demonstrating personal qualities

The fundamental underpinning of leadership development and medical professionalism is an understanding of the personal qualities that are important in the delivery of high standards of care. These qualities are closely linked with the qualities required to be a good doctor and are often part of personal and professional development modules or programmes. For example, students often keep a portfolio which includes a requirement for reflective writing. However, we cannot assume that students are fully able to reflect effectively; reflection is also a skill that needs to be taught and developed, so activities in the early years should be structured to facilitate this.

Working with others

Students on medical undergraduate programmes need to learn to cooperate and work collaboratively from the very start, both in the clinical setting and the classroom. All medical schools make extensive use of small group teaching and for those who use problem-based learning, the collaborative nature is even more formally embedded. Interprofessional learning can also be effective in helping students to work more collaboratively with other health professionals (World Health Organization, 2010).

Managing services

Understanding how services are managed is vital but becomes even more important in the current climate of structural reorganisation and cutbacks in public spending. Students need an understanding of health-care systems and organisations coupled with opportunities to engage in management activities (see case scenario 8.1).

Case scenario 8.1 managing services

While on placement at their local hospital, students C and L are invited to work with managers in the hospital complaints department to help investigate and respond to a patient complaint relating to a refusal by the organisation to prescribe an expensive drug. The students review the letter of complaint, seek advice on the hospital policy for prescribing and how this relates to National Institute for Health and Care Excellence guidelines, and discuss the case with members of the clinical team. They help to draft a letter of response to the patient, and write a summary report which they present to their clinical supervisor and peers, highlighting the management issues that arose.

Improving services

As well as the core curriculum and the clinical context, specialist student selected components can enable students to take part in service improvement activities or clinical audits. In some schools, student selected components include an intercalated degree. For example, the Imperial College London MBBS/BSc programme has offered a very popular BSc in Health Management option (run in conjunction with the business school) since 1998. Students from this and similar programmes have gone on to undertake academic foundation programmes in clinical leadership and management (see case scenario 8.2).

Case scenario 8.2 improving services

Students in the early years of the curriculum meet with patients in the ward to implement the use of patient safety tools and medicine reconciliation in the clinical setting, having learned about and practised using simulation activities. Students record and critically evaluate the different challenges of using these in clinical practice, and explore the links from this to possible audit of patient safety.

Case scenario 8.3 setting direction

Sheffield Medical School offers a leadership in the NHS symposium for graduating final year student doctors, where speakers with international reputations offer personal perspectives on clinical leadership. The symposium provides an understanding of different leadership styles, the role of emotional intelligence in leading and managing others and the role of 'nearby leadership' in the NHS. It also allows students to analyse their own experiences of leading and being led during clinical rotations. Students particularly value the emotional intelligence component and the exercises intended to develop self-awareness.

Acknowledgements to Pirashanthie Vivekananda-Schmidt for this example

Setting direction

It is often hard for undergraduates to think about more 'senior' aspects of leadership such as vision setting or setting direction. Exposing them to different leaders and hearing their stories can help students see how such leadership works in practice, see case scenario 8.3.

Liverpool Medical School offers fellowships for students who have been elected to lead the student medical society, during which the students undertake a research project on an aspect of medical leadership and write a reflective report discussing their own leadership development during the fellowship (see case scenario 8.4).

Case scenario 8.4 A student-led leadership initiative at Swansea
Paul O'Connell, final year GEM student

As a graduate entry medical student with experience of leadership and management it occurred to me that the existing curriculum content in medical leadership and management at Swansea's College of Medicine might be augmented through student-led, extra-curricular activities. The idea was to initiate a student society and enable first-hand medical leadership and management experience so that leadership behaviours might be embedded before commencing work as a junior doctor. Additional support for this idea came via my role as Swansea University's student representative for the Faculty of Medical Leadership and Management.

An initial open meeting was arranged and an invitation emailed to all current Swansea medical students. Twenty people attended and a broad-ranging discussion was held around the concept of the society, its scope, aims and objectives and organisational structure. The society was named CLIPS (Clinical Leadership – Improving Patient Services) with aims and objectives to teach, support, inspire and encourage active cooperation through educational events, workshops and health-care improvement projects. In order to reflect the multidisciplinary nature of the profession, it was decided that the scope of the society would include all students of health-care-related subjects.

(continued overleaf)

Case scenario 8.4 A student-led leadership initiative at Swansea (continued)

Two further events were organised, the first of which was an evening of talks on medical leadership and management by experienced speakers and the second was an event called 'Placement 101' aimed at dispersing the apprehensions of 1st year students about to commence their first clinical placement. Lessons learned from the first event were applied to 'Placement 101' which was held in a venue outside the university and designed to be light-hearted and loosely educational with a quiz and prizes at the end. Feedback from both events was unanimously positive; attendance at the first was 11 medical students compared to 35 at the second.

The current committee of president, treasurer and secretary will be replaced before the year-end through an application and interview process for which several students have expressed an interest.

Introducing the concepts of mutual support and leadership behaviours through student-led activities may be a powerful way of augmenting the taught elements of medical leadership and management in medical schools. A wider audience can be reached through events which are framed as light-hearted and perhaps held in a venue outside the university so as to be dissociated from formal teaching and assessment. Student-led extra-curricular activities may catalyse inter-cohort education and foster an environment of mutual encouragement and support.

A diverse audience can be reached through events which are fun, educational and which address pastoral issues such as student apprehensions. Affiliation to a body such as the Faculty of Medical Leadership and Management lends legitimacy to the society's brand while providing networking support and advice for committee members.

Assessment

The literature on developing leadership and management skills in undergraduate curricula provides very little discussion on how to assess these skills within undergraduate programmes. There is, however, an extensive literature on assessing professionalism (e.g. Arnold, 2002; van Mook et al, 2009b) and many of the issues are common to both. The guidance for integrating the

MLCF into the undergraduate curriculum suggests using a range of existing formative and summative assessment methods including portfolios, reflective writing, multisource feedback, structured clinical assessments (e.g. objective structured clinical examinations) and written examinations. Peer assessment is also being used more widely in the assessment of professionalism (Garner et al, 2010) and could be adapted to assess leadership and team-working skills (see case scenario 8.5).

Conclusions

The MLCF has proved a powerful and highly useful tool that enables medical educators to structure leadership and management development in medical students. However, we need to keep a critical eye on the debate about the ultimate effectiveness of a competency-based approach to leadership development (Alimo-Metcalfe et al, 2008) and to ensure that introducing leadership along with other new requirements such as research and teaching skills does not further overburden curricula. More consensus and research needs to be

---

Case scenario 8.5 Assessing leadership

The Liverpool curriculum has introduced an innovative assessment tool for leadership and team working. A prototype was created using focus group data, literature review, analysis of current existing tools (e.g. anaesthetists' non-technical skills; Fletcher et al, 2003) and expert review of measured domains. Final year students' team working and leadership skills were assessed using a standardised clinical set up and scenarios in a patient simulation centre. The scenario had several components including testing for the ability to challenge a senior when they were clearly in the wrong and when patient safety was compromised. The scenarios were video recorded and independently evaluated. Project results showed that the Liverpool tool was easy to use in a simulated clinical environment with satisfactory inter-rater congruence and validity. In addition, the project highlighted issues with challenging authority in decision making and leadership (see Chapter 14).

---

undertaken on what the theoretical basis should be underpinning the leadership curriculum, who should deliver leadership training and how to ensure teachers are appropriately equipped.

Further work on developing innovative ways of developing and assessing leadership skills for large cohorts of students, coupled with research evaluating the effectiveness of the MLCF, will ensure that the next generation of doctors are fully equipped to meet the challenges of maintaining effective patient care in conditions of ongoing change and resource constraints.

Key points

- Doctors and medical students are required to demonstrate leadership and management skills
- The Medical Leadership Competency Framework sets out competencies and suggestions for undergraduate medical education
- Developing competence in understanding yourself, personal qualities and working with others are already embedded in personal and professional development programmes, but not always 'labelled' as leadership
- Some challenges remain in introducing leadership development and appropriate assessments in already crowded curricula with large numbers of students
- Leadership development needs to be seen as part of lifelong learning.

CHAPTER 9

Towards a better understanding of clinical leadership

Steven A Burr, Yee L Leung

Why is clinical leadership important?

The effectiveness of leadership is important to everyone, yet it is frequently misunderstood and often represented as undesirable. Many theoretical models extol the virtues which make a good leader, yet there is comparatively little practical advice. How well do you understand your ability to influence others? How could you improve?

Clinicians are best placed to understand the needs of health-care systems. Yet it is unusual for clinicians to take leadership positions within organisations in the UK, compared with elsewhere in the world. Management often has negative connotations and appears removed from caring for people. The Care Quality Commission (2014) has found hospitals with good care, but inadequate leadership. The NHS is organised in a way which inevitably causes leadership to be hierarchical. Disconnect between senior management and front-line clinical service has highlighted inadequate governance procedures, requiring the implementation of special measures (Hawkes, 2014). Current medical leaders are concerned about who will succeed them (Hay Group, 2014). Moreover there is a general perception among doctors in training that being a director, executive, specialty lead or commissioning chair is not a positive career move (Limb, 2014a). Doctors need to reflect on their ambition to help improve the health of the maximum number of people possible (Moberly, 2014).

Effective leadership has long been known to improve care outcomes; for example, the bystander effect (failure of groups to respond to others who are in difficulty) is significantly reduced in groups with a leader (Baumeister et al, 1988). Consequently leadership has been given more prominence by the creation of the Faculty of Medical Leadership and Management in 2011, and the publication of standards for medical leaders (Faculty of Medical Leadership and Management, 2015). There is a drive to foster a culture of positive leadership attitudes and behaviours for staff at all levels from 'ward to board' (Department of Health, 2014). Quality of care correlates with having clinician engagement, stable top leadership, strategies for improvement, supportive learning cultures, accountability frameworks, and regular performance review. To achieve this it is now clearly recognised that investment is required at an institutional level (Limb, 2014b). Apart from optimising the working environment, effective clinical leadership requires the application of emotional intelligence at the personal level (*Table 9.1*).

Table 9.1 Suggestions for leaders to maximise success

	Need	**Value**	**Behaviour**
1	optimise teamwork	pride	Promote team identity and vision, carefully select team members, align roles to needs, clarify priorities and degrees of autonomy, elicit feedback from all individuals, resolve conflicts openly
2	support team members	committed advocate	always put needs of team first, empower team, ensure cross-cover and succession, identify problems (e.g. fatigue, regression and disengagement), intervene to reconcile burdens, involve and inform those most affected first, give genuine and targeted feedback, provide meaningful training and teambuilding opportunities
3	solve problems	resolve	encourage initiative and improvisation where appropriate, seek advice, evaluate risk-benefits, consult team, decide

Table 9.1 Suggestions for leaders to maximise success (continued)

	Need	Value	Behaviour
4	introduce changes	confidence	encourage challenge, ensure change is necessary before acting, model effects, identify resistance and motivate, resource appropriately, act with conviction, re-evaluate
5	communicate effectively	integrity	be transparent and honest, foster a 'no blame' culture, ensure complaints go up and not down, act on evidence, dispel uncertainty, deliver news personally
6	act with equality	humility and respect	treat others as you would wish to be treated, value everyone equally
7	manage authority	loyalty	be loyal to the team, encourage dissent before deciding and solidarity afterwards, do not undermine the authority of others
8	set an example	moral courage	always act in the best interests of the team, be even-tempered, envisage success, use failure constructively
9	avoid known delusions	selfless	guard against all forms of self-interest and exploitation
10	undertake regular evaluation	reflective	determine the effectiveness of team performance in achieving the vision

Know what leadership is

A coordinator organises and communicates, while a manager makes decisions and delegates so as to allocate resources. In contrast, a leader successfully initiates and motivates change in the activity of others so as to achieve a vision (*Figure 9.1*).

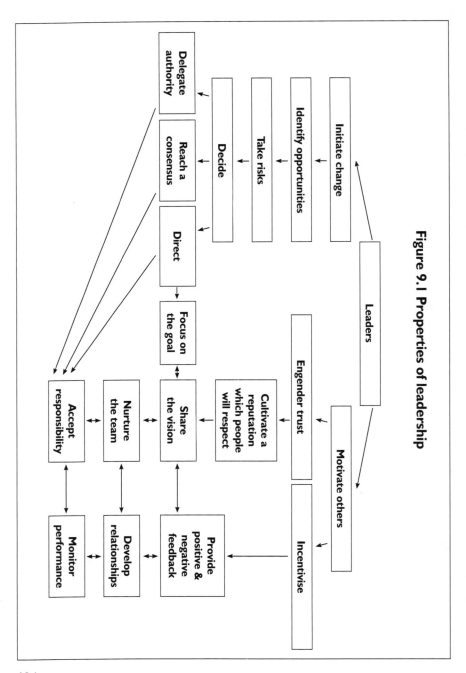

Figure 9.1 Properties of leadership

To initiate change you must identify an opportunity, decide to take a risk, and act upon it; while to motivate others, you must engender trust and incentivise. To engender trust you must act as an example and cultivate a reputation which people will respect, while having a shared vision, accepting responsibility for your decisions and owning the changes you promulgate. It is necessary to protect and nurture the team. However, it can be difficult to choose between the vision and team when their needs conflict. If the success of one is at the expense of the other then which to prioritise depends on their relative impacts. To incentivise you must provide feedback, the effectiveness of which can be maximised by a combination of both constructive criticism and reward.

Understand the theoretical approaches to leading

Temper your natural strengths according to circumstances to adopt the most appropriate leadership style (Schaeffer, 2002). In a crisis it is necessary to be authoritarian, when a consensus is required be democratic, and when empowering team members it is appropriate to take a more laissez-faire approach and delegate decision making among the group (Lewin et al, 1939; Van Wormer et al, 2007). For any given situation a leader will be either task-orientated to focus on clarifying the work which needs to be undertaken by different individuals to achieve the goals of the team, or relationship-orientated to focus on supporting the social interactions and concern for satisfaction of the team (Fleishman, 1953; Griffin and Ebert, 2010). Similarly, a leader's intervention can be either transactional when the leader has the authority to reward and punish, or transformational when team members are cared for, stimulated and developed (Burns, 1978; Bass et al, 1996; Bass and Riggio, 2005). Team cohesion can also be improved by adopting a functional approach which compensates for weaknesses by monitoring conditions, directing, motivating, teaching and coaching team members, and actively participating in the team's work to maximise achievement (Hackman and Walton, 1986; House 1996). The Healthcare Leadership Model postulates nine dimensions to effective leadership: inspiring shared purpose, engaging the team, holding to account, influencing for results, evaluating information, sharing the vision, connecting service, developing capability, and leading with care (NHS Leadership Academy, 2013).

Achieving effective leadership

A pragmatic approach to achieve effective leadership is to attempt to distil the essence of what needs to be applied from all of the above. With this in mind, it is necessary to consider how to: optimise teamwork, support team members, solve problems, introduce changes, communicate effectively, act with equality, manage authority, set an example, avoid known delusions, and undertake regular evaluation.

Optimise teamwork

Foster pride in the distinctiveness of the team identity as greater than any individual (i.e. be elite, not elitist). This improves a sense of belonging and motivates individuals to reflect on their contributions and improve performance. Successful teamwork requires sharing the same vision and this in turn often involves recruiting team members with the same values. Team members should be selected judiciously (Hackman, 2009). Roles need to be transparent, aligned to strengths and weaknesses, and the limits of authority for independent decision making must be clear. Conflict resolution requires constructive democratic discussion allowing team members to be empowered to take responsibility and lead if necessary. Where success has occurred then opportunities should exist to congratulate and further empower members.

Support team members

It is crucial to have an approach which facilitates learning from mistakes and the ongoing development of professional competence. A leader should be a committed advocate for the team. Credibility depends on being engaged in understanding the conditions affecting the team so as to better tailor solutions to needs (McKimm, 2004). A good leader understands the needs of the team, is able to delegate responsibility for tasks to team members, empowering them to achieve goals, and intervening to lead by example when necessary. How one leads a team depends on the qualifications and experience of team members. An established cohesive team will often only require instructions to achieve a goal, deputising roles if necessary, while a relatively new group will require more guidance from the leader, often supported by mentoring.

Ensure cross-cover and succession planning to avoid single points of failure, by sharing experience to enable contingency and continuity in case of losing a team member. Being conferred responsibility without also having control can cause stress. In individuals it is possible to identify problems of: fatigue through avoidance of responsibility, regression to earlier goals through aggressive violation of rules, or disengagement through attempts to justify inappropriate actions (by diminishing consequences or undermining opposition). When necessary intervene in workload and work relationships to reconcile burdens, but ask their consent where appropriate, and inform those most affected first. Feedback needs to be genuine so as to not be devalued, and targeted to have maximum benefit. Be aware of support networks and refer onwards if beyond your own capacity to handle. Training should be realistic and relevant for practice and experimentation, to reduce unfamiliarity and stress. Team building by away day training and competitive activities can be used to appraise capabilities, optimise team interactions, and promote retention and recruitment. It is also possible to gauge individuals' work capacity and problems during opportunities for relaxed conversations unrelated to work. Overall, be proactive and compassionate in your support (Burr and Leung, 2013; see also Chapter 13).

Solve problems and introduce changes

The role of a leader is to clarify direction and goals and this requires both confidence and resolve. Confidence is needed to seek the initiative, project inspiration and be assertive. Resolve is needed to take reasonable risks and be sufficiently assured for robust constructively debated planning.

Problem solving

Problem solving requires logical and sometimes innovative thought processes which are adaptable according to circumstances and scenarios. Permutations of potential obstacles to the goals should be predicted, with contingency planning for possible alternative solutions. Perfection should be aimed for but there should be an understanding that it may not be achieved. Ensure that you understand the mechanisms of decision making so that you are able to improve your choices (Leung et al, 2011). Leaders should then ask questions, seek advice, and ask for help as necessary (Offerman, 2004). When consulting the team, allow the most junior member to speak first to encourage honesty and discourage 'group thinking'. Hidden disagreement can undermine implementation later on (Offerman, 2004). After all have contributed, the leader should summarise options, determine any consensus, and decide a course of action (see case scenario 9.1). If most decisions are negotiated, cooperatively planned and fully explained then there will be greater ownership and likelihood of success, as well as a greater probability of acceptance on the rare occasion that a direct order is needed. Circumstances requiring direct orders

---

Case scenario 9.1 Obstacles can be opportunities

Problem

A project to transfer care from an inpatient to a day case setting required the collection of evidence: that patient safety would not be compromised, that a good patient experience would be maintained, and that there would be no increase in complication rates. The resources required to collect and collate such data were unavailable. The additional burden of attempting to acquire evidence without allocated resource increased stress within the team, and the impetus for the vision became lost.

Solution

A junior member of the team was able to suggest that a separate case needed to be made for dedicated support for the project. The project lead developed a business case to secure software, hardware and staff time to collect and process the data and quantify the risks. This in turn justified the resource expenditure, facilitated the transfer of care and ultimately ensured the success of the project.

Lessons learnt

Leading requires change, change involves risk, and taking risks is stressful. Remaining calm enables rational decision making based on the best available information. Ensuring everyone involved is empowered to share their ideas, increases the possibility of identifying the best-fit solution. Problems which are shared and overcome can both clarify the vision and bring the team closer together.

---

which are to be unquestioningly obeyed should be exceptional and reserved for handling unexpected dangers. Understanding the leader's vision empowers team members to use their initiative if the situation changes. Team members should only relinquish their responsibility to make a decision when the leader has more expertise in the matter (Chomsky, 1999; Dannhauser, 2007).

Introduce changes

Ambiguity and challenge provide freedom for change and opportunity for innovation. Discouraging challenge can perpetuate errors (see Chapter 14), stifle innovation, cause disenfranchisement and damage morale. Know the hierarchy of authority and processes for change, in particular who is entitled to: debate, take responsibility for making a decision and disseminate information. Before introducing change, consider why the thing you propose to change was set up the way it was originally. Is change necessary, and what needs must be met? Don't reinvent the wheel, or take action for the sake of being seen to take action. Nevertheless, when change is necessary then welcome and direct change while maintaining or improving standards. Prepare for change by planning and investing in research and development wherever possible before taking action. When the need for change is uncertain then, as Nelson Mandela said, 'may your choices reflect your hopes not your fears'. Beware that comfort of certainty and effort of change will cause scepticism, and vested interests will cause resistance.

Resistance to change needs to be recognised and any potential for conflict proactively managed. Individuals who are reluctant will go through the well-established stages of change (i.e. denial, anger, bargaining and depression, before acceptance). Engagement can be leveraged by identifying the motivations of different individuals, such as financial (e.g. one-off bonus or consolidated reward) (see case scenario 9.2), status (e.g. bestowing authority or enhancing reputation), or moral obligation (e.g. repayment of personal debt). It is often necessary to use a combination of example, persuasion and compulsion to get others to do what you want. Avoid micromanagement by devolving leadership of elements. Set targets and leave implementation to the team in order to disseminate ownership. Individuals should be autonomous within clearly defined parameters (of who, what, where, when). To set these parameters it is necessary to understand the resource implications of decisions. By ensuring that you are not fully occupied with routine work it is possible to protect a reserve in capacity which can be used to exploit opportunities. In any case, be prepared to incorporate changes as new information, or a new perspective on old information, comes to light. As required, this should lead to recalibration of the vision and purpose of the team so as to maintain momentum and quality.

Case scenario 9.2 Engage all stakeholders

Problem

An improvement project to change the way patients are moved through a care pathway required lots of steps involving lots of staff from a variety of disciplines. The main stumbling block was that no-one knew who did what or when, consequently patients never knew where they were in the care pathway.

Solution

Consultants, junior doctors, nurses, allied health professionals, administrative and other ancillary staff were all invited to a meal at a local restaurant to discuss their role in the care pathway. The vision for change was reiterated, and each step in the care pathway was openly discussed, along with potential problems and their possible solutions.

Lessons learnt

Do not underestimate the potential to motivate others by arranging a meeting for a luxury experience (e.g. an expenses-paid meal at a reputable restaurant or use of conference venue facilities). The meeting should be at a neutral territory which doesn't discriminate or deter participation. This provides an opportunity to exclusively focus on the vision: to identify and prioritise the resolution of potential problems, creating a sense of shared ownership to win over sceptics, while rewarding engagement at the same time. Encourage all to get involved so that you can gain insight into their perspectives. Such information should be used to refine your planning so as to increase the probability of acceptance, and thus maximise overall success.

Communicate effectively

Leaders behave with integrity, being honest and fostering an open 'no blame' culture. Ensure that complaints are dealt with appropriately by those who have the ability to bring about change within the hierarchy. Any changes should be based on available evidence and not rumour. The vision should be clearly established and not subject to unjustified change as this will engender distrust among the team.

Act with equality

Treat all people equally as you would wish to be treated yourself (Luke 6:31). Leaders should act with humility and respect for others, suffering the same privations as the team. Full transparency discourages sycophantic behaviour (which in itself can foster distrust and decrease team cohesion). Additional benefits and detachment associated with being a leader can be resented, although transparency can lead to an appreciation that additional responsibility deserves recognition (Berkowitz, 1953; Stewart and Manz, 1995). Individuals will vary in the type of exchange that they develop with their leader (Graen et al, 1982), and it is important not to undermine the status and confidence of any team member. The development of 'in-group' members who have high-quality exchanges with the leader at the expense of other 'out-group' members who have low-quality exchanges with the leader (Howell, 2012) should be avoided. Supporting and relying on individuals perceived as being more experienced, competent or willing to assume responsibility will disenfranchise other members of the team, although their input should be recognised and appreciated.

Empathise with the aspirations and concerns of all team members to understand how best to influence their commitment. As team members develop, each individual's contribution to any debate evolves, increasing team empowerment. In turn, value those who express individuality as they are more likely to hold themselves accountable for their actions. Avoid generating a perception of leaders and non-leaders (i.e. them and us), and don't use information to hold power over others (e.g. claiming that they don't need to know). Successful leadership is not established by exerting power over people, but by sharing power with people in a reciprocal relationship between the leader and all other individuals in the team (Forsyth, 2013). It can be helpful for leaders to think of themselves as serving the team, by ensuring all individuals have the means to realise their potential and improve collective performance. Remember that all individuals in a team including the leader are interdependent.

Manage authority

By acting with integrity and thinking flexibly, a leader gains respect and loyalty from their followers and thus authority to direct the team to achieve a vision. Fear of failure and thus risk aversion promotes the adoption of behaviours not in keeping with being a good leader (e.g. concealment of shortcomings by ill treatment of team members). By recognising and understanding one's own weaknesses, a leader can delegate certain tasks to people who are best suited to resolve those problems. This promotes attainment of the vision by the appropriate use of team resources without detriment to morale.

Set an example

A leader requires the moral courage to always act in accordance with appropriate values, and be resilient in the presence of adversity. So as to not undermine morale, an even temperament should be maintained under all conditions and feedback should not be responded to emotionally. Nevertheless feedback should be provided in an empathic manner. Success should be recognised and celebrated, while mistakes should be dealt with in an open and non-discriminatory manner with proportionate sanctions.

Avoid known delusions

Leadership requires intelligence, trustworthiness, humaneness, courage and discipline. Excessive reliance on intelligence leads to rebelliousness, humaneness to weakness, trust to folly, courage to violence, and discipline to cruelty. To maximise effectiveness a leader requires all five virtues together, each appropriate to its function (Sun Tzu, circa 500BC). A leader also requires selfless commitment to place the collective interest of the team before his/her personal interests. It is necessary to guard against self-interest and exploitation

(Kellerman, 2004). A self-important leader will undermine team performance. A leader should avoid:

- Thinking that he/she is worth more than those he/she works with (egocentric)
- Aligning the team's interests with his/her own to exploit the team (narcissistic)
- Believing that he/she knows and sees everything (omniscient)
- Believing that he/she is clever enough to achieve what-ever he/she wants (unrealistic optimism)
- Believing that he/she has the power to do whatever he/she wants (omnipotent)
- Believing that he/she can get away with doing whatever he/she wants, because he/she is either too clever to be caught or too important to be punished (invulnerable).
-

If the achievement of the team deteriorates because of any of these delusions then the leadership has become toxic.

Undertake regular evaluation

Encapsulating the essence of leadership is elusive, but it is possible to recognise limitations and identify opportunities for improvement for yourself and others by undertaking reflective appraisal. Contemplate your involvement with clinical leadership in the workplace (e.g. undertaking quality improvement projects, facilitating service transformation, rota redesign), and consider taking up opportunities for further relevant training (e.g. 'Darzi' Fellowships in Clinical Leadership, postgraduate courses such as an MSc in Professional Leadership). Regular anonymised 360° feedback improves self-awareness (Atwater et al, 1995; Walker and Smither, 1999). Appraisal can be augmented by using a managerial grid model (Blake and Mouton, 1985) and/or an attribute pattern approach (Zaccaro, 2007) to assess concern for people (relationship-orientated leadership) *vs* concern for production (task-orientated leadership). Team performance requires regular audit to evaluate the alignment of practice with purpose. Overall it is important to make the distinction to measure leadership performance by the success of the team relative to key outcomes of the vision, rather than by the success of the leader or whole organisation.

Conclusions

This chapter has explored how a greater understanding of leadership can be achieved by providing insights and advice to help maximise team effectiveness in order to achieve a vision. Effective leaders use different aspects of communication, interaction and action judiciously, with varying degrees of emphasis, so as to initiate and motivate change in the activity of others. Leaders develop respect and trust through facilitating conviction to a shared vision, by taking responsibility for accepting calculated risks and learning from mistakes while striving to achieve that vision. Key is the establishment of values within the team, being an advocate for the team, and reflecting on outcomes to bring about improvement. Above all else, the vision needs to be clear so that leadership can provide focused direction.

Key points

- Staff-sensitive, patient-centred leadership is an opportunity to magnify your values and improve outcomes for more people
- Leadership gives you the authority to make decisions, delegate, initiate and motivate change to achieve a vision
- Leadership requires being a committed advocate for the team, and exhibiting: confidence, resolve, integrity, humility, respect, loyalty, moral courage and pride
- Leadership can be improved by learning how to: optimise teamwork, support team members, solve problems, introduce changes, communicate effectively, act with equality, manage authority, set an example, avoid known delusions and undertake regular evaluation.

Section 3 – Leadership in practice

Doctor as professional and doctor as leader: same attributes, attitudes and values?

Helen O'Sullivan, Judy McKimm

Introduction

This chapter, based on O'Sullivan and McKimm (2011b), examines the links between medical professionalism and medical leadership and discusses how the values that are required to be a 'good doctor' are the same as a 'good leader'. The potential of this overlap to inform the debate on developing and assessing both medical leadership and professionalism is evaluated.

The 'professionalism movement', as defined by Hafferty and Castellani (2010), has existed in the medical education literature for about 15 years. The reasons for the rise of professionalism are varied and conflicting, with many commentators citing the medical scandals such as Shipman (Shipman Inquiry, 2002–5), the Bristol Royal Infirmary heart scandal (Department of Health, 2001) and the Alder Hey organ retention case (Royal Liverpool Children's Inquiry, 2001) as the underpinning reasons for the focus on professionalism (see case scenario 10.1).

However, changes in society and expectations from doctors and the medical profession have also led to an acceptance of the need for a changed informal contract between society and doctors (Cruess and Cruess, 2010). In addition, researchers have demonstrated a link between unprofessional behaviour and complaints against physicians (Ginsburg et al, 2000) and a link between disciplinary action against doctors and unprofessional behaviours exhibited at medical school (Papadakis et al, 2004). In the last decade, considerable effort has been devoted to defining medical professionalism (van Mook et al, 2009b) and looking at ways to develop and assess it in medical students and junior doctors (van Mook et al, 2009c).

Case scenario 10.1 Royal Liverpool Children's Inquiry (2001)

'Would any parent not have objected if told that every organ of their child would be taken and in most cases left untouched for years without even an attempt at a clinical histopathological examination? (Royal Liverpool Children's Inquiry, 2001, p3)'

This inquiry was held into the joint practices of the Royal Liverpool Children's Hospital and Liverpool University (via Alder Hey Institute where the collections were held) regarding non-compliance with the Human Tissue Act and other major managerial, supervisory, clinical and professional failings. The overall aim of collecting the tissues was for research, primarily into sudden infant death syndrome, but what began as misguided paternalism in the 1940s, led to poor custom and practice which resulted in an abuse of individual doctors' powers and to the subsequent inquiry by the late 1990s. The 'Redfern Inquiry' exposed horrendous practices at all levels (including the Coroner's Office) including large-scale retention of children's organs without parental consent or knowledge, failure to maintain accurate records and failure to provide even a basic histopathology service for children who had died of sudden infant death syndrome or cardiac failure, leading to inaccurate recordings of the cause of death.

Such inquiries heralded a review of the role of the doctor in society, questioned the foundations of the doctor–patient relationship and led to a reform of the legislation around human tissues, the establishment of clinical governance processes and a reform of the role of the General Medical Council in regulating doctors' performance.

Professionalism definitions and frameworks

One of the most influential definitions of professionalism is that set out in a report by the Royal College of Physicians (2005), *Doctors in Society: Medical Professionalism in a changing world*:

> 'Medical professionalism signifies a set of values, behaviours, and relationships that underpins the trust the public has in doctors.' (Royal College of Physicians, 2005)

Other authors have attempted to define these values, behaviours and relationships in a number of overlapping frameworks (Ginsburg et al, 2000; Swick, 2000; Hilton and Slotnick, 2005; Jha et al, 2006). In addition, national competency frameworks such as the CanMEDS framework (Royal College of Physicians and Surgeons of Canada, 2005) and the General Medical Council's *Good Medical Practice* (General Medical Council, 2013) include specific competencies related to professionalism.

Approaches to developing and assessing professionalism

The development and assessment of professionalism is now well established in the undergraduate medical curriculum. The General Medical Council's (2009) document *Tomorrow's Doctors* prescribes outcomes for all medical curricula in the UK leading to an MBChB (or equivalent) in three categories:

1. The doctor as a scholar and scientist
2. The doctor as a practitioner
3. The doctor as a professional.

A survey of the literature on assessing professionalism (van Mook et al, 2009c) analysed the types of assessment methods that are being used. This work is supported by a study (Levenson et al, 2010) that asked medical students what sorts of assessments they were being exposed to. The most common types are portfolios, objective structured clinical examinations, peer appraisal, clinical and faculty staff appraisal of professionalism and reflective writing.

As doctors progress through foundation and speciality training, professional behaviours are also assessed through a range of workplace-based and written assessments including case-based discussion, mini clinical evaluation exercise (mini-CEX), team assessment of behaviour (TAB) (see case scenario 10.2), objective structured clinical examinations and e-portfolios. Fully qualified doctors are also required to demonstrate and evidence a range of professional behaviours through revalidation, including multisource feedback from patients, colleagues and peers. Reflective writing is seen as one of the core tools through which students and doctors both learn and demonstrate their understanding of what being a professional means in practice.

Case scenario 10.2 Team assessment of behaviour

Lucie had been working hard as an F2 academic leadership fellow and had introduced two new quality improvement initiatives in the department. She was looking forward to see how her newly-honed leadership skills had been assessed by her colleagues. She was disappointed to see that, although the team assessment of behaviour included some skills and behaviours that aligned with leadership, there was nothing that specifically asked colleagues to evaluate her leadership skills.

The items on the team assessment of behaviour (The Foundation Programme, 2012) were:

- Maintaining trust/professional relationship with patients • Listens • Is polite and caring • Shows respect for patients' opinions, privacy, dignity, and is unprejudiced
- Verbal communication skills • Gives understandable information • Speaks good English, at the appropriate level for the patient
- Team-working/working with colleagues • Respects others' roles, and works constructively in the team • Hands over effectively, and communicates well • Is unprejudiced, supportive and fair
- Accessibility • Accessible • Takes proper responsibility. Only delegates appropriately • Does not shirk duty • Responds when called. Arranges cover for absence

How could Lucie get routine, multi-source and meaningful feedback on her leadership?

Leadership, as a defined set of specific skills or competencies, is not currently routinely assessed in either undergraduate or postgraduate contexts. Given some of the overlaps between professionalism and leadership, it is possible to use some of the methods used to assess professionalism to assess leadership. Conversely, many leadership programmes use a combination of multisource feedback, reflective writing and workplace-based assessment to formally assess leadership development. The Medical Leadership Competency Framework (MLCF) (NHS Institute for Innovation and Improvement and Academy of Medical Royal Colleges, 2010a) provides many examples at all stages of education and training of how competencies might be learned and assessed, and it is therefore feasible to explore how current assessments of professionalism might easily incorporate elements of leadership development.

Mapping professionalism frameworks with the Medical Leadership Competency Framework

In order to understand more fully the overlaps between professionalism and leadership, aspects of the MLCF are compared with some of the key professionalism frameworks and the General Medical Council's (2013) *Good Medical Practice (Table 10.1)*. From this analysis, some clear areas of overlap occur, such as ethics, integrity and high moral standards; respect for patients, communication and building relationships with patients; reflection, self-awareness and self-management.

In a report on the views of professionalism and leadership in medical students, Levenson et al (2010) comment that students accept and understand that leadership is a part of every doctor's professional practice but that there is ambivalence towards the role of management. Colleagues who had taken on significant management responsibilities were seen as having 'gone over to the dark side'. Although working in the context of a US health-care system, Souba (2011a) effectively summarizes the dilemma:

> 'The ethical foundation of the medical profession, which values service above reward and holds the doctor–patient relationship as inviolable, continues to be challenged by the commercialisation of healthcare.' (Souba, 2011a)

Table 10.1 Comparison of notable definitions and frameworks of medical professionalism with key aspects of the Medical Leadership Competency Framework

Medical Leadership Competency Framework* **(NHS Institute for Innovation and Improvement and Academy of Medical Royal Colleges, 2010a)**		**Hilton and Slotnik (2005)**
1. Demonstrating personal qualities	1.1 Developing self awareness	Reflection and self awareness
	1.2 Managing yourself	Responsibility/ accountability for actions
	1.3 Continuing personal development	
	1.4 Acting with integrity	Ethical practice
2. Working with others	2.1 Developing networks	
	2.2 Building and maintaining relationships	Respect for patients

*indicates that not all elements of the framework have been included in the table. Brackets indicate that some interpretation was used by the authors in placing the particular element in the table

Swick (2000)*	Jha et al (2006)*	Arnold and Stern (2006)*	General Medical Council (2013)*
Reflection	Personal awareness	(Excellence)	Recognize and work within the limits of your competence
Accountability	Management	Accountability	You are personally accountable for your professional practice and must always be prepared to justify your decisions and actions
			Keep your knowledge and skills up to date
Adhere to high ethical and moral standards	Compliance to values	Ethical and legal understanding	Be honest and act with integrity
	Doctor–patient relationship	Communication skills	Listen to patients, take account of their views, and respond honestly to their questions

Table 10.1 Comparison of notable definitions and frameworks of medical professionalism with key aspects of the Medical Leadership Competency Framework (continued)

Medical Leadership Competency Framework* (NHS Institute for Innovation and Improvement and Academy of Medical Royal Colleges, 2010a)		Hilton and Slotnik (2005)
2. Working with others	2.3 Encouraging contributions	
	2.4 Working within teams	Working with others
		Social responsibility

Souba goes on to argue that it is the fundamental personal values of a leader that can safeguard the longstanding ethical basis of medicine. He suggests four (ontological) pillars of leadership that anchor leadership to professionalism:

1. Awareness – the ability of a leader to be a perceptive observer, with a knowledge of his/her own biases and weaknesses, who is able to perceive, feel and be conscious of events, object and sensations
2. Commitment – this is a commitment to a purpose larger than ourselves, to not be focused only on ourselves or self-fulfilment
3. Integrity – sticking to one's word and honouring promises – being transparent
4. Authenticity – acting as being in a manner that is consistent with your own beliefs – avoiding the lure of desire for approval or needing to look good (Souba, 2011a).

These four pillars are strongly reminiscent of the main areas of overlap between the MLCF and the professionalism frameworks, suggesting that these are the main areas of interest that demonstrate the relationship between professional values and behaviours and medical leadership. This is supported by *indicates that not all elements of the framework have been included in the table. Brackets indicate that some interpretation was used by the authors in placing the particular element in the table

Swick (2000)*	Jha et al (2006)*	Arnold and Stern (2006)*	General Medical Council (2013)*
			Work with colleagues in the ways that best serve patients' interests
Respond to social needs	Motivation (altruism)	Altruism Humanism	Never abuse your patients' trust in you or the public's trust in the profession

empirical work that has looked at leadership qualities that support leadership effectiveness (Alimo-Metcalfe and Alban-Metcalfe, 2001; Souba et al, 2007; Alimo-Metcalfe et al, 2008).

Wise leadership and phronesis

Writing from a broader leadership perspective, Nonaka and Takeuchi (2011) have argued for a reinstatement of the ability to lead wisely. They suggest that leadership knowledge is not enough to ensure success in an increasingly complex set of challenges and that wisdom is the essential missing element. They also argue that wise leaders are able to practise moral discernment, quickly sum up a situation and grasp the key essence of a problem, that they can create a context that promotes organisational learning, that they can communicate in a way that everyone can understand, that they can exercise political power judiciously and that they can foster practical wisdom in others. Wisdom is not present explicitly in any of the leadership or professionalism frameworks that have been examined in this article. However, Hilton and Slotnik (2005) discuss the concept of 'phronesis' in their writing, this being a Greek word for practical wisdom. They argue that phronesis is about much more than attitudes, referring also to insights and judgements based upon experiences of dealing with uncertainly and complex situations. They contend that this stage of phronesis can only be acquired after a period of experience and therefore medical students, while capable of exhibiting exemplary professional values and behaviours, can only be considered as 'proto professionals' (Hilton and Slotnick, 2005).

Turning the good doctor into a good leader

If we accept the concept of phronesis as an essential component of both the doctor as a professional and the doctor as a leader, it seems that doctors need a period of time working on the front line delivering a relevant service before they can become effective leaders. Learning to be a medical professional and a leader takes time, and both learning and assessment need to be relevant and timely. Medicine is unique among the traditional professions for being managed by managers who are not part of the profession but who are often drawn from wide-ranging managerial or commercial backgrounds. In education, head teachers and vice chancellors invariably start out as teachers or lecturers, the military is led by former soldiers, sailors and aircrew, and bishops and archbishops start out as vicars or priests. In these professions, leadership is often learned 'on the job', whereas for doctors, opportunities for learning leadership and management skills have been scarce and the prevalence of 'professional managers' in the NHS has been a disincentive for doctors to fully engage in managing and leading clinical services (see case scenario 10.3).

However, times are changing and with the widespread implementation of the MLCF and other frameworks, opportunities for management and leadership development are rapidly increasing. Such opportunities include academic foundation programmes, Darzi fellows and clinical leadership postgraduate programmes. The establishment of the Faculty of Medical Leadership and Management provides further opportunities for development and acknowledgement of leadership and management roles. But, in order to ensure that doctors develop leadership and management skills and 'learn leadership' as part of their emerging professional development and identity, this needs to be embedded into all curricula at all stages. In other chapters (8 and 17 for example) examples are provided of how such development might be included in undergraduate and foundation programmes; however, this has often been considered more as a bolt-on for small numbers of students or doctors in training rather than as an integral part of professional development. Management skills, for example, are often not explicitly taught even though students and trainees are expected to self-manage, to project manage and to carry out management tasks such as clinical audit.

Conclusions

The relatively recent focus on teaching, learning and assessing professionalism provides an opportunity to embed leadership development within these aspects of programmes. Ensuring that doctors can effectively lead as well as follow, and can distinguish when to step up and when to step back is all part of becoming an effective team player, particularly in interprofessional teams.

Case scenario 10.3 Service improvement

Ravi and Desi, two ST2s with an interest in leadership and management had been asked to work with two clinical directors, the director of nursing and the head of medical imaging and support services, to investigate and make recommendations on expanding the ambulatory care service at the hospital. Because of the lack of support and imaging services to the clinics, doctors (particularly doctors in training) were tending to admit patients rather than send them home with an outpatient appointment as the inpatient services were prioritised. The team spent three months investigating services in other locations (including overseas), reading up about service pathways and design, meeting key groups of stakeholders, considering financial options with the director of finance and the department managers and eventually produced a report and recommendations for the chief executive and her team.

After the project, all the team felt they had learned from the experience and were starting to develop some understanding of service redesign, but realised that their real 'practical wisdom' would be learned through engaging with the implementation of the new services.

Understanding your impact on others and developing insight helps ensure emerging leadership behaviours are appropriate, but also helps relationships with patients, colleagues and peers.

If we look from the other side of the coin, maybe it is equally timely for those developing and implementing professionalism programmes to take a look at the leadership literature and ways of developing future leaders, because many of the skills, behaviours and qualities that make a good leader are those required by doctors as professionals. As Souba (2011a) highlights above, what makes a good doctor and a good leader is intrinsically about personal behaviours, qualities, insights and maturity. It is vital that students and doctors have the time and opportunity to learn about and develop personal insight and skills that enable them to work with and relate to others appropriately and effectively. This involves knowing the limits of competence, the roles and responsibilities of the health-care team, enabling effective communication (especially in times of crisis or conflict) and ensuring patient safety. Just as Cruess et al (2014) remind us that professionalism is about 'being a physician' as much as 'doing' doctor activities, Alimo-Metcalfe and Bradley (2009) emphasise that the 'how' of leadership (the practical wisdom) is as vital as the 'what' (the skills), and it is in this area that the overlap of leadership with professionalism is most profound.

Key points

- Medical professionalism has been the focus of attention in the literature for the past 15 years with a large body of work on defining professionalism
- Professionalism is now an established part of undergraduate and postgraduate curricula
- Evidence is starting to emerge on the most effective ways to develop and assess professionalism
- Significant overlaps exist between professionalism frameworks, the MLCF and other leadership frameworks
- Studies of medical professionalism and medical leadership have much to offer one another in terms of identifying appropriate values and behaviours as well as methods of developing and assessing what makes a good doctor and a good leader.

CHAPTER 11

Clinical leadership effectiveness, change and complexity

Judy McKimm, Alex Till

*With acknowledgements to Dr Naomi Chinn, Core Medical Trainee
and Dr Sally Simpson, Paediatric Speciality Trainee, Yorkshire
and the Humber Deanery for their input*

Introduction

The philosopher Heraclitus of Ephesos, who lived in 500BC, noted that 'life is flux'. Commonly translated as 'change is the only predictable constant', Kouzes and Posner (2007) remind us that effective leaders are those who are comfortable with and understand change.

Traditionally, change itself has been described as being either 'developmental', 'transitional' or 'transformational', each of which can be relevant in different contexts for individuals, teams and organisations in response to external and internal demands, pressures and drivers. Without such responsiveness, there is likely to be stagnation or even failure to achieve the vision. This requires leaders to demonstrate the willingness and capability to be flexible, to scan the horizon, and pay attention to political, economic, sociological and technological trends. Establishing and maintaining this 'adaptability' is crucial for change leaders and an understanding of the change literature, theories and models will be core to maintaining leadership effectiveness. This chapter is based on the article by McKimm and Till (2015).

The more traditional, or 'linear' models, focus on helping people and organisations plan for and 'manage' change. This is useful when changes are small-scale, relatively straightforward or can be approached using project management techniques. Often, however, particularly within health care, leaders often face more complex changes or those with unclear or uncertain features. In these situations, alternative approaches, such as those from systems thinking and complexity science, may be more helpful as they help to facilitate 'emergent' change. Each type of change requires different styles, approaches and behaviours from leaders, which must be used effectively to successfully manage its implementation (Goleman, 2000).

This chapter explores how an understanding of approaches to leading and managing change and complexity science can help clinical leaders engage with and manage change in complex environments and systems more effectively.

Psychological aspects of change

At individual, team or group level, leaders need to pay attention to the psychological aspects of change. This can greatly impact on people's ability to cope with and adapt to changing situations, structures or physical relocations. All change, even when positive, such as taking up a new job or moving to a new locality, involves some loss or grief related to what went before. Responses to change can therefore be compared to Kübler-Ross' five stages of grief during which an individual loses competence (albeit often temporarily) as they progress and come to terms with the change. Periods of denial, anger, bargaining and depression may need to be worked through before the new situation is finally accepted and full competency is resumed (Kübler-Ross, 1975).

Fisher's personal transition curve also considers the internal reaction to change (Fisher, 2005). The suggestion here is that people's motivation and outputs can (and should) be anticipated to decline in times of transition and change, and that these are largely dependent on their own perception of historic, current and anticipated experiences. Fullan (2004) reminds leaders to 'appreciate the implementation gap', whereby as people learn new skills by engaging in innovation, they may lose performance, confidence and become reluctant to take on new activities or roles to try and protect this (see case scenario 11.1).

Maintaining an awareness and understanding of the stages of loss, transition or competence curves therefore helps leaders to consider how responses to planned or unanticipated changes may affect the implementation timeline and when support mechanisms may be required to help individuals progress and work through this.

Categories of change

Alongside the psychological effects of change, leaders must also consider the exact type of change itself that is required. Ackerman (1997) categorised change broadly into 'developmental', 'transitional' and 'transformational' efforts:

- Developmental change: involves emergent, continually incremental change which enhances a pre-existing state
- Transitional change: involves staged progression from a pre-existing state to a newly desired state

> **Case scenario 11.1 'Mind the gap'**
> Karen and Rakesh have just moved into the last rotation of this year's training programme (CT2). Talking in the canteen, Karen said 'I am feeling so stressed about being on Ward 15, I'd just learned where everything was and who was who on Ward 8 and now I have to start all over again. It's so frustrating and I miss the lovely team on Ward 8!'
>
> Rakesh replied 'I know, and Dr Barley, the consultant, expects me to know all my patients just like that. I can barely find my way round the ward notes system as it's completely different from the Acute Admissions Unit. Don't they realise we're not stupid (though I feel like I am) but we need a bit of time to adapt to the changeover – I feel I am rushing around and worried I'm going to make a major mistake. This morning I got two patients both called Mrs Morgan mixed up when I was checking results, luckily the staff nurse pointed it out before I did anything'.
>
> In times of regular and routine transition, such as changing rotations, even within the same hospital, clinical leaders need to expect and anticipate the 'implementation gap'.

■ Transformational change: involves radical change, which shifts drastically from a pre-existing state to realise a new state, which may require ongoing adaptation and improvement until the overall vision is realised.

Whatever the context, when a leader is able to identify the type of change needed, he/she can more precisely select an appropriate change model or theory to help guide the development of the implementation strategy. If appropriate, the speed and success of implementation can then be maximised with the resistance and psychological distress minimised where possible.

Linear models of change

Although not exclusively, developmental or transitional change is often planned and can be considered 'managed'. In these situations, 'linear models' are most suited and while numerous strategies, frameworks and models exist, we discuss two widely-known models.

Lewin's model of change

Kurt Lewin was one of the early change theorists and described the three basic steps involved in any change: 'unfreezing', the 'change' itself (often referred to as the transition period) and 'refreezing' (*Figure 11.1*).

Within this model, Lewin (1948) discusses 'drivers' and 'resistors' – drivers are factors that push for change (e.g. a new government policy) and resistors are factors which fight against it (e.g. human factors whereby people do not understand the policy or they cannot see how to implement it locally). Lewin suggests that effective change leaders should focus on limiting and overcoming resistors, rather than persistently adding drivers.

One of the strengths of Lewin's model is its application as a concept rather than a direct implementation strategy. By thinking about what needs to be done in each of the three steps and how to limit resistors, change leaders are better able to initiate, progress and sustain change and understand when to implement more direct strategies as necessary.

Figure 11.1 Lewin's three step change model (Lewin, 1948)

- Unfreezing: Involves breaking the status quo whereby driving forces for change are met by counteracting restraining forces. Removing resistors and understanding the human behaviour behind these are key to unfreezing and providing the motivation for change.
- Change/Transition: Once unfrozen, these driving forces must be enacted, directed and controlled to bring about the required change. This often requires a transition period.
- Refreezing: Once the desired new direction is reached, stabilisation must be sought to embed the change and prevent regression.

Figure 11.2 Kotter's eight accelerators (adapted from Kotter, 2014)

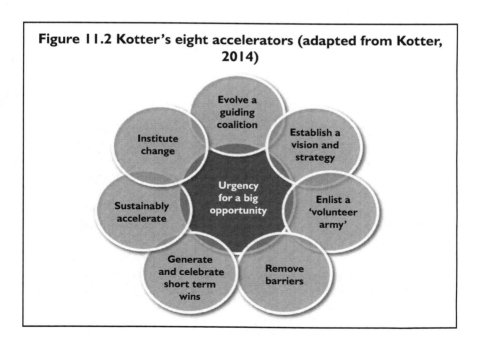

Kotter's eight accelerators

Rather than conceptual, John Kotter's work is more pragmatic, directed towards the required action to achieve change successfully. Those familiar with change management may be aware of Kotter's 'eight steps' (see Chapter 17 for an example of how this was used in practice). These were revitalised and modernised into 'eight accelerators', which are self-perpetuating and dynamic in nature (Kotter, 2014). Kotter outlines his vision for a 'dual operating system' within organisations. The first: a more traditional hierarchical management structure, the second: a dynamic system free from bureaucracy capable of rapidly adapting to change. Facilitating this approach are core principles and eight accelerators, which act as the practical activity undertaken, see *Figure 11.2.*

Kotter's 'eight accelerators' can be applied to any situation where change is required, for example, introducing a new ambulatory care pathway or home-based clinical service. Using the accelerators in an iterative way (rather than as a checklist) helps emphasise the need for proactive, agile responses to implementing change in rapidly evolving clinical environments and highlights the leader's role in maintaining and injecting momentum or energy to the change process.

Understanding change, complexity and adaptive leadership

Unlike with developmental and transitional change, transformational change is often more complex and requires alternative approaches to that which linear models can offer. The complexities that change leaders working within modern organisations encounter often stem from multifaceted inter-connected systems, not just internally, but externally. Taking a systems' perspective is crucial for leaders, for without it, they are unlikely to generate the unique tailored approach which is often required to create the innovative solution to overcome that particular problem, in that particular context. For example, if trying to reduce inpatient stays for older patients, taking a systems' perspective may require making changes to emergency admissions, GP referrals, ambulatory care services, increasing point of care diagnostics, training new health workers, improving links between social services and hospital on discharge, and so on.

'Chaotic systems flit a bit too readily from novelty to novelty; living systems need to consolidate gains. Predictable, stable systems, by contrast, display none of the panache needed to create new order or even to respond adaptively to creature environments. Complex systems lie between these poles, at the edge of chaos; and they have both panache and stability sufficient to sustain life' (Marion, 1999).

To aid our understanding further, Bar-Yam (2004) discusses complexity theory which draws from a variety of scientific disciplines and concepts, including physics, chaos theory, eco-biology and mathematics to formulate four key underlying ideas:

1. 'The mechanisms of collective behaviour (patterns)
2. A multi-scale perspective (the way different observers or stakeholders describe a system)
3. The evolutionary process that describes complex systems
4. The nature of purposive or goal-directed behaviour'. (Bar-Yam, 2004)

Adaptive leadership

Within this complexity, a number of writers have considered the types of leadership behaviours and styles that might be most effective. Heifetz et al (2009) discuss the concept of 'adaptive leadership', which acknowledges that leaders work within systems where inherent challenges and political dimensions are faced both internally and externally. Adaptive leaders recognise this and hold an ability to create a culture enabling both the organisation and the individuals within it to remain responsive and resilient to them in order to 'thrive' (Heifetz et al, 2009). This concept of 'thriving' is drawn from evolutionary biology which suggests that successful adaptation preserves the essential DNA of a species, discards or regulates DNA which is non-essential or inhibiting, and creates DNA arrangements that enable responsive adaptation to new situations (Heifetz et al, 2009). For health-care leaders, this requires thinking purposefully about what 'thriving' actually means in terms of various stakeholders and the organisation itself. Depending on the organisation and circumstances, thriving may include: financial efficiency or making a profit, meeting the needs of patients and populations, demonstrating core values or delivering excellent patient care (case scenario 11.2).

Adaptive leaders are able to build on successes of the past, while simultaneously recognising what is outdated and unnecessary when determining the current and future focus for change. One such technique is to view change from different perspectives and recognise when different approaches or models are needed to diagnose 'problems' and develop strategies to overcome them. Returning to the organisational vision, mission and values are often useful here and tools such as stakeholder analysis, driver diagrams, PESTLE (political, economic, sociocultural, technological, legal and environmental driver), and SWOT (strength, weakness, opportunity and threat) analysis can help systematise and inform the direction of travel.

For the above reasons and more, public expectations and health-care opportunities are rapidly shifting. Leaders need to be mindful and highly tuned into external factors to avoid becoming an 'outlier' and to ensure that their organisation remains 'thriving' within the current climate. However, the inevitable innovation and change required for this must be balanced against conservatism and stability; while vital, innovation implemented too extensively and too quickly can be destabilising, discourage individuals and alienate them from the 'next big thing' as they feel undervalued and displaced when it comes

---

Case scenario 11.2

'Researchers in England used complex adaptive systems thinking to explore why the effect of a single intervention incorporated into a complex clinical environment may be different from what is expected. Demographic and health information were collected from all patients admitted to a UK hospital between January 2003 and June 2004. Continuous process monitoring was undertaken using charts to detect planned or unplanned organisational process changes affecting mortality outcomes' (Cockings et al, 2006).

'A systematic review examined whether organisational interventions that build on the principles of complex adaptive systems thinking improve outcomes for people with type 2 diabetes. Of the 32 studies included, most used at least one complex adaptive system characteristic in their intervention designs and 91% were deemed to be effective or have mixed effects. The greater the number of complex adaptive system characteristics present in each intervention, the greater the effectiveness. Interconnections between participants and co-evolution were most likely to be associated with success'. (Leykum et al, 2007).

along. When facilitating organisational change, it is essential to attend to the underlying culture and not simply focus on structures and systems.

Fullan (2004) suggests six key principles underpinning adaptive leadership:

1. The goal is not to innovate the most: Consolidating fewer changes sustainably is preferable to implementing multiple innovations too quickly which are likely to be short lived
2. It is not enough to have the best ideas: Remaining insightful so as not push own ideas onto others and understanding the importance of providing ongoing motivational support for good ideas (no matter who generated them)
3. Appreciate the implementation dip: Understanding and managing the loss of competence and dip in performance which occurs with any change
4. Redefine resistance: Listening to different perspectives, build good relationships and working with the creative side of conflict and resistance
5. Reculturing is the name of the game: Restructuring is powerful but without addressing the required cultural shifts, sustainable change is unlikely to be achieved. Reculturing challenges the way things are done
6. Never a checklist, always complexity: Even when linear, change often becomes complex and new patterns emerge as a result of environmental factors and the unpredictable interaction between 'agents' within it (Fullan, 2004).

More recently, Obolensky (2010) has suggested that those working within such complexity should consider shifting from a more traditional oligarchical approach (in which leaders carry out a number of tasks or functions) to one which is polyarchic (in which leaders delegate functions to 'followers' and attend to the process of leadership). His 'four by four' model (below) sets out eight principles, which at first glance seem paradoxical, but when set in place, create a culture within which change can emerge (*Table 11.1*).

This view broadly coincides with the current conceptions of future leadership within the NHS; one of shared, distributed, collective leadership (West et al, 2014, 2015) and similar reflections by others, stating that we should be focussing more on leadership development (social capacity), rather than leader development (individual expertise) (Yukl, 2002; Bolden et al, 2003).

Within complex, post-modern health care, we must shift the rhetoric away from one whereby the NHS exists as a machine bureaucracy, focussing on standardising functions with linear relationships, towards a system with interconnectivity, individual agency and variation (Plsek and Greenhalgh, 2001; Kernick, 2011). Leaders should not be impartial observers, but part of a dynamic system with an underlying purpose and internal order, focussed on building relationships, tolerating ambiguity and facilitating the emergence of new ideas and innovation (Plsek and Wilson, 2001).

Decision-making

The complexity of health care requires leaders to juggle competing pressures and demands which evolve rapidly on an almost daily, if not hourly basis. To sustain safe health-care delivery we must understand this complexity and shift the conceptualisation of leadership and decision making away from a 'one-size-fits-all proposition' to a more considered responsive approach.

Adaptive leaders need to have the skills to evaluate contexts so as to create the conditions in which the organisation (and those who work within it) can cope with change and develop resilience. Snowden and Boone's (2007) Cynefin framework can be used to evaluate conditions and contexts and help us to operate and make decisions in what is often an unpredictable and sometimes seemingly irrational world. The organisational or system landscape is contextualised into one of four domains to help conceptualise the current situation: 'simple', 'complicated', 'complex' and 'chaotic'. When none of these appears predominant, an additional fifth domain: 'disorder' can be used, as summarised in *Table 11.2*.

Table 11.1 Leaders' tasks, adapted from Obolensky (2010)

Define an underlying purpose	Set clear objectives at individual and group level
Give discretion and freedom to act	Set boundaries to enclose actions
Ensure everyone has the skills and motivation to work	Identify a few simple rules
Build in tolerance for uncertainty and ambiguity	Provide continuous and unambiguous feedback

Table 11.2 Decision-making, adapted from Snowden and Boone (2007)

Simple domain	*Actions – Sense: Categorise: Respond* Stakeholders hold a shared understanding and parties readily agree to implement a self-evident change. Risks include stifling of innovation, oversimplification of situations and complacency. Leaders unaware of these pitfalls may plunge into a chaotic environment
Complicated domain	*Actions – Sense: Analyse: Respond* The required change, while obvious to some, risks complication. Stakeholders raise multiple options demanding expertise to analyse the complicated context in which the proposed change occurs. Risk-averse leaders may stifle progression secondary to innovation appearing controversial
Complex domain	*Actions – Probe: Sense: Respond* Constant flux exists within the unpredictable complex environment therefore single or simple solutions will probably not work. Courage and confidence is needed to 'probe, sense and respond' allowing a resolution to emerge organically. Without tolerance for experimentation, over controlling toxic or destructive leadership may evolve
Chaotic domain	*Actions – Act: Sense: Respond* Turbulence secondary to an indiscernible relationship between cause and effect creates chaos. Stabilising the environment through autocratic direction (coercive leadership) while not ideal, is necessary to prevent further deterioration. Somewhat ironically, the desperation for resolution impels innovation and transformational emergent change may result
Disorder domain	Fortunately rare, true disorder exists where the current context is indiscernible and multiple factions emerge. Leaders must dissipate these factions and identify smaller isolated elements within the disorder where the context can be identified and subsequently managed

Snowden and Boone's domains provide leaders with a tool to analyse their context so they can adapt appropriately to make decisions and select relevant leadership styles and change management techniques for success. Understanding that within individuals, teams and organisations these contexts exist on a dynamic spectrum is crucial to facilitate a system with the fluidity to adapt and respond to multiple external and internal changes and drivers.

When operating within the complex domain, Bak et al (1987) suggests that organisations or systems function with 'self-organised criticality'. Here the leader's role is more about containing boundaries, creating the conditions that help guide the process and letting solutions evolve, rather than trying to control everything by 'managing' the change, such as in a frantically busy emergency department or 'failing' clinical service.

Another useful tool is Stacey's (2002) 'certainty-agreement matrix'. Here, the closer the leader can get people towards agreement about the change and what the impact will be, the closer they are to working in the simple domain (above). As such, leaders must work with followers to obtain agreement and provide certainty where possible. Conversely, leaders who wish to push for change can 'perturb the edge' of chaos and help transformational change emerge by working in the complex zone where there is uncertainty and disagreement (so-called creative conflict). However, this requires experience as leaders need to be confident, courageous, adaptive, and responsive to listen to their followers; leaders need to have 'energy, enthusiasm and hope' (Fullan, 2003).

Conclusions

This article has explored one of the essential requirements of effective leaders: the ability to manage, work with and be comfortable with change, particularly in complex contexts. There are many ways of viewing change and we have considered some of the predominant theories and models for managing linear, developmental or transitional change. Such models are very useful for project-based initiatives or when changes need to be made within stable organisations or systems (e.g. relocating a ward or introducing a new IT system). When systems are more complex or when there is little certainty or agreement about the change and its impact, then leaders need to adopt different styles and approaches, many of which are derived from complexity theory and systems thinking. Here, adaptive leadership which is responsive, flexible and open to change is more useful so that change can emerge rather than be directly controlled. As health care operates in a state of constant change and complexity, health-care leaders need to draw from such theories in order to help stimulate innovation and emergent change.

Key points

- The ability to manage and be comfortable with change is a defining leadership characteristic
- All change involves some loss and grief, leaders need to be aware of the 'implementation dip' during which confidence and competence falls
- A range of models exist to help leaders manage and plan for change, linear models are useful for planned change
- Complexity theory and systems thinking provides us with different ways to facilitate emergent or transformational change, this needs adaptive leadership.

CHAPTER 12

Personality, self-development and the compassionate leader

Judy McKimm, Helen O'Sullivan, Charlotte Messer

Introduction

This chapter discusses how the publication of the Francis report stimulated increased debate on medical leadership, highlighted alignment with contemporary thinking on leadership development and professionalism, and foregrounded that development and demonstration of appropriate personal qualities is central to effective medical leadership. It is based on the article by McKimm and O'Sullivan (2013).

> 'Patients must be the first priority in all of what the NHS does by ensuring that, within available resources, they receive effective care from caring, compassionate and committed staff, working within a common culture, and protected from avoidable harm and any deprivation of their basic rights' (Francis, 2013).

This quotation from the Francis report highlights as vital that all staff working in health care, whatever the difficulties, constraints and circumstances, need to deliver compassionate care. The report goes on to note that, while health workers at all levels must display the values of the NHS, leadership and role modelling is essential: 'The common culture and values of the NHS must be applied at all levels of the organisation, but of particular importance is the example set by leaders' (Francis, 2013).

These sentiments are echoed in other guidance and policy documents. For example the General Medical Council (2012a) notes that:

'...being a good doctor means more than simply being a good clinician. In their day-to-day role doctors can provide leadership to their colleagues and vision for the organisations in which they work and for the profession as a whole. However, unless doctors are willing to contribute to improving the quality of services and to speak up when things are wrong, patient care is likely to suffer.' (General Medical Council, 2012a)

Such statements reiterate common themes running through contemporary literature, the findings of inquiries and the media response: that the public and professional bodies expect doctors and other health professionals to consistently provide good, compassionate care for patients and families, to strive actively to improve services and to lead by example, including speaking out when care fails to meet acceptable standards. This poses leadership challenges for organisations and individuals alike, challenges which are explored in this article.

A culture of engagement

Since the publication of the Darzi (2008) review, a number of writers have tried to tease out what medical leadership might be and explain why many doctors do not see themselves as leaders. One of the issues identified is that many doctors see moving into a leadership role as becoming more managerial, and that moving into 'management' involves moving to the 'dark side' (Spurgeon et al, 2011). The divide between managers and medical or clinical leaders is longstanding, based partly on the power and perceived autonomy of the medical profession and the appointment of non-clinical managers who are often seen (by applying targets, protocols and guidelines) as threatening professional expertise.

Forbes et al (2004) suggest that there are two types of doctor-manager: the 'investor' and the 'reluctant'. Investors move into management in order to achieve particular agendas or change, some see themselves as natural leaders and accept that effective management is needed to make significant health innovations and improvements. Reluctants have not moved into management through conscious choice and see their role as more negative (the dark side), often conflicting with their clinical role. Many doctors are reluctant to give up clinical work, as this is central to their professional identity and is also perceived to give credibility. Dickinson et al (2013) showed that while there have been improvements in the involvement of doctors in medical leadership and management, a gap still exists between doctors in leadership positions and their medical colleagues. The report recommends increasing the number of doctors in formal leadership roles and improving the culture of engagement. In order for this to happen, doctors and other health professionals need to work together to establish the elements of this engaging, caring culture. The Francis (2013) report suggests that: 'the common culture of caring requires a displacement of a culture of fear with a culture of openness, honesty and transparency, where the only fear is the failure to uphold the fundamental standards and the caring culture'.

At the heart of developing this culture must lie demonstration of doctors' personal qualities and values as they apply in practice, however busy and time pressured. All working in health services also need to acknowledge that the vast majority work with the patients' best interests at heart, even though their roles may be very different.

Personal qualities that make a good leader

Early theories of leadership considered that personality traits and qualities were fundamental to effective leadership, with the emergence of the heroic leader (or 'great man') as the archetype. While traits such as integrity, drive, inspirational, authenticity and approachability seem fairly stable across all contexts, writers now see this as only one element to leadership and that listing personal characteristics does not really help explain why different leadership works better in different situations and how leadership can be learned.

Trait theory

Although trait theory has been criticised, there is increasing evidence that certain personal qualities in leaders can have an impact on personal effectiveness and leadership success. In a review of empirical studies looking at the link between traits and leadership effectiveness, Zaccaro (2007) identified studies that showed a link between such attributes as optimism, proactivity, adaptability and nurturance. The paper also identifies a meta-analysis of 78 studies that linked one or more of the 'big five' personality factors (extroversion, conscientiousness, neuroticism, openness and agreeableness) to leadership. Although extroversion showed the strongest correlation, openness was also positively correlated. While this conceptualisation of openness is not exactly the same as the construct of openness mentioned in the Francis (2013) report, being open to different experiences and people fits with the distinction Forbes et al (2004) make between the investor and the reluctant doctor-manager. Zaccaro (2007) lists several personal qualities where there is some form of evidence linking that quality and effective leadership:

1. Cognitive capacities: general intelligence, creative thinking capacities
2. Personality: extroversion, conscientiousness, emotional stability, openness, agreeableness, Myers–Briggs type indicator preferences for extroversion, intuition, thinking and judging
3. Motives and needs: need for power, need for achievement, motivation to lead
4. Social capacities: self-monitoring, social intelligence, emotional intelligence
5. Problem-solving skills: problem construction, solution generation, meta-cognition
6. Tacit knowledge (Zaccaro, 2007).

Emotional intelligence

Qualities that can be categorised as 'social capacities' have received much attention. The role that emotional intelligence plays in medical leadership and medical professionalism has been demonstrated to be linked to effective leadership in the general leadership literature (Mayer et al, 2008). However, a limited amount of evidence exists that emotional intelligence (as measured by a range of validated instruments) can be increased through educational interventions during medical training (Cherry et al, 2012). Although emotional intelligence is linked to improved communication skills in medical students and junior doctors (Cherry et al, 2013), further research is needed to make a direct link between emotional intelligence and being an effective medical leader.

Even though there is no clear link between emotional intelligence and 'being a good doctor', interest is growing in using aspects of emotional intelligence testing in medical schools admissions. So far studies of this have been done in the USA and a review of best practice in UK medical admissions found no evidence of current use of personality or emotional intelligence testing (Cleland et al, 2012). Despite this, current shifts in selection methods at all stages of a doctor's career are placing more emphasis on trying to assess characteristics including caring, resilience, prioritisation, ethical decision-making and motivation through the use of methods such as multiple mini-interviews, extended interviews and situational judgment tests. The discourses in professional guidance also state attributes such as compassion and empathy and the role of the doctor as leader and manager more explicitly (General Medical Council, 2012a), see also Chapter 10. Case scenario 12.1 describes how easily someone can get 'derailed' when things are busy and they feel pressured.

Case scenario 12.1 'Getting derailed'

We all have strengths and areas for improvement based on our personality traits and preferences. Here, a psychiatry specialty registrar (SpR) tells us about an incident where her strengths (being focussed, delegating, pace-setting) actually became overplayed when she was stressed and caused problems for her, her colleagues and the patient.

'I was leading an afternoon ward round when a new junior doctor wanted to discuss Mr X with me. Mr X was under a different team and I was not involved in his care. The junior doctor informed me that his long-term catheter had become damaged so it had been removed, he was now in urinary retention. The junior doctor asked me for advice which surprised me because it seemed obvious that Mr X should have a new catheter inserted and I would expect a doctor at that level to be competent in this procedure.

An hour later, the junior doctor told me that he had tried to catheterise Mr X 4 times unsuccessfully. I then asked detailed questions which revealed a complicated urological history with previous catheterisations requiring specialist input. I became angry and asked him why he hadn't told me this in the first place. The catheter had been removed in the early hours of the morning and now Mr X had now been in retention for over 12 hours. He said that he assumed I knew about all the patients on the ward because in his previous job the SpRs looked after all the patients, despite being split up into different consultant teams.

I advised the junior doctor to contact the urology SpR on-call to organise transfer of the patient to have his catheter inserted urgently. The junior doctor returned 45 minutes later to say that he could not get hold of the urology SpR. By this point Mr X was in discomfort and relatives were complaining that my ward round was over-running. I asked the junior doctor to contact the nurse in charge of the urology unit because the urology SpR on-call was not responding. The junior doctor then returned to say that the nurse had authorised Mr X to be transferred for a catheter insertion.

Continued overleaf

Having the self-insight and emotional intelligence to recognise this is part of becoming both a better leader and doctor.

Engaging leadership

Other studies also show the importance of personal qualities to clinical leadership. Alimo-Metcalfe and Alban-Metcalfe (2006) carried out a large scale,

---

Case scenario 12.1 'Getting derailed' (continued)

I thought this was the end of the matter until 30 minutes later the junior doctor returned to inform me that he had received a very irate phone call from the urology SpR who was unhappy that we had organised an admission through the nurse, and not through him. He had therefore blocked the admission and advised that I try to insert the catheter myself! At this point I suspended the ward round and took over from the junior doctor. I contacted the urology SpR on-call and explained the situation. He was very critical of me on the telephone, said that we should have contacted him much earlier as we knew about his urological complications and that the junior doctor should not have tried to insert the catheter four times as this could have led to even more complications. I tried to explain my position, however, he started making derogatory comments about psychiatry and psychiatrists. I became defensive and we got into an argument. I then reminded him that the focus should be on the patient, and Mr X needed his catheter re-inserted urgently. He eventually agreed for the patient to be transferred and we ended the conversation on hostile terms.

What occurred after the event?

Once I'd organised the transfer, I spoke to the junior doctor about not recognising the importance of Mr X's complicated urological history much earlier and not giving me all of the relevant details at our initial encounter. I also told him that he should not have attempted catheterisation on so many occasions and he should have been able to organise the transfer himself. I was angry and this reflected my communications with him. I had to postpone seeing some patients and relatives until another day which I had not had to do before as I pride myself on running organised, efficient ward rounds. The following day I spoke to Mr X's consultant about how the events unfolded.'

---

empirical, longitudinal study of multi-professional teams working in the NHS and found evidence of a cause–effect relationship between clusters of leadership qualities and objectively measured productivity. They describe the possession of a combination of these qualities as an 'engaging leader' who is someone who encourages and enables the development of an organisation characterised by a culture based on integrity, openness and transparency, and the genuine valuing of others (Alimo-Metcalfe et al, 2008). Alimo-Metcalfe and her group have amassed significant empirical evidence about the factors that are important in engaging leadership and overall leadership effectiveness. Her team have developed the research tool into a diagnostic tool that can be used in leadership development. They suggest that identifying the presence of qualities that are rated highly and negatively can have a powerful impact and can direct personal development activities (Alban-Metcalfe and Alimo-Metcalfe, 2013).

Case scenario 12.2 Deep and surface acting

'The latest research on the link between burnout and emotional labour suggests that it's the way you try to act that predicts whether you are going to suffer from burnout or not. In some jobs it is the high emotional labour that actually predicts a greater sense of personal accomplishment. So the key seems to be whether at work you are performing emotional labour requiring superficial acting or deep acting.

Superficial acting is where you just pretend to be pleased to see someone while deep down you can't stand them.

Deep acting is where you try to change your basic attitudes towards the people you interact with by positively altering your thoughts and deeper feelings you have about them. So, for example, if you are in child care work and some of the children you are looking after annoy you, you make a conscious effort to remain positive and not snap at them because deep down you believe that this is a better emotional state to be in than showing how irritated you are. Engaging in deep acting seem to find jobs that demand high levels of emotional labour more personally rewarding. You learn the skill of deep acting by using the same techniques as Hollywood actors who seriously research a part. For example, if an actor is to play the role of a policeman or policewoman, he or she will go and hang out with real police staff, adopt a role model, and immerse themselves in that world.'

(Persaud, 2004) http://careers.bmj.com/careers/advice/view-article.html?id=394

Emotional labour

In other professions, there is an increasing emphasis on acknowledging the impact of 'emotional labour' – 'a requirement to produce emotional states in others or exercise a degree of control over the emotional activities of others' (Crawford, 2009). Held and McKimm (2012) suggest that the more congruent and authentic leaders' emotional displays are and the more skillfully they can use affect (expressed emotion), the more at ease they are with their actions and the more impactful they are on those around them. 'Leaders and followers constantly balance the tensions between rational thought, emotion and intuition' (Held and McKimm, 2012) (case scenario 12.2).

However, Alban-Metcalfe and Alimo-Metcalfe (2013) argue that it is useful to distinguish between the activities leaders perform, e.g. leading a team (as defined by a competency framework) and how they act or behave (as defined by a leadership style), in other words the way they lead the team (assertively, through delegation). They also suggest that a combination of competence assessed using a competency framework combined with what they term an 'engaging' style of leadership produces effective clinical leadership. How this research evidence translates into developing good medical leadership is open to debate. Souba et al (2007) argue that teaching doctors about leadership is different from creating doctors who are leaders and that we will not create good medical leaders by imparting a series of behaviours and traits. Rather we should be creating a culture where there are opportunities to develop leadership deep into the organisation through it being a 'lived' experience: ontological leadership.

A note about dark personality and leadership

In a book that launched a proliferation of headlines such as 'Is your Boss a Psychopath?', Babiak and Hare (2006) argue that while only about 1% of the general population are psychopaths, the figure is about 3% for those in high level management positions in organisations. This work is part of a wider interest in the impact of what is known as the 'dark personality' in leadership. Dark personality is often defined as the subclinical level of the personality characteristics of the 'dark triad': narcissism, Machiavellianism and psychopathy (Paulhus and Williams, 2002).

Narcissism is derived from narcissistic personality disorder which is diagnosed on criteria such as a sense of entitlement, requiring excessive admiration and a belief that the person is special (American Psychiatric Association, 2013). According to Babiak and Hare (2006) 'Narcissists think that everything that happens around them, in fact, everything that others say and do, is or should be about them' (p. 40). Other authors have provided several sub-definitions of narcissism (for a review see Spain et al, 2014). Interestingly, there appears to be a relationship between narcissism and leadership emergence but not leadership effectiveness (Grijalva et al, 2015) and this illustrates one of the dilemmas of the dark triad – that at first there may be positive outcomes with these personalities – at first narcissists may seem charismatic, dynamic and confident.

Jones and Paulhus (2008) describe Machiavellianists as being motivated by 'cold selfishness and pure instrumentality' (p. 93) While Machiavellianism does not seem to be related particularly to the emergence or effectiveness of leadership, the main issue is that Machiavellianism is related to unethical behaviour as well as persuasion, making it problematic in the workplace. Jones and Paulhus (2008) point out that Machiavellianism is related to behaviour such as cheating, lying and betrayal. There seems to be less of an 'upside' to Machiavellianism and less clear evidence of its impact on leadership. Babiak and Hare (2006) describe the psychopath as being 'without conscience and incapable of empathy, guilt, or loyalty to anyone but themselves' (p. 19). Psychopaths (being clear that we are refereeing to sub-clinical levels of psychopathy) are likely to be attracted to positions of influence and thus might be slightly over-represented in leadership, however, the potential damage done by psychopaths in positions of power is huge. As with narcissism, it has been argued that some characteristic of psychopaths are linked to positive outcomes such as communication skills, but the evidence suggest that psychopathy is mainly toxic in the workplace (Smith and Lilienfeld, 2013).

This book focuses entirely on the positive aspects of leadership and on how we develop the positive leadership characteristics that will transform the health service of the future However, we need to keep in mind the impact of dark personality and toxic leadership and find ways to mitigate its effects when we find it.

Personal development in medical leadership

Given the importance of personal qualities in what is required and expected of doctors as professionals and as leaders, it should be possible to integrate professional development activities towards both those ends. Until relatively recently, the development of 'professionalism' was seen as something that occurred through maturation, and learning was primarily through exposure to positive role models and socialisation into the profession. However, now professionalism is actively taught and assessed at all stages and increasingly so is leadership and management, sometimes as part of 'professionalism', sometimes separately.

Leadership and management theories can help us develop clinical leadership understanding and skills, develop as a professional and usually underpin development programmes. At whatever level or context in which a student, trainee or doctor is working, it is helpful to think of developing leadership and management under three headings as many of the theories place their emphasis on one of these:

1. Developing and building on the personal qualities or personality of the leader as an individual
2. Developing skills relating to the interaction of the leader with others
3. Learning about leadership in relation to the environment or system (Swanwick and McKimm, 2014).

What is also vital, as described above is that, while we tend to use the word 'leadership' and not 'management' to refer to medical leadership and management, leadership is not better than management – most activities involve a combination of both, and doctors need to learn to manage as well as lead. Accepting that systems, services and people need to be managed as well as led (and that doctors can and should do both) will help to address the divide discussed earlier.

Self-insight

Because effective leadership draws on personal qualities as well as understanding of other people, systems and organisations, development of self-insight is essential and thus leadership cannot be wholly learned through online courses or readings. The most effective leadership programmes provide opportunities for reflection, gaining feedback from others and a safe place to practice skills and test out ideas. Assessment is a key driver in ensuring that performance across domains is both measured and improved. It is important that assessment of leadership and management moves away from self-assessment (useful though that is) and that robust assessments involving other people (including patients) are used in development programmes and in the workplace. Tools such as multi-source feedback or 360° appraisals, measuring health innovations, audits and efficiency savings and assessing application of health improvement tools (e.g. the Productive Ward; Quality, Innovation, Productivity and Prevention; and Situation, Background, Assessment and Recommendation) are examples of effective assessment methods used in leadership and management development. The Francis report suggests that mandatory annual performance appraisals should be introduced and 'each clinician and nurse should be required to demonstrate their ongoing commitment, compassion and caring shown towards patients, evidenced by feedback of the appraisee from patients and families, as well as from colleagues and co-workers. This portfolio could be made available to the General Medical Council or the Nursing and Midwifery Council, if requested as part of the revalidation process' (Francis, 2013).

The Medical Leadership Competency Framework (MLCF) suggests that medical leaders should be able to demonstrate the following personal qualities:

- Developing self-awareness by being aware of his/her own values, principles and assumptions, and by being able to learn from experiences
- Organising and managing him-/herself while taking account of the needs and priorities of others
- Continuing personal development by learning through participating in continuing professional development and from experience and feedback
- Acting with integrity by behaving in an open, honest and ethical manner.

The increasing importance of enabling health professionals and doctors to develop leadership skills and understanding and provide fora for debate, development and resources led to the establishment of the NHS Leadership Academy and the Faculty of Medical Leadership and Management which work across the UK, as well as other bodies and activities in the devolved countries (see Chapters 2 and 6). Organisations are now starting to reframe models and rhetoric and qualities such as compassion, caring and courage are now explicit in frameworks such as the Healthcare Leadership Model (NHS Leadership Academy, 2013) which also emphasises personal qualities throughout the nine dimensions.

'The way that we manage ourselves is a central part of being an effective leader ... personal qualities like self-awareness, self-confidence, self-control, self-knowledge, personal reflection, resilience and determination are the foundation of how we behave. Being aware of your strengths and limitations ... will have a direct effect on how you behave and interact with others, and they with you. Without this awareness, it will be much more difficult (if not impossible) to behave in the way research has shown that good leaders do. This, in turn, will have a direct impact on your colleagues, any team you work in, and the overall culture and climate within the team as well as within the organisation. Whether you work directly with patients and service users or not, this can affect the care experience they have. Working positively on these personal qualities will lead to a focus on care and high-quality services for patients and service users, their carers and their families' (NHS Leadership Academy, 2013).

However, while reports and frameworks emphasise the importance of shared, collaborative, collective leadership, at all levels, that is dispersed throughout the organisation, more person-centred leadership theories such as authentic (Gardner et al, 2005), relational (Tepper et al, 2006), servant (Greenleaf, 2002) or ontological (Souba et al, 2007) leadership are not explicitly drawn from. Case scenario 12.3 describes some of the realities of clinical practice and how 'emotional labour' works in real life. Medical leaders are well placed to truly understand the service pressures of their colleagues and, if given the right tools, should be able to develop service improvements and leadership skills to help doctors deliver 'care and compassion' while avoiding burnout or mistakes.

Conclusions

Developing and demonstrating appropriate personal qualities is central to effective clinical leadership but that does not mean that there is no room for individual difference, indeed this must be nurtured. However, the Francis report and other inquiries into sub-standard health care have brought into sharp relief that clinical leadership and doctors' engagement in management is vital to maintain the focus on providing compassionate care to all through demonstrating behaviours that patients and the public expect. As Bass (2008)

Case scenario 12.3 'The emotional labour of care'

'This week aged 42, I finished my morning GP duty session at 1.30 pm after taking 53 calls from anxious patients, seeing 10 patients face-to-face and doing one home visit. I sent one woman to hospital with an infected knee, spent 30 minutes with a man who since his teenage daughter was diagnosed with schizophrenia has lost his job, been arrested for drunk driving and bought rat poison with the intention of suicide, and stopped half the regular prescriptions for an elderly woman who told me she wanted to stop postponing death. I was just about to slip out to get some lunch when the practice manager called to ask if she could speak to me urgently, one of my patients had complained about me and had written to the local newspaper, the MP and the parliamentary health ombudsman. I opened my door to find one of our trainees waiting outside – 'Please can you help me?' she asked. My next session was due to start at 2 pm, there were 15 patients booked in, I had 43 blood results to check, a boxful of hospital letters, and a message from a social worker about a patient that was expected to die. I hadn't had anything to eat or drink, or even time to pee since I left home at 7.15am.

Work like this constitutes a normal working day for health professionals, but at the same time it is completely abnormal. To do this, and to engage seriously, compassionately and with full attention and moral seriousness demands what Iona Heath has described with eloquent passion as a "labour of love". It is emotional labour. If we expect health-care professionals to treat care as a vocation and patients with empathy and compassion, we need to appreciate the enormous burden of patient-centred care. We must treat carers with the kindness and respect we expect them to treat their patients. We must make time to help them give the personal care their patients need and time to listen to them. We must listen to their concerns, their doubts, fears and distress.

Not a day goes by without someone in health policy or politics claiming that the NHS has put professionals before patients for too long, or that public service propagates professional complacency or that the threat of competition or prison is needed to improve care or compassion. These claims are profoundly depressing and so far removed from my experiences of 25 years of personal care, so insulting to all the dedicated, caring professionals I've worked with, and so, so wrong for patients.'

From Tomlinson (2013)

suggests '…the most important element [of leadership] … comes from a combination of emotional expressiveness, self-confidence, self-determination and freedom from internal conflict.'

Whatever form development and assessment of leadership takes, it is very similar to developing professionalism in that embedded, integrated approaches are needed that incorporate workplace-based assessments, appraisals and professional reviews, and encourage long-term development and reflective practice. Many medical schools and training programmes now include specific activities designed to develop leadership skills and the personal qualities that are required from a compassionate and clinically effective doctor. In addition, many medical educators are exploring how assessments can be made more robust both in selecting suitable applicants for the medical profession and assessing their personal development once they are there. We must be cautious, however, not to use validated tools that assess such factors as personality and emotional intelligence until we have more secure evidence about the role that these characteristics play in being a good doctor and a good medical leader. Self development aligned with robust measures will enable a culture shift in the NHS, and we should in future see more doctors engaging in leadership and management at all levels to improve health services and the patient experience.

Key points

- The publication of the Francis report stimulated a reframing of medical leadership that incorporates care and compassion
- Personal qualities are central to medical leadership and clinical engagement
- The qualities that underpin effective, value-led leadership are closely aligned with qualities that underpin professionalism
- A wide range of development programmes, resources and organisations is available to support the development of leadership and personal development
- Some evidence exists that desirable personal qualities such as emotional intelligence can be improved through a development programme
- Assessment of behaviours based on demonstration of personal qualities should be embedded in multisource feedback, appraisals and performance reviews as well as in routine workplace-based assessment for trainees and students.

CHAPTER 13

The role of emotion in effective clinical leadership and compassionate care

Helen O'Sullivan, Judy McKimm

Introduction

This chapter explores the role of emotion in clinical leadership and medical practice and suggests that the Francis report and subsequent debate provide the opportunity for a reframing of how doctors and leaders might engage in 'emotion work'. It is based on the article by O'Sullivan and McKimm (2014).

The circumstances and consequences of the Mid Staffordshire scandal and the Francis report are well documented (Thorlby et al, 2014). It is striking that the Francis report acknowledges that the words suffering, dignity, respect, compassion and sensitivity are highly emotive, yet they are used liberally throughout (Francis, 2013). This contrasts with Shapiro's (2011) suggestion that not only do official reports sanitise emotions, but the processes of professional medical socialisation systematically blunt learners' emotional reactions. The commentaries and debates that followed the Francis report and subsequent inquiries and reviews focussed not only on seeking to understand why health workers, leaders and managers behaved as they did, but in preventing this in future across the NHS and related public services. In a health-care environment in which resources (people, time, funding) are increasingly constrained, a key challenge for clinical and other health-care leaders is to enable health professionals to provide compassion and care while meeting organisational demands, all of which take time. If we are to avoid doctors' stress and burnout, then meeting this challenge is essential. Howe (2008) suggests that in the people-oriented professions, staff 'inevitably find themselves working daily with people whose needs are pressing and whose emotions are disturbingly aroused ... It is critical that ... workers understand the part that emotions play in the lives and behaviour of those who use their services...Practitioners need to understand how emotions affect them as they work with users and engage with colleagues'.

This chapter explores how doctors have traditionally been trained to set aside the emotions they may feel with a view that, by so doing, the 'clinical care' they provide will be better. However, the Francis report and subsequent debates raise questions as to whether this 'scientific' and 'objective' approach, the medicalisation of health and disease and the compartmentalising of tasks to different health professionals contributed to some doctors failing to take responsibility for addressing the poor care at Mid Staffordshire. While all health- and social-care professionals need to protect themselves psychologically from others' suffering and pain, doctors need to be trained to balance scientific objectivity with the risk of objectifying patients by taking a narrow, disease-focussed interpretation of what medical care means.

Emotions and empathy

Until relatively recently, although 'empathy' has long been viewed as a core professional attribute, doctors have not traditionally been taught to use their emotions actively in clinical practice. Thus doctors tend to intellectualise emotions, which helps them remain objective about what they do. Doctors (unlike other health- and social-care professionals) are not traditionally taught or formally equipped to work with their emotions as part of clinical decision-making and care. Medical schools have included constructs such as 'empathy' in selection and assessment processes for many years, but related emotional constructs including 'suffering', 'compassion', 'care' and 'sensitivity' have not been routinely and overtly addressed and, when they are, are framed as a set of cognitive and behavioural skills that can be taught and assessed objectively (Shapiro, 2011).

The words 'emotion' and 'empathy' are closely linked. The Oxford English Dictionary (www.oxforddictionaries.com) defines 'emotion' as a 'strong feeling deriving from one's circumstances, mood, or relationships with others' and an 'instinctive or intuitive feeling as distinguished from reasoning or knowledge'. It states that the word is derived from Latin and French meaning excite or move. The word 'empathy' means 'the ability to understand and share the feelings of another', derived from German philosophy, translated from the Greek 'empatheia' – 'passion, state of emotion'.

When looking at the concepts from this perspective, it seems difficult to understand how a doctor could be truly empathic without engaging in emotional connection and an internal discourse about the emotions being felt. The notion that emotions are not an integral part of the clinical reasoning process therefore appears fundamentally flawed, yet (unlike professions such as psychotherapy) students and doctors in training are not taught to actively surface and work with these emotions (case scenario 13.1). Indeed, a number of studies have demonstrated that measurable levels of empathy decline over the time that students spend in medical training (Hegazi and Wilson, 2013).

McNaughton (2013) makes the point that emotion has been 'either elided as part of a larger construct of values, attitudes and beliefs, or falsely dichotomised with "reason", making it largely invisible as a valuable form and source of knowledge'. She identifies 'emotional intelligence' as particularly relevant to a discourse of emotion as skills. Emotional intelligence, discussed below, is an emotion theory, and is 'a dependable method for measuring and judging capacities seen as not otherwise amenable to reliable capture' (McNaughton, 2013).

If doctors' compassion is to be taught, learned and assessed, it must be measurable and from a skills approach, currently only two things can be measured: the quality of communications and emotional intelligence. McNaughton (2013) criticised the skills approach to emotion for emphasising performance rather than 'reaching inside the boundaries of the individual', citing a review by Lewis et al (2005) which criticised emotional intelligence for trying to measure the immeasurable and perpetuating an individualised rather than

---

Case scenario 13.1 Learning from peers

Sam (a second year medical student) is working on the care of the elderly ward with Ffion (a foundation doctor). They both attend a particularly difficult case conference about what end-of-life care should be provided for Mrs Hawthorn, a 95-year-old woman with dementia and advanced bladder cancer in which her daughter broke down in tears. Afterwards, Sam says to Ffion 'that was really upsetting, how do you cope?' Ffion shrugs her shoulders and replies, 'well, you've just got to toughen up, there are so many patients, you can't get involved as a doctor'.

Does this (fairly widespread) belief that objectivity is protective partly explain the 'empathy decline'?

collective model of emotion. Given these comments, perhaps we should be exploring how to teach and assess the unpacking of emotional processes in clinical reasoning as well as focussing on 'measurable' performance.

Emotional intelligence

What is emotional intelligence?

The concept of emotional intelligence gained prominence with the publication of Daniel Goleman's book *Emotional Intelligence: Why It Can Matter More Than IQ* (Goleman, 1996). With this book, Goleman succeeded in bringing to the general population the idea that having a high emotional intelligence was 'a good thing'. Mayer and Salovey (1997) first sought to explain why some individuals are more capable than others of processing emotional information and use it to guide their behaviour by proposing a social interaction model of emotional intelligence. In this model, emotional intelligence was defined as:

> '...a type of social intelligence that involves the ability to monitor one's own and others' emotions, to discriminate among them and to use this information to guide one's own thinking and actions' (Mayer and Salovey, 1997).

Mayer et al (2003) later criticised the representation of emotional intelligence as a set of interrelated mental competencies because it could lead researchers to consider it a blanket term for interpersonal skills. They refined the construct to encompass the abilities to:

1. Perceive emotions – to detect and read emotions in self, in faces, pictures and voices
2. Use emotions – to harness emotions in thinking and problem solving
3. Understand emotions – to comprehend emotion in language, perceive nuance and track emotions over time
4. Manage emotions – the ability to regulate emotions in self and in others.

Emotional intelligence thus became a skill set including empathy, the ability to solve problems, optimism, and self-awareness. Since their initial conceptualisation, a number of alternative definitions of emotional intelligence have been proposed (Goldenberg et al, 2006). Davies and Stankov (1998) and Law et al (2004) define emotional intelligence as an abstract construct with four components:

1. Appraisal and expression of emotion in self
2. Appraisal and recognition of emotion in others
3. Regulation of emotion in self
4. Use of emotion to facilitate performance.

Bar-On (1997) defines emotional intelligence as a set of non-cognitive skills, abilities, competencies and capabilities that allows individuals to cope with environmental pressures whereas Kasman et al (2003) describe it as 'the means to perceive and express emotions and regulate emotions in self and others'. These multiple conceptualisations may seem to 'blur' emotional intelligence as a construct, but models of emotional intelligence can be split into two broad types: ability models, and trait and mixed (dispositional) models. Ability models (such as Salovey and Mayer's model) are extensions of information-processing theories of intelligence and conceptualise emotional intelligence as an 'intelligence'. Emotional intelligence comprises a set of cognitive abilities relating to perceiving, understanding, using and managing emotional information and as a further dimension of intellectual competence not considered by traditional conceptualisations of intelligence.

Trait models (such as Petrides' model (Petrides and Furnham, 2003)) and mixed (dispositional) models (such as Goleman's (1996) model and Bar-On's (1997) model) view emotional intelligence as a set of interrelated competencies, skills, abilities, personal qualities and personality traits. There is some overlap between the main components of the two types:

- Emotional intelligence is seen as a multidimensional construct with both cognitive and affective elements, consisting of the ability to recognise, deal with and apply emotional information to everyday decision making and behaviour
- A person with higher levels of emotional intelligence is seen as being able to join together emotions and reasoning, use emotions to facilitate such reasoning, and reason intelligently about emotion
- Standardised, self-report questionnaires are used to measure emotional intelligence.

The reliability, validity and cross-cultural applicability of the tools differ, however, as does the degree of overlap between individual questionnaire items. It is important to stress that an individual's emotional intelligence is distinct from a predisposition to experience certain types of emotions, which is related to the personality traits of positive and negative affectivity (George, 2000). Also an individual's emotional intelligence does not relate to how intensely emotions are experienced. Instead, emotional intelligence represents the extent to which an individual's cognitive capabilities are informed by his/her emotions, and the extent to which emotions are cognitively managed (George, 2000).

Benefits of emotional intelligence

The benefits to lay people of having high levels of emotional intelligence have been demonstrated. For example, emotional intelligence positively influences the ability to identify others' emotional expressions and makes people more satisfied with their interpersonal relationships, more flexible in social interactions, better able to manage their moods and more adaptable when under stress (Ciarrochi et al, 2000, 2002). Emotional intelligence has also been demonstrated to be a desirable attribute of good leaders and team-workers in a non-clinical setting (Goleman, 2000). The popularisation of emotional intelligence as 'mattering more than IQ' has promoted it as a crucial attribute for successful psychological and social functioning.

It could be argued that the importance of emotional intelligence may be stronger for professionals and leaders in professions whose everyday work is highly emotionally charged and particularly in contexts where there are higher levels of emotional labour (Held and McKimm, 2012). It is therefore logical to conclude that emotional intelligence may have face validity for use in medical education and development of medical leadership and practice, particularly given that an awareness, and understanding, of the role and influence of the multiple emotional experiences faced on a daily basis is integral to becoming and being a good doctor (Weng et al, 2011).

A note of caution

One of the main concerns about applying general theories about emotional intelligence to medical education and medical leadership development is whether tools designed to measure emotional intelligence can be reliably applied to medical populations. Medical students differ from the general population because their age range is narrow and they are a highly selected population of high academic achievers, with a socioeconomic background narrower than that of the general population. The reliability and validity of some, but not all tools, have been confirmed in medical student samples (Brannick et al, 2011) so anyone deciding to use a particular tool to measure emotional intelligence as part of a development tool for medical leadership would need to carefully check the validity of such a tool in that population.

Another concern about using emotional intelligence in this way is whether there is a 'minimum' level, after which emotional intelligence stops having an influence on medical leaders' practices. Given that emotional intelligence research is still in its infancy, there are limited data available to answer this question, which makes it particularly difficult to know how to use it as a selection criterion for other medical education or leadership development.

Finally, what are the potential negative or unintended outcomes of applying emotional intelligence to medical education and leadership? Two obvious concerns are that labelling a student or doctor as emotionally 'unintelligent' could become a self-fulfilling prophecy, while labelling one as highly intelligent could set up tensions in the competitive setting of a medical school or among trainee leaders. Measuring emotional intelligence will inescapably focus people's attention in a way that could, ultimately, trivialise the very quality that it was intended to strengthen and distract attention from other qualities that are not measured or fed back to people, which might be every bit as important to patients and colleagues.

Emotions and clinical leadership

The Francis report not only gave tacit permission for leaders and health professionals to use emotive language but moved towards mandating health service providers at every level to consider and use emotions as a routine part of their work. For example, while it may seem somewhat contrived to tell 'patient stories' at every NHS trust board meeting, this does ensure that the patient voice is heard, including the emotions and feelings that individual narratives involve and 'stir up' in others. Throughout history, hearing of the plight and suffering of others moves people to action, and in the case of UK health care, the Francis report and other reviews (see case scenario 13.2) stimulated what will hopefully be meaningful, long-lasting and truly patient-focussed changes. Clinical leaders are vital in sustaining this momentum and improving care.

The leadership and other literature offer some insight into how leaders can create a culture of compassion and care through the appropriate use of emotion. Early work on leadership focused on personality traits, and psychologists identified leadership traits such as emotional stability, conscientiousness, intuitiveness and empathy as key to leadership effectiveness (Cattell and Stice, 1954). In 1973, Mintzberg identified that leadership success was based on ability to establish social networks, work effectively with subordinates and the facility to empathise, all key skills for the collaborative leaders needed by contemporary health services (Mintzberg, 1973).

Case scenario 13.2 The Francis report (2010)

Based on evidence from over 900 patients and families, Sir Robert Francis reviewed the failings in care at Mid-Staffordshire NHS Foundation Trust between 2005-2009. The report, published in 2013, found evidence towards a culture that perpetuated conditions of appalling care. It was found that 'the system as a whole failed in its most essential duty – to protect patients from unacceptable risks of harm and from unacceptable, and in some cases inhumane, treatment that should never be tolerated in any hospital'.

Harrowing stories were heard of failings in even the basics of care including situations where 'patients were left in excrement in soiled bed clothes for lengthy periods', 'water was left out of reach', and 'assistance was not provided with feeding for patients who could not eat without help'. These findings sent shock waves throughout the NHS and have called for a 'relentless focus on the patient's interests... with frontline staff that must be empowered with responsibility and freedom to act in this way' under strong and stable leadership in stable organisations.

Regulating and containing emotions

Stevenson (2007) questions whether the current health service orthodoxy addresses the impact of emotions on professionals. She asks: 'how can organisations ... run on principles of order and rationality take into account the underlying emotional dynamics which profoundly affect the behaviour of their staff?'. Effective collaboration must create space to understand the emotions vested in the work. Stevenson (2007) suggests that 'these emotions should not be viewed in solely negative terms; they are the drivers of positive and negative behaviours and they underpin purposeful behaviour'.

The concepts of emotional competence and self-awareness need to be defined carefully in medicine which has a high emotional 'load' with routine emotion displays from patients, relatives and colleagues. When defining and promoting what is meant by emotional competence, leaders and practitioners need opportunities to address their own emotional vulnerabilities and fallibilities (Heron, 1992; MacCulloch, 2001). This where medicine can learn much from other professions around professional supervision and support. The emotional intelligence literature identifies the need for leaders to control, regulate or manage disruptive emotions and Goleman implies a causal relationship between disruptive emotions and negative behaviours (Salovey and Mayer, 1990; Goleman, 2000). All emotions are disruptive by their very nature, however, and authentic and congruent leaders (highly valued in complex professional fields) need to establish an atmosphere which both contains emotion yet enables people to express emotions safely. Iszatt-White (2009) suggests that leaders need to be able to allow 'emotional displays' which are part of 'the proactive use of emotion-based work in the accomplishment of leadership work'.

Morrison (2007) suggests that emotional intelligence competence is 'pivotal to gaining the co-operation of other colleagues and services ... to achieve their outcomes'. He argues that competence is not based on control but on awareness of the emotional dimension and the ability to use emotions positively. Yukl (2002) notes that most contemporary leadership theories involve a process of social influence. Avolio et al (2004) suggest that authentic transformational leaders are able to instil hope, trust and positive affectivity in their followers via personal and social identification, and George (2000) concludes that:

'...emotional intelligence contributes to effective leadership as leaders must be able to anticipate how followers will react to different circumstances and effectively manage these reactions'.

This reflects a shift in the way that leadership is being conceptualised around emergent change and shared leadership (Morrison, 2010). This shift acknowledges that individual personality traits (including emotion, integrity and empathy) are important but need to be contextualised within complex systems, networks and interdisciplinary collaboration (Bolden et al, 2003).

Emotional labour and emotion work

The emotions that drive positive and negative behaviours are both drivers and constrainers within dynamic systems. Emotions may be positive or negative, depending on how they are handled. Clinical leaders need to be comfortable with emotional labour and affective leadership, and able to tolerate ambiguity.

Waddington (2005) defines emotional labour as 'paid work which requires a person to express and manipulate emotions as a part of their job'. Crawford (2009) describes emotional labour as 'a requirement to produce emotional states in others or exercise a degree of control over the emotional activities of others', going on to note that good leaders create the conditions for the safe expression of emotion. Expanding the concept of 'patient safety' to include the need for leaders and individual health professionals to 'hold' or contain emotions rather than control them will acknowledge this. This subtle shift highlights the key role of leaders in reading the emotional 'temperature' of patients and carers, within their team, department or organisation and outside it. Leaders who fail to do this rapidly fall out of step with their members or followers and lose credibility.

Doctors and other health workers routinely perform emotional labour. Hochschild (2012) proposes that emotion regulation is achieved in two ways. When employees change their outward emotional expressions without feeling emotions they are displaying, they are surface acting. In contrast, when they actually feel the emotions they display, they are deep acting. Emotion work is also performed through spontaneous and genuine emotion. Ashforth and Humphrey (1993) suggest that both surface acting and deep acting may have harmful psychological effects, depending on the degree to which the actor identifies with the role and occupation. 'If emotional labor is consistent with a central, salient, and valued social and/or personal identity ... it will lead to enhanced psychological wellbeing' (Ashforth and Humphrey, 1993). Generally, the more congruent and authentic leaders' emotional displays are, the more at ease they are with their actions.

Humphrey et al (2008) distinguish emotional labour performed by transformational leaders from other forms of emotional labour. They suggest that 'leaders who perform emotional labor will be more likely to be perceived as transformational leaders ... deep acting will be more effective than surface acting at increasing perceptions of transformational leadership' ... Leaders high on empathy will prefer to use genuine emotional expressions and deep acting instead of surface acting.' (Humphrey et al, 2008). See also Chapter 12 case scenario 12.2.

Leaders working in emotionally-charged contexts, who can draw on deep acting or spontaneous and genuine emotion, may therefore be considered most effective and gain the respect of followers (see Chapter 15). Such leaders need to draw on emotional intelligence competencies, demonstrate understanding of their context and networks, and be willing to perform emotional labour. This requires congruence between the leader's personality, behaviours and understanding that appears consistently authentic in a range of situations. Followers typically rate consistency, integrity, courage, enabling and role modelling as key leadership characteristics (Kouzes and Posner, 2007). Most leadership development activities acknowledge that a balance is needed between theory, building on innate personality traits, and developing practical and interpersonal skills and competencies associated with effective leadership (Bolden et al, 2003; Kouzes and Posner, 2007). Multi-source feedback can be very helpful in developing high-level interpersonal leadership competencies.

Affective leadership

Fineman (2004) refers to the recorded emotional narrative as a 'key subjective, biographical production, combining interpretation, embodiment and lived experience'. Doctors are highly familiar with listening to patients' narratives as part of history taking and increasingly urged to engage in reflective writing and practice, but are less familiar in terms of the art of leadership. Denhardt and Denhardt (2006) used the 'dance of leadership' as metaphor for the artful use of affect (expressed emotion) that shows situational awareness, contextual sensitivity and recognition of an individual's needs. 'Recognising the artistic dimension of leadership ... compels us to acknowledge and give further thought to the inner resources required by the leader' (Denhardt and Denhardt, 2006). The affective leader can rapidly assess the affective state of the other, analyse his/her own affective state, and from this select the appropriate affect to display in order to achieve the desired (or best achievable) outcome (Newman et al, 2009). 'It is a transactional process in that the followers agree to play their "role" as long as the "dance" steps are followed. For the skilled leader the process is one of rapid cognition. It happens intuitively, often outside conscious awareness, since the speed at which the various observations and decisions are made is greater than that of conscious thought. Leaders and followers constantly balance the tensions between rational thought, emotion and intuition' (Held and McKimm, 2012).

As services become more integrated, leaders must adopt an emotionally appropriate approach to managing different professional attitudes, expectations and stereotypes. The approach must match the affective expectations of the (often unequal) professional workforce, moderate their own and others' stereotypes and calm fears about professional identity and lack of control. This requires leaders to artfully use affect to enable professionals to work in an atmosphere of connectedness, tolerate uncertainty, and learn from positive and negative emotional experiences. One technique to facilitate reflection and build this cultural atmosphere is through 'Schwartz rounds', briefly discussed in case scenario 13.3.

Case scenario 13.3 Schwartz rounds

One way in which the NHS is trying to support staff working in emotionally-charged roles is through the introduction of 'Schwartz rounds'. These began in the USA in the late 1990s and in 2009, the King's Fund Point of Care programme began piloting these in two trusts in the UK. The rounds are multidisciplinary, open to all hospital staff and provide a safe place once a month for staff to discuss and reflect on the non-clinical (emotional and social) aspects of their work. Evaluation of the UK rounds in 2012 indicated that the rounds are appropriate for the UK NHS setting; they had support at all levels of the organisations; had huge personal impact on staff, relationships and team working, and impact on the wider organisational culture (Goodrich and Levenson, 2012). This evaluation echoed the impact the rounds have in the USA (Lown and Manning, 2010).

Conclusions

This article has explored some of the contemporary views relating to emotions, emotional intelligence, emotion work and emotional labour in clinical settings. An overriding message emerging from the literature is that how emotions are expressed and used is highly dependent on constantly changing social norms and expectations. Clinical leaders therefore need to be highly competent in acknowledging and containing their own and others' emotions safely and in reading the organisational and social 'mood' and 'temperature' accurately.

'Post-Francis', we are in the midst of a shifting landscape which provides huge opportunities to reconceptualise how doctors and health providers work with and acknowledge not only the emotions of those for whom they care, but those of health professionals themselves. For doctors, this also means rethinking the self-imposed boundaries between doctors and other health providers and in learning how to incorporate emotion work into education, training and everyday practice. For clinical leaders, supporting students and doctors in balancing organisational demands with caring, compassionate, safe patient care is essential but is one of the biggest challenges in today's resource-constrained environments.

Key points

- The Francis report and subsequent publications and debates have set the scene for a rethinking of how emotions are used as part of leadership, medical education and practice
- Emotion work and emotional labour have to be acknowledged as a routine part of doctors' work and doctors need to be trained and supported to use emotions effectively
- Clinical leaders need a high level of emotional intelligence, but emotional intelligence is only one component of 'emotion work'
- A key challenge for clinical leaders is to enable doctors to meet organisational demands while providing compassionate and safe clinical care in resource-constrained environments
- A key leadership skill is being able to accurately judge the emotional and social 'temperature' and 'mood' of situations, teams and organisations.

CHAPTER 14

Don't follow your leader: challenging erroneous decisions

Michael J Moneypenny, Arpan Gupta, Simon J Mercer, Helen O'Sullivan, Judy McKimm

Introduction

This chapter provides insight into how medical students and doctors at all levels can challenge decisions with a view to improving patient safety, discusses some of the difficulties and barriers in so doing, some of the underpinning reasons behind this and the important role of followership. It is based on the article by Moneypenny et al (2013).

A series of reports into failings in the NHS, including the Francis report (2013), the Keogh review (2013) and the Berwick report (2013), highlighted the role of leadership in establishing successful organisations with a culture that meets the public's expectations for high standards of compassionate care. Indeed, one of the recommendations of the Francis report states the need for 'strong and stable leadership in stable organisations' (Francis, 2013).

The Darzi review (Darzi, 2008) focused heavily on teasing out the qualities and requirements for successful health-care leadership. All the above reviews also emphasise the important role of medical students and doctors in training in foregrounding patient safety. Although the concept of 'followership' has traditionally received less attention and the word 'followership' only appears once in the full Francis report, the concept of effective followership implicitly pervades the recommendations. The Medical Leadership Competency Framework (MLCF) has been revisited by the NHS Leadership Academy and developed into a leadership framework for all practitioners in the NHS – the Health-care Leadership Model (NHS Leadership Academy, 2013). The underlying philosophy of distributed leadership that characterised the original framework has been extended into the concept of collective leadership (West et al, 2014). In models of distributed (shared, dispersed, collaborative or collective) leadership, the requirement on the team, as distinct from the leaders of that team, to take responsibility for patient safety and health improvement is paramount.

Ever since the landmark study by Milgram (1963), which examined the willingness of people to obey orders even when they thought they were actively harming people, there has been interest in many fields in the causes of failure to challenge authority and the potential damaging consequences of such failure. In medicine, which is a highly hierarchical system, this lack of challenge is a component of communication failures and a major cause of preventable patient harm and death (Kohn et al, 2000; Cosby and Croskerry, 2004; Firth-Cozens, 2004; Lingard et al, 2004; Sutcliffe et al, 2004; Makary et al, 2006; Belyansky et al, 2011). If we are to improve patient safety then it is vital that students and doctors in training are enabled and equipped with the skills and confidence to challenge perceived authority when working in health-care teams, while maintaining good working relationships. The ability for doctors to work effectively in teams is highlighted from the start of the educational process. For example, in *Medical students: professional values and fitness to practise*, the General Medical Council (2007) states that medical students should: 'develop and demonstrate teamwork and leadership skills'.

As we see in case scenario 14.1, although the traditional view of a team worker may be one of providing support for a leader, numerous instances exist where failure on the part of a team worker to challenge an erroneous decision by the leader led to an adverse outcome (Cosby and Croskerry, 2004; Gladwell, 2008; Bromiley, 2009). In contrast, Seiden et al (2006) discuss a number of cases where medical undergraduates prevented patient harm by speaking up. This emphasises the importance of enabling students to do this from the start of training.

We were interested in finding out why some medical undergraduates failed to challenge leadership decisions, while others were willing to do so. Although a number of writers have discussed the reasons for failure to challenge in a medical setting (*Table 14.1*) (Coats and Burd, 2002; Sutcliffe et al, 2004; Wachter, 2005; Kobayashi et al, 2006; Walton, 2006; Pian-Smith et al, 2009), there has as yet been no attempt to categorise and rank the most common reasons why medical undergraduate students fail to challenge more senior doctors.

Studies have also shown that there is a difference in perceived willingness to be challenged between seniors and juniors; seniors tend to believe that they encourage being challenged, a situation which is not corroborated by their juniors (Coats and Burd, 2002; Makary et al, 2006; Belyansky et al,

---

Case scenario 14.1 Confronting seniors

'Participants reported that they found it difficult to tell doctors if they thought they were doing something wrong and reported that it was easier to do something after the event. For example, one student was observing a senior house officer (doctor in training) putting in a dialysis line on a renal ward. The student had seen the procedure performed a number of times and was aware of the correct way of doing it. The senior house officer in question was performing the procedure differently from previous times and his technique was very poor but she felt that she could not do anything at the time as she was just a student. "Afterwards I went to my mentor who arranged for the senior house officer to be observed performing the procedure and so he was re-trained." Most participants agreed that a lot of senior house officers had bad techniques but as student nurses they felt they could not do anything. All agreed that senior nurses did tell the doctors'.

Extract from *Confronting errors in patient care*, Firth-Cozens et al (2002). The report describes a study using mixed nurse-doctor focus groups considering aspects of speaking up when mistakes were being made.

Table 14.1 Barriers to challenging adapted from Pian-Smith et al (2009)

Perceived barriers to action	Assumed hierarchy
	Fear of embarrassment of self or others
	Concern over being misjudged
	Fear of being wrong
	Fear of retribution
	Jeopardising an ongoing relationship
	Natural avoidance of conflict
	Concern for reputation
Additional barriers when challenging a teacher or mentor	Respect for the teacher–student relationship
	Violation of a special trust
	High value placed on experience
	Concern over being negatively evaluated

2011). Because failure to challenge erroneous decisions may contribute to patient morbidity and mortality (Belyansky et al, 2011), discovering the most common reasons for this failure should help to inform further research and practice into overcoming actual or perceived barriers.

This chapter reports the results of a small scale study investigating the nature of challenge among medical students at a UK medical school.

The research study

A high-fidelity simulated scenario was designed in which a faculty member, playing the role of the senior member of the team, made two erroneous decisions regarding the correct care of a critically ill patient (*Table 14.2*).

In deciding what the two erroneous decisions should be, the authors consulted medical students not involved in the study, the simulation centre staff and staff in the School for Medical Education. They wanted to incorporate two erroneous decisions which would be easily recognised as such by final year medical undergraduates. Making the errors 'obviously' wrong would allow the authors to avoid the problem encountered by Pian-Smith et al (2009) of being unsure whether the lack of a challenge was the result of a lack of knowledge rather than some other factor. The authors tested the scenario on a final year medical student not involved in the study and found that it worked as planned.

Table 14.2 Planned erroneous decisions

Erroneous decision 1	Delaying needle decompression of a tension pneumothorax in order to await a chest X-ray which will take 15–20 minutes to be carried out. Vital signs are: blood pressure 70/50 mmHg, heart rate 130 bpm, oxygen saturation 75%
Erroneous decision 2	Decompressing the wrong hemithorax. The 'senior' plans to decompress the wrong hemithorax despite the absence of breath sounds, hyper-resonance to percussion and deviation of the trachea away from the other (correct) hemithorax

If the participants failed to challenge the erroneous decision, they would be prompted to do so by being asked questions such as: 'That is right, isn't it?' If despite repeated (>3) prompts the candidate failed to challenge the senior then one of the other team members, also played by faculty staff, would challenge and the senior would change his/her mind.

A total of 18 final year medical students agreed to participate. The students were told that they would be involved in a simulated scenario which tested their team working and leadership skills. At the beginning of the session each medical student was welcomed, provided written consent, was briefed and given a routine introduction to the mannequin, its capabilities and limitations. This was followed by the scenario, which lasted up to 15 minutes. The scenario was video-recorded and the actions and oral communication of the participants noted. Immediately following the scenario, the participants participated in a debrief which involved using a think-aloud technique (Fonteyn et al, 1993) and viewing of the video recording to explain their thoughts and beliefs during the scenario. The actions and verbal communication of the participants were analysed in relation to students' reasoning during the debrief. The language used by the medical undergraduates in challenging the senior was coded according to a system used by Pian-Smith et al (2009) (*Table 14.3*).

Table 14.3 Scoring system for challenges

Type	Score	Example
Say nothing	1	
Say something oblique, obtuse	2	Really?
Advocate or inquire	3	Shouldn't we do something about the pneumothorax?
Advocate or inquire repeatedly, with initiation of discussion	4	Which way was the trachea deviated? and/or Is that not a tension pneumothorax? and/or Are you sure that is correct?
Use crisp advocacy-inquiry	5	Well he's still not stable enough to be honest to have an X-ray, so would you be able to release the tension pneumothorax?

What the study showed

With every candidate having the opportunity to challenge twice, 36 instances occurred where leadership could have been challenged. Twenty erroneous decisions were challenged without requiring a prompt, ten decisions were challenged after one or more prompts and six decisions were never challenged.

The talk-aloud recordings from the latter two groups were analysed to elucidate whether the candidates knew that the senior was making a mistake and what their reasoning was for delaying or failing to challenge. In 15 of the 16 decisions (94%) the candidates knew the senior was mistaken. Three of the 16 decisions could not be categorised as the candidates did not explain their reasoning. The remaining 13 decisions were categorised (*Table 14.4*).

In terms of the language used by the candidates, the authors found similarities with the post-debriefing cohort of Pian-Smith et al's study (*Figure 14.1*). The majority of candidates who did question the decision of the senior doctor used a combination of advocacy or inquiry language. Very few candidates used an obtuse method of questioning the erroneous decision.

Table 14.4 Reasons for failing to challenge

Reason	Number (%)	Example
Assumed hierarchy	10 (77)	'…because the anaesthetist had arrived and I felt that we'd kind of transferred responsibility to him…'
High value placed on experience	6 (46)	'…he's obviously had experience of this in the past…'
Fear of being wrong	2 (15)	'… I had to understand it before we proceeded cos we needed to get this right.'
Fear of embarrassment of self	1 (8)	'Didn't want to say something that was gonna to be completely ridiculous.'

Discussion

Although this study was small-scale, the findings are consistent with other studies and suggest that erroneous decisions remain unchallenged not because of a failure to notice that the decision is wrong, but because of reluctance to challenge the leader. The majority of failed challenges are the result of a perceived hierarchy, i.e. the senior is obeyed because he/she is senior rather than more experienced. This finding is backed up by other studies (Belyansky et al, 2011). It has also been suggested (Sydor et al, 2013) that the hierarchical nature of the medical profession might lead to reluctance to challenge leaders in critical matters of patient safety. This has been described by Cosby and Croskerry (2004) as the 'authority gradient' in medicine and the results of this study suggest that this gradient, whose negative effect is worst during high pressure situations, continues to exist. As Bromiley (2009) states: 'We are taught respect for our senior and/or experienced colleagues. It's often "simply not your place" to speak up. Again this deference to others is very common in incidents and accidents the world over.'

Figure 14.1. Comparison of scores from the study by Pian-Smith et al (2009) and the study of undergraduate medical students described in this chapter. The scoring system shown on the x-axis is outlined in Table 14.3.

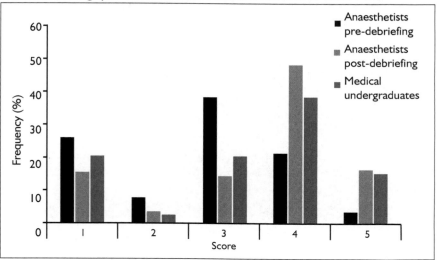

Effective team communication should be non-hierarchical (Mahlmeister, 2005), but this study shows that there is still an operating hierarchy within medicine which prevents medical undergraduates from speaking up, even in a simulated environment. What this demonstrates is how a follower's behaviour is influenced by his/her perception of how positional power and authority operates in the workplace. The perceived consequences of challenging a 'superior' from a professional perspective need further exploration to determine whether these beliefs are based on previous experiences, this specific relationship, rumour, or low skill or esteem levels of the learner. It is the case, however, that a senior who is responsible (for example) for a student or trainees' assessment or sign off has a high level of power over him/her and the consequences of challenging may be perceived to not be worth the risk

---

Case scenario 14.2

'I was a registrar on call in A&E [accident and emergency] when a young man came in with signs of fever. He'd been out to the cinema and had collapsed on his way home. He was obviously very sick. He had a high temperature and was hypotensive. As I examined him, I spotted a small black, boggy mark on his upper arm. He hadn't noticed this, and said it didn't hurt. I wondered whether it could be necrotising fasciitis. The clinical appearance fitted everything I'd read about the condition, and I sent blood samples to the lab. I then phoned the on-call surgical registrar. He looked at the mark, but didn't agree with my diagnosis and decided not to operate. I also spoke to the consultant microbiologist about the blood cultures. He thought the man probably had cellulitis, and he gave me antibiotic advice. But I still had a bad feeling about the man's case. I just knew that he was seriously ill. I tried to get a bed in ITU [intensive therapy unit], but it was full. So the man was admitted to an acute ward. During the night he had an arrest and went into septic shock. His skin continued to blister and discolour. He was taken to ITU and operated on in the morning. He did have necrotising fasciitis and needed to have several fingers and toes amputated. I felt awful. There was this poor young man with horrible scars and we hadn't treated him early enough. I learned a tough lesson that day. I should have questioned the surgical registrar's opinion and pushed harder for a bed in ITU. I was out of my depth and should have called my consultant, even though it was one in the morning'.

National Patient Safety Agency (2005)

(case scenario 14.2). From an intrapersonal perspective, by not challenging someone in power, the follower avoids being blamed, shamed or scared: all very powerful, core emotions which can highly influence behaviours, especially 'in the moment'.

Grint and Holt (2011) propose a typology of followership in which the students who did not challenge the decision in this study would be categorised as 'compliant followers'. The aim of medical education at the undergraduate and postgraduate level should be to develop what Grint and Holt refer to as 'responsible' followers – team members who have the interpersonal skills to challenge authority and decision making in a way that will not contribute to a defensive or risk-averse culture. Chapter 15 gives a more in-depth exploration of followership.

Conclusions

This was a small-scale study with a number of limitations, and further research is needed in this area to determine which factors may influence the decision to challenge leadership and what educational interventions, such as use of the 'two challenge' rule (Agency for Healthcare Research and Quality, 2008; Pian-Smith et al, 2009) or simulation sessions incorporating erroneous decisions, may be effective in promoting appropriate leadership challenges. Similarly training should be included for more senior doctors to enable openness to challenge, which might be more helpfully termed 'discussion' or 'input' to the decision-making process. If the use of these interventions could be instituted at the undergraduate level as well as more generally throughout the medical workforce, we would be one step closer to providing a culture that promotes safer health care.

Ethical approval for this study was granted by the University of Liverpool Medical School's Research Ethics Committee.

Key points

- A large body of work identifies the difficulties and barriers of challenging the decisions or behaviours of those in authority
- A small-scale, simulation-based study involving medical students produced similar findings to those involving senior doctors and in other settings relating to reluctance to challenge seniors
- The concept of 'followership' provides an explanatory framework through which the relationship between students, doctors in training and senior doctors can be explained
- Serious implications for patient safety arise if teams and cultures are based on hierarchies, over-reliance on positional power, and command and control leadership styles
- More work is needed to determine the most effective ways of developing confidence and skills so that students and doctors in training can have clear, consistent and listened-to input into decision making.

CHAPTER 15

Followership, clinical leadership and social identity

Hester Mannion, Judy McKimm, Helen O'Sullivan

Introduction

This chapter explores how the concepts of followership, social identity and social influence help clinical leaders and followers better understand how leadership processes function within and between individuals, teams and complex organisations. It is based on the article by Mannion et al (2015).

Health professionals commonly work in teams to deliver health care to patients and communities across various organisational, professional, service and social settings. West and Lyubovnikova (2013) describe real team working as an 'illusion', the idea that teams work effectively as stable entities is a misconception, as in reality they are fluid and differ greatly in character depending on the situation and team composition, with most health workers working in 'pseudo teams'. As health and social care service delivery becomes more complex, the traditional hierarchical uni-professional structures and lines of authority are becoming increasingly ineffective and outmoded (Martin, 2011). The doctors' role as 'head of the healthcare team and commander of considerable resource' (Tooke, 2008) does not necessarily apply in all situations which means that traditional conceptions of 'command and control' type leadership are rarely applicable.

This fluid, dynamic reality makes leading and working in teams more difficult and complex than may appear on the surface and for which formal medical and health-care education poorly equips students (Barrow et al, 2014). Recent studies and policy rhetoric emphasise a shift towards collective or shared leadership (West et al, 2014) but in practice there is a lag between expectations and practice, with ineffective teamworking contributing to the majority of patient safety concerns and medical errors (Studdert et al, 2002).

In the light of this, we explore whether too much emphasis is being paid to the development of clinical 'leadership' without due consideration for 'followership'. A similar question has been posed in the generic leadership literature (Oc and Bashshur, 2013; Uhl-Bien et al, 2014) and a deeper understanding of the importance and impact of followership may well enable doctors (and other health workers) to work more safely and effectively in a range of teams and situations. Without followers, there would be no leaders and followers' relationship with and influence on leaders is currently the subject of much research and scrutiny. How professionals conceptualise themselves in terms of both their professional identities (e.g. as doctors, as anaesthetists, as midwives) and as leaders, managers or followers is an essential consideration in working with others in intra- or inter-professional teams. This chapter describes the interlinked concepts of followership, leadership and social identity formation and how our understanding of these applies to clinical practice and leadership.

Understanding followership

'Our understanding of leadership is incomplete without an understanding of followership' (Uhl-Bien et al, 2014, p.84).

Leaders need followers; followers can be seen as not only influencing leaders' behaviours but as actively co-constructing and moderating leaders' behaviour and the leadership process (Uhl-Bien et al, 2014). The vast majority of leadership research is 'leader-centric', i.e. it sees leaders as having organisational and group power which they use to affect outcomes and change processes. This leads to stereotypical (but widely held) views of effective leaders being inspiring, motivating, charismatic individuals, followers as passive, obedient subordinates and organisations as designed in terms of formal hierarchies, with roles or positions reflecting status as a leader or follower. The term 'follower' (rather like the term 'manager') is then perceived as somewhat derogatory or secondary to that of 'leader'. From this perspective, leader effectiveness is explained in terms of personality traits, behaviours or styles and contexts or situations and the most dominant theories used to explain or research leadership are those of charismatic and transformational leadership (Bass and Riggio, 2005). In practical terms, leaders need to learn which behaviours are most helpful and which are not in working with their followers. Leaders will be adaptive and modify their behaviours depending on the relationship between the leader and follower(s), what they want followers to do and in different situations. Case scenario 15.1 demonstrates how easily a leader can get 'out of step' with followers which can lead to unintended (often unrealised) consequences.

The 'romance of leadership'

Research into followers considers the way in which followers construct leaders and leadership, these are 'follower-centric' approaches. From a follower-centric perspective, it seems that followers need leaders just as much as leaders need

---

Case scenario 15.1 'Such a nice guy, but...'

Graham, a care of the elderly consultant, was waiting in the queue for morning coffee when he overheard two foundation doctors talking, clearly about one of his colleagues.

'I hate working with Dr X, he is so nice to everyone, all the patients and relatives love him and he swans around the ward smiling. Everyone says what a fantastic doctor he is, well, they clearly haven't worked on the ward. He makes out that he does everything but in reality it is the poor trainees and nurses running around behind the scenes'.

'Well, it's that old-fashioned type of consultant leadership isn't it, they sort of think they're gods and because the patients revere them as well, it all goes to their heads. I don't think they realise that it isn't how we work now and what we expect of leaders, we need them to roll their sleeves up and value everyone for their work – it just isn't respectful to take all the credit. Anyway, I've heard they're really struggling to recruit trainees now as word has gone round, I certainly wouldn't apply while he is in charge.'

Graham was a bit taken aback, he hadn't realised how people felt about Dr X, he just labelled him as a bit 'old-school' – might this help explain the trouble they were having with recruiting? He resolved to keep his eyes and ears open and see if what the foundation doctors were saying was true or just hospital gossip.

followers, particularly in times of crisis, instability or rapid change. Uhl-Bien et al's (2014) review of the research on followership described two theories that help explain this: the 'romance of leadership' and 'implicit leadership theories'. The romance of leadership concept (Meindl et al, 1985) suggests that Western cultures often focus on the leader as the main element in group processes and that there is a fundamental attribution error in that followers may over-attribute causality for group outcomes to the leader. Charismatic leadership theory and attribution processes are linked to help explain the 'social contagion' that happens when followers are stressed or excited – they imbue leaders with more charisma, importance and influence than they may actually have – similar to a hero leader (Bligh et al, 2004). Of course, as long as the leader is functioning as followers expect, then these processes are positive for all involved. However, leaders are human and therefore fallible, they make mistakes and they may not act or look as followers might expect. This can lead to problems, mistrust, a perpetuation of certain leader types and, in extreme cases, the downfall of leaders.

Implicit leadership theories

Just as leader-centric views are widely held, which diminish the influence and importance of followers, so too are preconceptions of what leaders should be like. Implicit leadership theories suggest that followers have beliefs and schemata for leadership behaviour that influence their perception of 'good' and 'bad' leaders. These schemata or prototypes are developed through experiences, the media and socialisation and are used to match leaders' behaviour or attributes against. These 'folk theories of leadership' (Sivasubramaniam et al, 1997) or 'philosophies of leadership' (Schyns and Meindl, 2005) are highly influential in shaping followers' acceptance and tolerance of different types of leader (Uhl-Bien et al, 2014). Implicit leadership theories help to explain some of the struggles faced by leaders who do not 'fit' into their followers' schemata, based not on leadership skills but on general attributes such as gender, profession, sexuality, disability, age or race. In practical terms, this means that some leaders may have to work much harder to overcome deeply held (but not always articulated) beliefs about what leaders should look like and behave. Over time, as health professionals (and their leaders) are drawn from a more diverse pool and leadership is dispersed at all levels of organisations, these attitudes should change.

Constructing leadership

Finally, more recent research has shifted from a focus on individuals to exploring followership behaviours as they help to co-construct leadership processes, these include the social identity and relational approaches (Hogg, 2001; Uhl-Bien, 2006) and complex adaptive leadership (DeRue, 2011). These theories see leadership and followership as socially constructed processes, mediated through relational interactions between people (Oc and Bashshur, 2013). The organisation is therefore best understood in terms of a complex, dynamic system (DeRue, 2011; McKimm and Till, 2015). Hollander (2012) suggests that from this perspective, the leader is part of the collective leadership process (and may be highly influential) but is only one of possibly many individuals involved. From a systems perspective, leadership is the product of the interaction between leaders' and followers' self-schema, culture, and relational, information-processing and task systems. Understanding this complexity is essential if the NHS is to support both leaders and followers to deliver the huge culture shifts required in the wake of the raft of reports into poor care (West et al, 2015). Followers may need to be prepared to follow non-traditional leaders as work patterns and roles change, leaders may need to be adaptive and change their ways of working to attract, motivate and retain a range of different followers and all may need to be able to shift rapidly between both leader and follower roles as leadership becomes more collective and dispersed.

Professional and social identity, followership and the clinical environment

Despite the need for fluidity of health systems and health workers described above, roles in the health professions remain well-established along traditional lines both professionally and socially, with expectations inside and outside the clinical environment mutually influencing one another. For doctors, these expectations typically involve competition with their peers, authority over other professionals in the workplace and some relative autonomy in decision-making once in positions of seniority (Horsburgh et al, 2006). This cultural dynamic is reinforced in undergraduate and postgraduate training, as medical students and doctors are encouraged to stand out, compete for positions and aspire to leadership roles (Barrow et al, 2014). This fundamentally informs and influences relationships between doctors as well as relationships between doctors and other health professionals.

Professional identity

Professionals work hard to maintain their social identity which is intrinsically tied up with strong emotions relating to 'selfhood' (Croft et al, 2015). If this is perceived as being threatened, then defensive behaviours and 'group-think' can emerge which can lead to difficult challenges for both leaders and followers. Souba (2011b) suggests that one way of addressing these issues is for health-care leaders to use an ontological perspective which involves developing action-focussed access to human nature, this is about being a leader, not simply focussing on doing leadership activities. 'Action focussed access to leadership allows leaders to get their head around the essence of leadership and their arms around the way it is exercised' (Souba, 2011b). This involves paying purposeful attention to language and meaning, your own and others' behaviours, thought patterns (e.g. stereotypes or schema about other health professionals) and self-limiting beliefs ('I can't possibly be a leader/follower/manager, I'm too young/old/different etc.') and may help to address some of the issues encountered in clinical practice.

Although the General Medical Council (2007) states the importance of both teamwork and leadership skills in medical students, the culture within the medical profession actively encourages aspiration to leadership and personal career progression over team success, with many teams existing in name only (West and Lyubovnikova, 2013). As a result, doctors become very experienced in self-promotion but are not encouraged to engender the attributes that will make them effective followers. This has important implications not just for efficient service provision but also for patient safety (Moneypenny et al, 2013). While a team cannot function without leadership, leadership cannot exist without followership. As Lee (2010) notes 'working in teams does not come easily to physicians, who still often see themselves as lone healers. Nonetheless, developing teams is a key leadership function for healthcare providers of all types'. Case scenario 15.2 shows how difficult it can be to 'fit in' to a group or team even when you are doing things with the best intentions.

The role of the follower

Understanding the motivations and composition of followers in the clinical environment can serve to inform more effective leadership, more cohesive team working and, ultimately, better patient care. Tee et al (2013), in their discussion of followership from a social identity perspective, describe the 'high-identifying' follower as one who identifies closely with the leader and the rest of the group, socially and professionally. High-identifiers have high expectations of their leaders in terms of procedural fairness, they also 'are more likely to be

---

Case scenario 15.2 Looking after number one?

Ramesh is a third year medical student, he's grown up with social media, and in light of his intended career as a doctor, is very careful about photos and comments that make their way on to the internet. His family already treat him as though he is a doctor in spite of his reluctance to look at their lumps and bumps and listen to their complaints. He has also found that patients in the hospital often call him 'doctor' even when he has introduced himself as a student. He has become increasingly aware that people have higher expectations of his behaviour outside the hospital, he hardly ever gets visibly drunk on nights out in public and has stopped illegally downloading music and films.

Ramesh is sitting an end-of-year written paper with the rest of his year group and a little way in to the exam he looks up and notices a renal physiology poster on the wall which contains some of the answers in the paper. He raises his hand to alert the invigilator to the problem. The poster is immediately removed. Ramesh assumes he is the only person who noticed the poster until after the exam when he encounters unexpected reactions from his student colleagues. 'You shouldn't have mentioned it' said one student 'that information was available to everyone and if people are too stupid to look around themselves then they don't deserve the free marks'. When Ramesh said that he thought it was cheating, some agreed while others said that it was simply making the most of the resources available and taking opportunities as they arose.

The related questions were subsequently removed from the exam. The incident leaves Ramesh less sure than ever that he has found the balance between being driven to achieve academic success and engendering probity in his choices.

---

affected by group level emotions, attitudes, and behaviours' (Tee et al, 2013). As it is the cultural norm in the medical profession to aspire to leadership roles, most doctors following a clinical leader may not only identify closely with their clinical lead but imagine themselves in their superior's shoes at some point.

Multi-professional teams

The situation for nurses may be somewhat more complex, where they may identify closely with fellow nurse in authority but are unlikely to identify closely with medical clinical leadership. Barrow et al (2011) describe how nurses were more resistant to the 'sovereign' power wielded by their medical colleagues and use sophisticated knowledge of systems and hierarchies to find their way around it. In spite of the high social and professional identification, doctors who are trained to stand out and get ahead, perhaps at the expense of their colleagues, are arguably less likely to show group loyalty, not least because they aspire to lead from the front rather than be part of an influential followership, driving for a personal rather than a group goal. Nurses have a strong collective professional group identity and solidarity, perhaps leading to a stronger more cohesive followership (Barrow et al, 2011; Croft et al, 2015). Both groups of professionals however, consider their 'home team' to be constructed of their professional peers, not of an interprofessional group and are less likely to identify (and indeed value) leaders outside their home team/ profession (Barrow et al, 2011). A greater recognition of the importance and influence of followership as well as leadership in the training of health professionals may encourage doctors to appreciate the influence they can have as followers, promoting team goals of delivering good service as well as personal professional achievement. For nurses, an understanding of influential followership might help to foster a more cohesive and equal working relationship with doctors they may find it otherwise difficult to relate to.

Followers' influence

It would be unfair, however, not to recognise as qualities some of the drive and aspiration particularly espoused by medical students and doctors in training; these characteristics need not be at odds with good followership. Kelley (2008) describes five basic styles of followership: the sheep, the yes-people, the alienated, the pragmatics and the star followers:

> 'Star followers think for themselves, are very active, and have very positive energy. They do not accept the leader's decision without their own independent evaluation of its soundness. If they disagree, they challenge the leader, offering constructive alternatives that will help the leader and the organization get to where they want to go. Some people view these people as really "leaders in disguise", but this is basically because those people have a hard time accepting that followers can display such independence and positive behaviour.'

Motivated and engaged doctors may fulfil such followership roles, provided it was culturally acceptable to put energy and time in to a pursuit that might not result in a leadership role or personal recognition over team success.

Oc and Bashshur (2013) propose that 'followers with higher position or personal power exert greater social influence on leaders' (p.924). If doctors are indeed high-identifiers who engage closely with their leadership, and perhaps star followers who are active in their influence over decision-making they are more likely to fall in to the category of persuasive rather than supportive followers. However, supportive followers may exert greater influence over time as they are rewarded by their leader for loyalty and consistency. Where the leader is a doctor the role of supportive follower in location-based teams is more likely to be fulfilled by nurses who stay, having completed their training, unlike doctors in training who are relatively transitory (Barrow et al, 2011). This may lead to difficulties for trainees who are trying to develop leadership roles while still moving locations on a regular basis when many of their potential followers are nurses who have a great influence both on the environment and more senior leaders.

In-groups, out-groups and 'prototypicality: why leaders need to maintain clinical work

In-groups and out-groups

In light of the apparent importance of social and professional shared identity within teams, the concepts of 'in-groups' and 'out-groups' in the clinical environment is also relevant. Tee et al (2013) assert that not only do groups turn against members who are perceived as dissimilar but also that a group will support a leader more strongly when they explicitly oppose an out-group. In the context of clinical medicine, this concept can be applied to the attitude of health practitioners to non-clinical management (Barrow et al, 2011). The perceived close proximity of leadership roles and management, still viewed as the 'dark side' in clinical culture, results in a reluctance of clinical leaders to be identified with their management colleagues (Spurgeon et al, 2011).

Group identity is reinforced by the clinical expertise that set clinical leadership apart from management, it is further reinforced by the identification of an out-group who are not only very different but who can be blamed for service failings. It is reasonable to suggest that the identification of a non-clinical out-group may in fact improve team cohesiveness between doctors, nurses and allied health professionals, and further bolster interprofessional working; however, it is questionable whether, in this context, a shared 'clinical identity' is enough to overcome more powerful differences in professional identity. Dangers exist in maintaining an out-group to sustain group identity, particularly if health services require a collective leadership approach in order to make fundamental culture changes.

Gosling and Minzberg (2003) remind us of the risks in separating leadership from management in that leaders may become disconnected and arrogant and managers may stifle innovation, but the risks in separating clinicians from management and leadership roles are equally (if not more) important in health care. These risks are well documented in reports into failing health services and calls for doctors and other clinicians to engage fully in leadership and management (Spurgeon et al, 2011; West et al, 2014).

Identity shifts

Croft et al's (2015) study of nurses on a leadership development programme highlighted the tension, identity conflict and emotional transition needed to construct leader identities. As the nurses moved into their new roles, they struggled to maintain their identity as nurses and credibility of their followers as their leader identities were not congruent with the nursing social group (Croft et al, 2015). These issues pose some key questions:

1. Might health professionals, and clinical leaders and managers have more than one social identity, some more predominant than others at various times?
2. Is belonging to one's 'own' professional group more important in maintaining identity than other social identities?
3. If there were a better rapport and working relationship between clinical leadership and non-clinical management, might there be a threat to clinical group identity (if such a thing exists)?
4. Is it necessary to have an opposing force or can a new group identity be fostered from a positive common goal: to provide a service of excellent, timely and safe care to patients.

The latter is what West et al (2014, 2015) would hope for in their call for collective leadership in the NHS.

Prototypicality

The concepts of social identity, in-, and out-groups provide some answers to these questions as they serve to explain the importance of clinical work to health professionals in clinical leadership. More than simply staying in touch with the reality of service delivery and innovations and medical technologies, maintenance of clinical expertise reinforces what is described as 'prototypicality'.

> 'To date, robust evidence exists to support the proposition that leadership effectiveness, under the social identity model, is dependent on the extent to which followers perceive leaders (1) to be representative of the group's identity, i.e. prototypical... and also (2) to be engaging in behaviours that are perceived as being beneficial to upholding the salient group identity, i.e. group-serving behaviour...' Tee et al (2013) p.904.

This may be particularly important in health-care environments where social and professional identity are so deeply connected.

Tee et al (2013) go on to say that leaders who fail to preserve salient group identity through prototypicality will be collectively disapproved of by their followers. However, prototypicality is not enough to constitute leadership. Procedural fairness by the leader and the attribution of successes to followers are both essential for group loyalty, particularly for 'high identifying' followers. This exposes a contradiction in professional culture particularly among doctors. While the implicit emphasis is on personal professional success, once in a position of authority, a leader who is perceived as self-serving will fail to gain the trust of the followership. With regard to social identity, the increased focus on professionalism (Hafferty and Castellani, 2010) has shone a spotlight on values, behaviour and public trust in doctors. Doctors are very sensitive and aware of the importance of the perception of integrity and probity in their practice, as such, leaders who fail to behave in an exemplary manner do more than just alienate individuals who have lost out but threaten the salient identity of the entire group. Case scenario 15.3 highlights how personal characteristics (such as height or gender) may lead to leaders not been seen as prototypical by followers or the rest of an in-group.

Conclusions

This chapter has explored specifically how an understanding of followership, prototypicality, social identity and social influence theories can help us understand the roles and difficulties of individuals, teams and organisations as they strive to provide high quality care. Research into followership has been ongoing for some time and the importance of followers to leaders' effectiveness (and even existence) is well recognised, but new approaches, drawing on a range of theories, are now providing additional insights. We argue that clinical leaders and those responsible for leadership development need to focus on these insights and theories as they provide ways forward for addressing key health-care issues and assisting teams, health professionals and managers to work more effectively together. In particular, raising awareness of the relational nature of leadership and followership and the influence followers have on leaders can help leaders adapt and develop new ways of working in complex systems and organisations.

Key points

- Leadership cannot be understood or explained without consideration of followership
- Leaders need followers, but followers also need leaders, especially in times of crisis, rapid change or excitement – leadership-followership is relational
- The social identities of different professional groups provide powerful forces both for support and for resistance to leaders
- Leaders who do not meet followers' expectations or beliefs as to leadership attributes or actions (i.e. are not prototypical) may be collectively disapproved of by followers
- Maintaining clinical work contributes towards prototypicality, social identity and leadership acceptability.

Case scenario 15.3 Looking the part

Emma is an ST3 in general surgery and stands at 5ft 3inches tall. She is average height for a woman but significantly smaller that most of her colleagues (all male). Emma works hard, gets on well with her colleagues and feels respected and supported by her seniors but sometimes feels frustrated by the seemingly constant reference to her stature, frame and small hands in theatres. These comments are always made humorously and affectionately….'someone fetch Emma a stool, I can only see her eyebrows from here'… but Emma has noticed that one male colleague who is barely an inch taller is never subjected to this kind of 'banter'.

Emma also suspects that junior clinical staff, while always polite, do not consider her an authority in the same way. As a result, friends notice that she is dressing and standing differently at work, she has swapped her comfortable flats for high heels on the wards, stands with her legs further apart and one commented on how she deepens her voice when talking to surgical colleagues and patients.

One senior consultant organises an annual training day for local specialists, which always coincides with a prominent football tournament. Emma does not follow football and is not interested in socialising in that way but wants to attend the training day and network with the group. She is left with a difficult decision. Should she complain about the exclusive nature of the training day and risk alienating her colleagues; should she make her excuses and miss valuable training and networking; or should she go and endure the day while feeling and looking out of place?

Section 4 – Leadership development

CHAPTER 16

Developing and assessing medical leadership

Judy McKimm, Helen O'Sullivan

In *Leadership and Management for all Doctors* the General Medical Council (2012a) sets out the wider management and leadership responsibilities of all doctors in the workplace:

> 'Being a good doctor means more than simply being a good clinician. In their day-to-day role doctors can provide leadership to their colleagues and vision for the organisations in which they work and for the profession as a whole. However, unless doctors are willing to contribute to improving the quality of services and to speak up when things are wrong, patient care is likely to suffer'.

It is probably safe to say that the case for all doctors, not just those in formal leadership roles, to be trained in leadership and management competencies has now been made. The real issue is how to achieve demonstrable improvement in these attributes, competencies and skills in order to improve patient safety, health outcomes and organisational achievements We have to be able to teach and facilitate the learning of leadership understanding, skills and behaviours and develop and implement more robust assessment methods. This chapter, based on the article by McKimm and O'Sullivan (2012), considers some of the ways in which doctors are now acquiring and extending their leadership and management skills and how these may be assessed.

Developing leadership

The Keogh review (2013)

In February 2013, the Prime Minister announced that he had asked Professor Sir Bruce Keogh, NHS Medical Director for England, to review the quality of care and treatment provided by those NHS trusts and NHS foundation trusts that were persistent outliers on mortality indicators. A total of 14 hospital trusts were investigated as part of this review (Keogh, 2013). Keogh was asked to review and find out whether existing action by these trusts to improve quality was adequate and whether any additional steps should be taken, whether any additional external support should be made available to these trusts to help them improve, and whether any areas required regulatory action to protect patients.

The review considered the performance of the hospitals across six key areas:

- Mortality
- Patient experience
- Safety
- Workforce
- Clinical and operational effectiveness
- Leadership and governance.

The review found an urgent need for all trust staff to understand the importance of managing and leading for quality improvement. For example, the review found insufficient evidence that board and clinical leaders were effectively driving quality improvement. In a number of trusts, the capability of medical directors and/or directors of nursing was questioned by the review teams. Common areas of concern across the affected trusts included:

- Poor understanding across the organisation of the strategy for improving quality
- Several trusts had recently undergone quality and safety reviews undertaken by internal and external groups, but could not show an efficient and effective approach to learning from these

- A significant disconnect between what the clinical leadership identified as the key risks and issues and what was actually happening in the hospitals.

Weaknesses were also caused by a lack of appropriate data being available to boards and even when it was available, it was not acted on effectively. The review recommended that all trusts needed to review their quality performance reporting to ensure that it measured the right things effectively to ensure that risks were identified and acted upon. After the reviews, 11 of the 14 trusts were placed into special measures by Monitor and the NHS Trust Development Authority.

Collective leadership

The shortcomings identified in the Keogh review could be argued to be the result of dysfunctional culture in the trusts involved. In their paper *Developing Collective Leadership for Healthcare*, West et al (2014) suggest that the most important indicators of culture in an organisation are the leadership style and the behaviours displayed throughout the organisation. Effective health care nurtures cultures where prominence is given to performance measures of patient safety and where continuous improvement is valued. Case scenario 16.1 outlines a system-wide example of developing and embedding a quality improvement culture across a large organisation. The paper discusses the concept of 'collective leadership' where patient safety and continuous improvement is the responsibility of everyone and where there is leadership at all levels. This can be achieved by empowerment and promoting autonomy.

West et al (2014) also recommend that more clinicians need to be involved in leadership and that there needs to be more diversity in clinical leadership in terms of women and black and ethnic minority doctors. In addition, they recommend programmes of leadership development that transform leadership styles to deliver the culture that is needed. Key features of this culture are speaking up when poor behaviour is observed, working across boundaries to deliver patient care, encouraging proactivity and innovation – moving away from a command and control culture to one that focuses on learning, and having the courage to deal with rude and aggressive colleagues and poor performance. They comment that culture is all about values, and those values are important to human communities. Of course, the NHS is a series of human communities and all human communities are kept going by warmth, optimism, humour and a sense of wonder. They conclude by asserting that the NHS needs leadership that embodies those values to take it forward.

As outlined in Chapters 2 and 3, the NHS has taken an increasingly structured and strategic approach to developing leadership. The Medical Leadership Competency Framework (MLCF), launched in 2010, provided a framework approach that could be used to scaffold leadership development in undergraduate and postgraduate education and post qualification continuing professional development.

The NHS Leadership Academy published the Healthcare Leadership Model in 2013 (see *Figure 3.3*) which is being used in England and explored in Wales and

---

Case scenario 16.1 Driving system-wide health care quality improvement at East London NHS Foundation Trust

East London NHS Foundation Trust is a typically complex health-care setting. Sixty-four different sites, many with high rates of child poverty and complex long-term conditions; a high proportion of ethnic minorities; 14 care commissioning groups and a focus on mental health and community care. East London NHS Foundation Trust has set itself the target of becoming the highest quality provider by 2020. They plan to achieve this by driving a systems-wide quality improvement process. It is championed from the top and the project lead is Dr Amar Shah, a consultant forensic psychiatrist and Associate Medical Director for Quality Improvement at East London NHS Foundation Trust, and the Faculty of Medical Leadership and Management London regional lead on quality and value.

The focus on applying quality improvement to mental health was new and so there was little evidence or data to start with and this has been built up through careful data collection and analysis. Individual projects are led by clinical colleagues as part of formal training programmes such as the Darzi Fellowship in Clinical Leadership. The focus has been on collaborative leadership through a team based approach to deciding how the projects run with quality improvement built in at the very beginning by choosing what measurements to take and how to use the data. The quality improvement culture is being reinforced with 500 front-line staff undergoing training and 250 clinical leaders gaining a deeper understanding of the methodology. The East London NHS Foundation Trust has embraced quality as its business model.

Adapted from Shah (2015)

Northern Ireland. This model comprises nine leadership dimensions, designed to provide a way of analysing current leadership behaviours and planning and evaluating personal and team-based leadership development programmes with the aim of improving NHS health-care leaders. These dimensions are:

1. Inspiring shared purpose
2. Leading with care
3. Evaluating information
4. Connecting our service
5. Sharing the vision
6. Engaging the team
7. Holding to account
8. Developing capability
9. Influencing the results

The dimensions include specific reference to personal qualities and there is a noticeable shift in emphasis to those personal qualities that have been shown to support a culture of compassion and caring in health services. The document outlining the model makes this specific connection suggesting that greater self-awareness, self-control, self-knowledge, determination, resilience and other personal qualities leads to more effective leadership behaviours. In turn, this leads to a more productive, care-focused and engaged team climate and an increasingly positive experience of care and service (NHS Leadership Academy, 2013).

Each dimension has a four-part scale against which leadership competence can be assessed. In comparison to the previous Framework, this Model is completely permeated by references to personal qualities, culture and value. Each dimension has a list of exemplars that describe behaviours that would not signify the dimension ('What is it not?'), for example:

- Hiding behind values to avoid doing your best
- Failing to understand the impact of your own emotions or behaviour on colleagues
- Reluctance to look for better ways of doing things
- Thinking politics is a dirty word
- Saying one thing and doing another
- Autocratic leadership
- Tolerating mediocrity
- Pushing your agenda without regard to other views.

NHS Education Scotland's Leadership Development Unit delivers a range of development programmes for leaders at different stages of their careers (see also Chapters 2 and 3).

The NHS Education Scotland Framework is also underpinned by personal qualities and values. An additional Code of Personal Governance spells out the values and personal behaviours that are expected of NHS Scotland's leaders and managers, which is supported by the model for leadership development illustrated in *Figure 16.1*.

Leaders'/Managers' Code of Personal Governance

As an NHS Scotland Leader / Manager I will:

Pursue service excellence by:

- Ensuring patients'/clients' needs are at the centre of decision-making
- Seeking to protect patients/clients and staff from clinical and environmental risk
- Encouraging service excellence and supporting changes to make this a reality.

Act with integrity and honesty by:

- Communicating with openness and honesty in all matters including handling complaints and giving feedback to staff
- Ensuring confidential and constructive communication
- Managing resources and financial risk effectively and efficiently
- Ensuring personal integrity and honesty at all times
- Seeking to protect patients/clients and NHS resources from fraud, inducements and corruption.

Account for my own and my team's performance by:

- Taking responsibility for my own and my team's performance
- Complying with all statutory requirements
- Providing appropriate explanations on performance
- Acting on suggestions/requirements for improving performance

- Supporting the Accountable Office of my organisation in his/her responsibilities.

Engage appropriately with others in decision-making by:

- Ensuring that patients, the public, staff and partner organisations are able to influence decision-making in relation to NHS services
- Supporting effective and informed decision-making by patients about their own care
- Seeking out the views of others and building mutual understanding
- Ensuring clarity and consistency in relation to dual accountability.

Figure 16.1 The Model for Leadership Development across NHS Scotland (Scottish Government, 2010a).

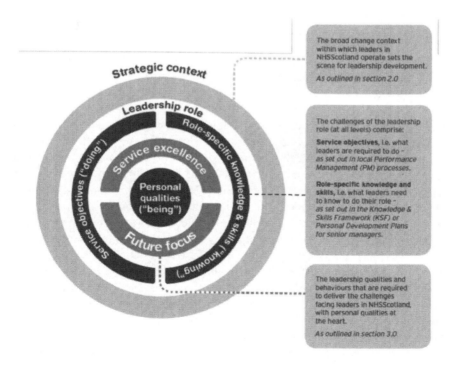

Develop my team and myself by:

- Building and developing effective teams, supported by appropriate leadership
- Instilling trust and giving freedom to staff/partners to make decisions within authority
- Being aware of and taking responsibility for my behaviour and continuous personal development as a NHS leader/manager, to ensure my fitness for purpose.
(Scottish Government, 2010a)

When the original MLCF was introduced, important work was carried out in undergraduate medical education to embed opportunities to develop relevant competencies from the Framework (see Chapter 8) and leadership and followership were included in the outcomes that all UK medical undergraduates must achieve set out by the General Medical Council in *Tomorrow's Doctors* (General Medical Council, 2009). The General Medical Council's 2015 consultation on Standards for Medical Education and training reinforces this by setting out the requirements for the learning environment which include:

'S1.1 The learning environment is safe for patients and supportive for learners. The culture is caring, compassionate and provides a good standard of care and experience for patients, carers and families' (General Medical Council, 2015, p12)

Case scenario 16.2 sets out four examples of how professional and regulatory bodies are increasingly recognising that leadership development needs to include human factors (ideally team-based) training. The Foundation Curriculum and all specialty training curricula include the requirement for foundation doctors to develop as leaders. For doctors who want to learn and study in more depth, one strand of the academic Foundation Programme focuses on clinical leadership and management. This has been extended in some regions by offering academic postgraduate qualifications (see Chapter 17 for one example). The NHS National Leadership Academy also offers places on the Clinical Leadership Fellowship scheme for clinicians who have been qualified for 4 years or more and an increasing number of relevant and credible in-house leadership development schemes and postgraduate programmes are available that prepare doctors for more senior leadership and service improvement roles. The NHS Leadership Academy runs a number of leadership programmes aimed at clinical leaders at various stages of their career and the Faculty of Medical Leadership and Management supports fellowships in leadership and management. These fellows are encouraged to take on leadership roles and run specific projects. For example, two clinical leadership fellows of the Faculty of Medical Leadership and Management arranged workshops at the Faculty of Medical Leadership and Management Welsh Regional Conference 'Prudent healthcare through excellence in clinical leadership' held in September 2014 in Cardiff. Another is developing a leadership development programme for her local education and training board (see Chapter 3 for more examples in the four UK countries).

Assessing leadership

Assessing leadership behaviours, understanding and skills is a crucial part of developing effective leaders. Without robust and meaningful assessments, it is impossible to tell if students and doctors in training are really achieving

---

Case scenario 16.2 Human factors in leadership development

(1) On the Clinical Human Factors Group (2011) website, Dr Ken Catchpole defines clinical human factors as:

'Enhancing clinical performance through an understanding of the effects of teamwork, tasks, equipment, workspace, culture and organisation on human behaviour and abilities and application of that knowledge in clinical settings'.

(2) NHS England (2013) published the Human Factors in Healthcare Concordat. The Concordat recommends that there is strong leadership and understanding for human factors in the NHS and that there is inclusion of human factors principles and practices in core education and training curricula for all health professionals and managers and to support ongoing professional development.

(3) The General Medical Council has confirmed the importance of recognising human factors in the development of generic professional capabilities for postgraduate medical curricula. This provides a reinforcement of *Good Medical Practice* (General Medical Council, 2013), which sets out what is expected of doctors, including communication and partnership working with patients.

(4) The NHS Leadership Academy is ensuring that human factors approaches are embedded in all of its programmes (NHS England, 2013).

---

required competencies and difficult to plan for improvement. Well-established ways to assess leadership include self-assessment and multisource or 360° feedback, which have been adapted from concepts developed in the general leadership literature.

The NHS Leadership Academy has developed its own 360° feedback tool that can be accessed online and used as part of an institution-wide leadership assessment process. The tool is managed online and participants can see how their assessment relates to the reference set for people in similar roles. See www.leadershipacademy.nhs.uk/resources/healthcare-leadership-model/supporting-tools-resources/healthcare-leadership-model-360-degree-feedback-tool (accessed March 2015).

Self-awareness is one of the key tenets of being a professional (Hilton and Slotnick, 2005) and being able to reflect, identify gaps in knowledge and skills and develop ways to address these are fundamental parts of the learning cycle. A self-assessment tool is very useful when a large system such as the NHS is attempting to develop clinical leadership on a huge scale. However, a wealth of empirical evidence demonstrates that self-assessment is not very reliable (Eva and Regehr, 2011) and therefore any self-assessment tool needs to be used as part of a range of pieces of evidence about leadership skills and/or performance, gathered over time. Evidence from the generic leadership development literature suggests that some of the most helpful assessments of leadership competencies, skills and attributes come from a combination of self-assessment; multisource feedback or 360° appraisal and objective assessment tools that use simulation, observed performance in the 'real world' context coupled with debrief, feedback and professional conversation.

Day et al (2014) reviewed the literature on leadership development and the methods of facilitating that development through feedback. Over the last 25 years, the majority of literature focuses on the role of 360° feedback as a method for gauging leadership development longitudinally. The authors differentiate between processes such as 360° feedback and personality type inventories and tools as mechanisms for gathering evidence on leadership performance. They suggest that the use of 360° feedback can be used as a measure of self-awareness and that individuals with self-ratings that mirror those provided by their followers are more self-aware. However, there is currently little research evidence relating self-awareness to effective leadership and further work needs to be carried out on a reliable measure of self-awareness and its link to effective leadership.

Evaluating leadership development programmes

There are many ways to evaluate the effectiveness of a leadership development programme including the four-level process developed by Kirkpatrick (1996). Leskiw and Singh (2007) propose six key factors that are vital for effective leadership development:

- A thorough needs assessment
- The selection of a suitable audience
- The design of an appropriate infrastructure to support the initiative
- The design and implementation of an entire learning system
- An evaluation system
- Corresponding actions to reward success and improve on deficiencies. (Leskiw and Singh, 2007)

By evaluating leadership programmes we can establish the most efficient and effective ways of developing the next generation of leaders.

Conclusions

So what does this mean for doctors working in today's health services who want to enhance their understanding and skills in clinical leadership and management? Appraisal and revalidation are part of the key to solving this problem. Thinking about all aspects of clinical leadership, be that at the frontline – at the bedside, in clinic or theatre – or in a more clearly defined management position, provides multiple opportunities for doctors to collect evidence about their leadership skills.

Using the NHS Leadership Academy's Healthcare Leadership Model or the Faculty of Medical Leadership and Management's Professional Standards as a baseline would enable doctors to cast a 'leadership lens' on daily activities and thus identify and accumulate 'evidence' of their leadership and management development, influence and impact over the longer term. The annual appraisal provides a good opportunity to take stock and set goals, including leadership or management training and development activities. Using established tools will give doctors insight into teamwork, communication skills and leadership style.

Seizing opportunities for engaging in specific leadership or management study (through workshops or e-learning), offering to lead or get involved in health innovation projects, reading about some of the theory and practice of leadership (in books, articles or reports) and finding a good mentor, coach or trusted colleague to provide honest and constructive feedback, will help all doctors to develop as leaders and make a difference in improving health-care. And for those who want to 'specialise' in leadership, national initiatives (such as the NHS Leadership Academy, Academi Wales, NI Deanery and the Faculty of Medical Leadership and Management, see also Chapters 2 and 3), regional deaneries, Royal colleges and universities provide multiple opportunities to take it further.

Key points

- Developing leadership and management skills and competencies is now an accepted part of training for all doctors at all stages of training and post qualification
- The NHS Leadership Academy and other national bodies such as the Faculty of Medical Leadership and Management are providing development opportunities and assessment methods based around the Healthcare Leadership Model and other leadership standards
- The most robust approach to assessing leadership involves using a range of different tools including multisource feedback, self-assessment and objective measures.

CHAPTER 17

Developing clinical leadership capacity among UK foundation doctors

Judy McKimm, Junie Wong, Richard Wright, Helen O'Sullivan

Active leadership and management is being called for from all professionals working in the NHS. Doctors are required to 'lead change as well as manage it', and medical leadership should be developed at all levels across the organisation (Department of Health, 2002; Darzi, 2008). This chapter, based on the article by McKimm et al (2011), provides a guide to how doctors in training can act as leaders within their workplace using various leadership and management tools. Here we discuss how the Medical Leadership Competency Framework (MLCF) and one of the first academic Foundation Programmes in clinical leadership and management in the UK benefitted doctors in training to learn and apply leadership to their own clinical setting.

Academic foundation programmes

The MLCF (NHS Institute for Innovation and Improvement and Academy of Medical Royal Colleges, 2010a) set out leadership competencies needed for doctors to become more involved in transforming health services. It was supported by a growing body of evidence that indicates that doctors' appropriate involvement in clinical leadership and management has a positive effect on organisational performance and health improvements (Hamilton et al, 2008).

In 2010, the MLCF competencies were developed into the Academic Foundation Programme competencies, a subset of which referred specifically to clinical leadership and management (UK Foundation Programme Office,

2010). Together, these documents provided a framework for training junior doctors in leadership and management. The original competencies were revised in 2013 to form the UK Foundation Programme Academic Compendium, with defined outcomes for research, education and leadership and management programmes (UK Foundation Programme Office, 2013). In leadership and management, the outcomes for foundation doctors are that the doctor:

- Identifies and articulates an opportunity for improvement in the health or social care or education environment in which he/she works
- Produces a plan for improving an aspect of the health-care or education environment in which he/she works through engaging individuals and teams from a range of backgrounds and professions
- Works effectively with a team to implement an improvement project in the health-care or education environment in which he/she works
- Evaluates the effectiveness of a project and develops recommendations for the future to further improve patient care
- Presents and disseminates learning from an improvement project (UK Foundation Programme Office, 2013).

Under each of the outcomes, competences are defined, plus examples of relevant supporting evidence and content suggestions for programme designers.

The MLCF and the 2010 Academic Foundation Programme framework and competencies both informed the design of a new academic programme in clinical leadership and management, a collaboration between the University of Leicester, East Midlands Foundation School and University Hospitals of Leicester NHS Trust. The programme is described in this chapter.

The Leicester academic foundation programme in clinical leadership and management

The Leicester one-year academic foundation programme in clinical leadership and management ran from 2009 until 2014, providing a cohort of twelve second year foundation trainees (F2s) each year with the opportunity to develop management and leadership practice alongside workplace-based learning (with two-thirds of time spent in the emergency department or acute medical services) and masters' level study (comprising one third of the time). All trainees were expected to achieve clinical competences as laid out in the foundation curriculum in addition to studying for a Postgraduate Certificate in Clinical Leadership and Management. They were selected following application and face-to-face interview. The Postgraduate Certificate curriculum was mapped onto the MLCF and was developed from an existing, successful Postgraduate Certificate in Higher Education Leadership offered by the University of Leicester. Successful participants could go on to study to masters' level if they chose.

Throughout the year, these selected foundation doctors attended eight contact days at the University which include aspects of leadership and management theory, health policy and organisational systems, self-development, group activities, case studies and action learning sets. Topics covered are set out in *Figure 17.1*.

Figure 17.1. The Leicester Postgraduate Certificate in Clinical Leadership and Management

The philosophy of the programme was that learners need to understand and engage with relevant underpinning theory which is applied to a wide range of clinical contexts to deepen awareness and recognition of how their own and others' leadership and management approaches affect clinical practice and health outcomes. Self-development and insight is fundamental to effective leadership, and the programme participants engage in a variety of self-development activities, at both individual and group level. Written assessments are closely aligned to workplace-based learning and reflect contemporary best practice in leadership and management development:

- An essay applying theory to workplace-based clinical practice (a national policy or strategy considered at local level, e.g. a service pathway or systems intervention)
- A workplace-based project management report (on a service or quality improvement)
- A reflective and evaluative portfolio (comprising a set of reflective, evaluative and analytical pieces on various aspects of medical, clinical and general leadership and management).

The workplace-based project is a vital part of the programme, requiring the development and application of leadership and management skills in a real-life situation. This takes place through engagement in supervised projects, predetermined by the trust, carried out across a range of hospital departments. The project is carried out over 6–8 months, supervised by a named supervisor in the trust who works with the trainee to identify and agree project aims, assists with access to people and departments, and provides support when things get tough. Health improvement projects included:

- Responding to the European Working Time Directive by reallocating roles in the trauma unit
- Improving the content, utility and timeliness of discharges in the emergency department to allow electronic delivery
- Improving practice in blood transfusion in a hospital medical directorate
- Lean working in the emergency department
- Exploring delayed discharges in the intensive therapy unit
- Improving theatre efficiency through establishing a 'day of surgical arrivals' unit.

The academic components of the programme provide doctors in training with the knowledge, skills, interpersonal approaches and support to take on leadership and management roles in the trust and successfully engage in change management and health innovation projects. Here, one of the trainees shares her experience of how the programme worked in practice using her work on implementing change at the trust's transient ischaemic attack clinic. She identifies issues and strategies for doctors in training taking on leadership roles within their workplace and how application of relevant theory and models enables more effective leadership at this level.

Case scenario – The transient ischaemic attack clinic project: a junior doctor's experience

This project was carried out over 7 months in parallel with clinical work in the emergency department and academic study for the postgraduate certificate. A performance audit had established that a limited proportion of patients were seen within national time targets, partly as a result of doctors' delay in triaging patients. Meetings with the project supervisor discussed results of analyses and suggested changes. An automatic nursing triage system was introduced and re-audit found this was successful in improving the proportion of transient ischaemic attack patients assessed in accordance with national guidelines.

Project initiation

Identifying a good project supervisor who can provide high level support and facilitate the progress of your project is vital. Support from the clinical lead within the Department of Stroke Medicine was invaluable in empowering me to introduce changes to the transient ischaemic attack clinic. Drawing up a project initiation document which incorporates the 'who, why and what' of your project and discussing it with your supervisor allows you to establish a clear understanding of the project's aim and scope. It also acts as a reference point throughout the project, preventing you from sidetracking from objectives or activities identified at the outset.

Effective leaders need to understand the working environment and identify why change is necessary. When planning for change, a SWOT analysis (listing internal strengths and weaknesses and external opportunities and threats) helps identify key issues, encouraging you to strategise your actions to exploit strengths and opportunities while minimising weaknesses and threats. Identifying external forces (which included national targets) coupled with internal audit (demonstrating lack of conformance with national guidelines) supported suggested changes in the transient ischaemic attack clinic.

Working with complex adaptive systems

Even small-scale health-care systems such as the transient ischaemic attack clinic can be complex. The large number of stakeholders (including doctors, nurses, patients) involved in running the clinic and the existing connections between them can result in constant and discontinuous change. It is a complex adaptive system (Marion and Bacon, 2000) and within such systems, there is a tendency to maintain generally bounded behaviour, or attractor patterns in response to change. Stakeholders may be attracted to some elements of the change and resistant to others, evaluating change from their individual perspective. As such, doctors in training need to recognise that implementing change in health systems can be extremely slow and, as even relatively small changes may impinge on many systems, multiple adjustments may need to be made to the original project plan.

Understanding and introducing change

Change can be viewed in four ways: psychologically, structurally, culturally and politically (Bolman and Deal, 2003). This 'framing' helps you consider multiple dimensions of change. Psychological aspects include personal feelings involved during a change process, e.g. uncertainty among nurses having to triage patients. Thinking structurally enables a consideration of formal roles and relationships. Cultural aspects include existing organisational values, beliefs and routines. Finally, when thinking politically, the arenas of competing interests and how to influence and negotiate change have to be considered.

With little affiliation to or influence on the department, the doctor in training's attempt to implement change may require a deeper understanding of the political and cultural context of change than first thought.

To plan, introduce and monitor the impact of change, Kotter's (1995) change model is helpful, particularly in helping to identify where things might be going wrong (*Table 17.1*).

Good leaders need to make sense of the work environment by understanding key issues, communicating these to colleagues and actively moulding their responses (McKimm and Phillips, 2009). This can be achieved by actively collaborating with others and building relationships to secure commitment and involvement to deliver sustainable change and improvement.

Table 17.1 Actions for leading change (From Kotter, 1995)

Kotter's change model	What was done
Creating a sense of urgency	Conducted an audit against national targets
Forming a powerful guiding coalition	Worked with clinical lead of the department and other key stakeholders
Communicating the vision	Created a proposal and presented to stakeholders
Empowering others	Introduced changes beneficial to stakeholders which they carried out
Creating short-term wins	Implemented small changes instead of big changes which could be quickly put in place
Building on change	Re-audit and proposing new changes
Anchoring changes in the culture	Proving to key personnel that changes worked and making these 'the way we do things round here'

Challenges and opportunities

Until recently, leadership and management were not necessarily seen as essential components of undergraduate medical programmes and there was little training in these areas at postgraduate level. The move to (re)engage doctors in clinical leadership has stimulated a wide range of initiatives, including doctors being involved in change management projects supported by e-learning and local training programmes. All foundation trainees are required to participate in short workshops and e-learning on management and leadership as well as carry out a clinical audit. Academic foundation programmes provide an opportunity for those with a particular interest in leadership and management to progress.

Academic foundation programmes

A number of deaneries and local education and training boards have introduced more comprehensive leadership development programmes as part of the academic foundation programme, including that of Leicestershire, Northamptonshire and Rutland Healthcare Workforce Deanery, one of the early proponents of clinical leadership and management programmes (Gallen et al, 2007). This programme was originally an interprofessional programme which enabled the participants to learn from other health professionals on an accredited programme while engaging in two 6-month rotations in general medicine and general practice. Evaluations of both programmes indicate that longer placements work best in ensuring some stability in the clinical environment (either a year-long placement or two 6-month placements would seem ideal) so that the doctors in training have the best opportunity to achieve the foundation competencies while undertaking an academic award-bearing programme.

Evaluation of the Leicester programme also indicates the vital importance of the workplace-based project to the trainees' success on the leadership programme and their subsequent learning for practice. Good supervision is required so that the doctors in training are fully supported in what is often a difficult task. The project and their specific role within it need to be clearly identified and communicated to all stakeholders. Trainees agree that the most effective role for them is as 'project champion' or 'little "l" leader' (Kelley,

1992; Bohmer, 2010) and for that they need to learn specific project management skills, how the organisation is structured and functions, and how people within it work and relate to one another. This is a key area of learning for the doctors in training and one which has not typically and explicitly been learned at medical school. The other learning gain of participating in the project is that of developing their own personal leadership style and approaches as they learn to navigate complex systems. Action learning sets, tutor and supervisor support and personal management skills are vital pieces of the jigsaw that enable achievement.

Challenges remain in applying the MLCF to the large number of foundation doctors and enabling them to develop appropriate leadership skills. Current foundation assessments do not specifically measure clinical leadership and management relating to health systems or organisations or intra- and interpersonal leadership skills (McKimm and Petersen, 2010). While the current understanding of clinical management and leadership among some doctors in training may be poor, many already participate in leadership activities, e.g. team leadership, management meetings or audits, but with little or no theoretical or practical underpinning.

Palmer et al (2008) investigated 196 second year foundation trainee doctors studying a team work and leadership module as part of the West Midlands foundation programme and found that the three competencies that were felt to be most important for the development of clinical leadership in the NHS were 'drive for improvement', 'collaborative working' and 'personal integrity'. They felt that the 'personal qualities' domain from the MLCF was the most important but did not mention 'self-management', 'political astuteness' or 'holding to account' at all.

Doctors in training tend to work within a transactional, or power and reward concept of leadership, associating leadership with the structure of the medical hierarchy (Barrow et al, 2011). Palmer et al (2008) suggest that 'the majority of them [second year foundation trainees] accept the system as it is at the moment, and are probably more concerned about the acquisition of clinical skills and the care of patients than about looking for improvements and change'. This perspective probably reflects their duties at the time and the demands of the foundation programme and, as Palmer et al acknowledge, the views of doctors about leadership will change with experience, maturity and seniority. This is very apparent when considering the changing perspectives and growth of the doctors in training on academic leadership programmes as they learn and reflect more about leadership in both theory and practice.

Looking back – six years on

'Before my enrolment into the Leicester academic foundation programme, I was in an early stage of clinical career and my focus at that time, naturally, was on honing my clinical skills. As I moved jobs as part of my training, I had adapted, without questions, to the local work practice even when I thought processes were less effective. It was during my participation in the programme that, for the first time, I took a step back from being at the frontline of health-care delivery and properly considered my understanding of health-care systems at a macroscopic level. I was prompted to question and evaluate the role doctors play beyond their clinical practice within the health system. More importantly, I was made to realise that junior doctors can be leaders and we can lead and manage changes within our work environment.

I built on this early introduction to clinical leadership and management by undertaking a master's degree in health-care management. Now back in clinical training, I continue to be actively involved in management projects, being focused on little changes while not being discouraged when progress is slow. I am inclined to think that my education in clinical management has equipped me with the willingness to understand when change is needed or why change is being proposed by the "management", and to work with change, which my peers at the clinical frontline may be more reluctant to consider. As a clinician equipped with leadership and management skills, I believe I am in a unique position to buffer the occasional disparate viewpoints of managers and health-care professionals. I believe the consideration of both viewpoints is required to balance the changes that may be necessary to improve health-care delivery to a population of patients.' Junie Wong

Engaging doctors in leadership development

The vast majority of doctors will not (and probably could not) engage in an intensive, supported exposure to leadership and management theory and practice as have the Leicester and other academic trainees. For many doctors in training therefore, effective leadership may more closely reflect Kelley's concept of active or exemplary followership which emphasises self-directed leadership in the absence of the power of a job title, encouraging the exploitation of the 'power of expertise, influence and persuasion' so that, through active participation and team-working, they become leaders at their workplace (Kelley, 1992; Fullan, 2004), see also Chapters 7 and 18.

As a range of guidance documents suggest, all doctors in training should be able to manage themselves, recognise their impact on others and work collaboratively in teams, while facilitating improvement and provision of high quality, safe health service delivery. This requires:

- A much greater awareness of leadership and management concepts and approaches from supervisors
- Robust and meaningful leadership development activities locked into organisational and health system needs and improvement
- Specific assessments of clinical leadership and management skills and behaviours which are not just tick box exercises or rather superficial multi-source feedback assessments
- A clearer definition of what doctors in training are expected to lead and manage (both within and outside purely clinical activities)
- The provision of supported opportunities for engagement in management activities
- Management training geared to improving services within the doctors in training's micro-environment.

Conclusions

Full engagement of doctors in leadership and management must include effective leadership and management being modelled 'at all levels' and leadership development which includes all students, doctors in training and practising clinicians across the NHS. Through a coordinated approach to such initiatives involving health-care and academic partners, doctors at all levels can take appropriate leadership roles in improving organisational performance and developing and sustaining wider health improvements and innovations.

Key points

- Current foundation programmes provide limited opportunities for trainees to develop leadership and management skills with a theoretical underpinning
- Clinical leadership and management are not assessed fully in the foundation programme
- Academic foundation programmes provide those with an interest in clinical leadership and management with opportunity to develop skills and gain an award
- Foundation doctors can make effective contributions to health improvements if given the right support and resources
- More work needs to be done to determine the most effective ways of developing leadership and management competencies in all foundation trainees.

Supporting the engagement of doctors in training in quality improvement and patient safety

Alex Till, Jay Banerjee, Judy McKimm

Introduction

This chapter, based on the article by Till et al (2015), discusses how routine, formal and meaningful engagement in quality improvement initiatives by doctors in training and medical students is a vital part of establishing a 'culture of care'.

One of the most dangerous phrases, particularly when patient safety concerns are raised, is 'we've always done it this way'. While evidence-based medicine requires clinical activity to be based on tried and tested proven evidence, reliance on often-unquestioned cultural assumptions about ways of working can pose real risks to patient safety. Medical errors are one of the leading causes of patient harm, with approximately 10–20% of patients seen in either secondary or primary care experiencing an adverse event (The Health Foundation, 2011a). A cultural shift is therefore needed which facilitates a questioning of assumptions, promotes system changes and locates patient safety and health improvement at the heart of all patient-centred care.

This cultural shift also involves enabling all employees of health-care organisations to realise their duty to identify and reduce the risks to patient safety (Berwick, 2013). It requires embedding systems of sustainable quality improvement into organisations' ethos (e.g. through Deming's 'System of Profound Knowledge') (Deming, 1993) with education and training provided at all levels to equip doctors with the understanding, skills and behaviours to effect widespread cultural change. This article discusses four interlinked themes identified from the literature and actual service changes that underpin this cultural shift in relation to educating doctors in training for health-care improvement.

A four-cornered approach

Contemporary international literature on service development, health improvement and patient safety and the dominant rhetoric in reports on poor or suboptimal health care highlight four recurrent organisational themes necessary to provide truly patient-centred care:

- The importance of culture
- Facilitating clinicians' active engagement in quality improvement
- Building sustainability
- Leadership and management development.

These themes will each be discussed in relation to how widespread and sustainable change towards a quality improvement culture might be implemented, with particular emphasis on doctors' education and training.

The importance of culture

Following a series of landmark cases (including the Laming report (Laming, 2003) and the Bristol inquiry (Kennedy, 2001)), UK public sector health and social care organisations and systems established much more robust systems of governance, quality assurance and monitoring. In 2013 and 2014, the Francis inquiry (Francis, 2013), the Keogh review (Keogh, 2013), the Berwick report (Berwick, 2013) and the Andrews report (Andrews and Butler, 2014) highlighted the need for even more stringent control systems. These calls have also been echoed internationally (Emslie et al, 2002).

In the NHS, clinical governance, quality assurance and clinical audit systems have been set in place to enable organisations to monitor, govern and improve health care. Quality assurance was intended to be 'the system through which NHS organisations are accountable for continuously improving the quality of their care' (Scally and Donaldson, 1998) and clinical audit has been described as 'a way to find out if healthcare is being provided in line with standards and where there could be improvements' (NHS England, 2014). Clinical audit is now routine throughout the NHS and all doctors in training and many medical students now engage in audit activities. However, Jamtvedt et al (2006) point out that the tendency to rely on clinical audit as an intervention to change clinical practice is misplaced and through using this alone, health-care organisations will only make improvements that are of 'small to moderate' effect.

While the now routine involvement of students and doctors in training in clinical audit is a very positive shift, the hierarchical nature of health care means that the culture of quality assurance is primarily driven from the top down. Clinical 'engagement', from the perspective of the student or doctor in training, is therefore typically limited to data collection and report writing on behalf of someone else (Nettleton and Ireland, 2000). Without their engagement from its conception, the majority of students and trainees are disinterested and unmotivated in the process and for many the system becomes a 'tick box' exercise (Hillman and Roueché, 2011). This means that potential innovation in practice is stifled and opportunities for a fresh perspective on health-care systems are limited. Bagnall (2012) goes further, suggesting that there is a widespread lack of interest in and disregard for doctors in training's innovative improvements. This suppresses their energy and willingness to contribute as agents for change and leaves them disheartened, disillusioned and ultimately, dangerously disengaged (Bagnall, 2012).

Creating a culture of health-care improvement therefore requires shifting the focus of attention beyond systems governed by quality assurance, towards a new culture of quality improvement (Dharamshi and Hillman, 2011). Defined by Øvretveit (2009) as 'achieving better patient experience and outcomes through systematic change methods and strategies which changes provider behaviour and organisation', this revitalized and proactive perspective should incorporate the recognition of doctors in training as 'valuable eyes and ears' on the frontline (Francis, 2013) and enable them to act as powerful agents for change throughout their careers by engagement in systematic quality improvement processes at an early stage. From an executive level this can be encouraged as we see in case scenario 18.1 through quality and safety walk-rounds

> **Case scenario 18.1 Quality and safety walk-rounds**
>
> Walk-rounds are an opportunity for senior managers and clinicians to visit a ward or department and, through conversations with patients and staff of all types and levels, and reading of documents, obtain a sense of key quality and patient safety issues from a 'bottom up' perspective. The rounds aim to promote a culture in which care is everyone's business and responsibility, coupled with a 'can-do' approach to making change. Ground rules are set in advance (including confidentiality and the topics to be considered), the rounds are led by the chief executive or most senior accountable person present. They occur regularly (e.g. monthly) and are located in the ward or department being discussed. Topics covered include communication, teamwork, risk management, prevention and control of care-associated infection, environment, equipment, process, continuing professional development and leadership.
>
> Before the round – information is reviewed such as quality and performance indicators; patient feedback; incidents/near misses; complaints/compliments; quality improvements, update since last round.
>
> Afterwards – an action plan is circulated and records updated, follow up where required by a senior manager.
>
> Adapted from Health Service Executive, Ireland (2013)

directly emphasising to senior leaders where improvements are needed and immediately implementing action plans to achieve them.

Facilitating clinicians' active engagement in quality improvement

Engaging students and doctors in training in real, systematic health and quality improvements is essential for effecting cultural change, however, many complex challenges exist in facilitating training and education in quality improvement (Mosser et al, 2009). Training requirements for career progression are already tightly defined and demanding. The high standards required and expected involvement in numerous extra-curricular activities, without formal time allocated in job plans, often force doctors in training to seek 'out of programme' activities to gain their Certificates of Completion of Training (CCTs).

It has been suggested that the training system needs to see quality improvement as a core responsibility intrinsic to professional values rather than an 'add on' for those who are particularly interested (Medical Professionalism Project, 2002). This point is reiterated in professional standards which require responsible and compassionate clinicians to help health-care organisations develop systems whereby safety and high quality clinical care supersedes all other priorities and is paramount in all clinical and management activities (e.g. General Medical Council, 2013).

A key challenge in fully engaging doctors in training involves generating enthusiasm among more senior clinicians for quality improvement initiatives. Often this can be problematic as a result of the 'time stealers' (e.g. staff shortages, out-of-hours' work, administrative burdens) in health service provision, therefore time must be made for mandatory quality improvement activities in already tightly scheduled postgraduate medical curricula (Gosfield and Reinertsen, 2003; Reinertsen et al, 2007).

Prochaska and Velicer's (1997) model of transtheoretical change highlights that without widespread practical training in quality improvement, the behaviour and attitudes of the majority of doctors in training will not progress beyond 'pre-contemplation' or 'contemplation', i.e. falling short of 'engagement'. It must also be recognized that while quality improvement activities will continue to attract 'innovators' and 'early adopters' (Rogers, 1962), the NHS will struggle to attract the mass 'early and late majority' required to enable it to survive, thrive and become one of the leading and safest health-care institutions in the world (Berwick, 2013; Keogh, 2013). To facilitate this improvement, existing health-care leaders, managers and educators need to synergistically work together to build a symbiotic relationship between leadership and quality improvement by transforming the education of doctors in training to one where they are all provided with the practical skills to directly implement quality improvement into clinical practice (Boonyasai et al, 2007).

Building sustainability

If a cultural shift which embraces and promotes a quality improvement culture and fully engages doctors in training is to become widespread and routine throughout the NHS, the shift needs to be managed at a national level with agreed quality improvement methodologies and curricula that requires training in such methodologies. The frequency with which doctors rotate through departments, trusts or health boards and regions throughout the UK and beyond is both a strength and a weakness. While this can facilitate learning and sharing of experiences (Dharamshi and Hillman, 2011) the danger is that, without establishing a sustainable, agreed methodology for quality improvement teaching and project coordination, it will be compromised by the same limitations impacting on clinical audit: sporadic, short lived and uncoordinated projects ('projectitis'). The situation is exacerbated for the current cohorts of doctors in training as many of their supervisors and seniors themselves have little experience in quality improvement.

While no single, simple initiatives are currently implemented across all NHS organisations, a range of activities is ongoing with central collation and evaluation of their effectiveness (e.g. the NHS Improving Quality activities www.nhsiq.nhs.uk). Other national initiatives provide excellent external quality improvement resources, e.g. those of the Institute for Healthcare and Improvement Open School (www.ihi.org/education/ihiopenschool/Pages/default.aspx) and rapidly growing project banks, such as BMJ Quality (http://quality.bmj.com) or The Network (www.the-network.org.uk).

Incorporating these resources routinely into training curricula would tap into doctors in training's extrinsic motivation and their desire to build competitive curriculum vitae through innovations, presentations and publications, as well as developing a quality improvement approach as part of everyday clinical practice. However, enabling individuals to engage in their own quality initiatives could potentially pose risks to organisations owing to a lack of alignment of quality improvement projects with the strategic vision and direction of the organisation. Working through quality improvement 'units' and organisational 'leads', with external advice and input, helps mitigate such risks and build sustainable improvements and learning organisations (Senge, 1990).

While 'disruptive innovation' can stimulate widespread change, a quality improvement approach primarily aims to instil 'adaptive innovation' through small-scale tests of change or plan-do-study-act cycles. Clinicians should therefore be encouraged and empowered to build on rather than disrupt existing practice by overcoming health-care problems on the frontline (Kenagy, 2009). This requires the formation of cohesive links between formal and informal networks within and between organisations, with connections extending to an executive level (Battilana and Casciaro, 2013). Internal quality improvement project banks are integral to this and must be coordinated carefully among not only doctors in training but all employees engaged in quality improvement. Establishing internal networks of key stakeholders can help turn vision into reality, and is another key factor in providing doctors in training with the support, mentorship and opportunities necessary to facilitate quality improvement. However, this does require senior clinicians to be enthusiastic about and ideally personally engaged in, innovation and improvement activities which is not always the case. Here, organisations may need to leverage regulatory requirements, such as the General Medical Council's mandate for quality improvement activity to be incorporated into doctors' appraisal and revalidation (General Medical Council, 2012b).

A combination of the activities outlined above can help engage doctors at all levels to build and embed sustainable, clinician-led health-care improvements (Tregunno et al, 2013). Salford Royal Infirmary NHS Foundation Trust is excelling in this area through its 'TICKLE' programme outlined in case scenario 18.2.

Case scenario 18.2 Local quality improvement and leadership development initiatives

Salford Royal Infirmary NHS Foundation Trust is a leading example for others looking to engage doctors in training with quality improvement initiatives. 'Junior doctors are encouraged to participate in quality improvement projects as well as contributing to quality assurance and clinical governance meetings. There is also strong support from the North West Local Education and Training Board. The trust is currently seeking to extend the engagement of all junior doctors in service improvement projects. To facilitate this, the trust has worked in partnership with junior doctors to set up "TICKLE" (Trainees improving care through leadership and education). The core emphasis of this group is to educate, build capability and facilitate the practice of non-consultant grade doctors in quality improvement and healthcare management and leadership' (Clark and Nath, 2014).

Combining didactic and experiential learning, both inside and outside formal teaching programmes, trainees are able to begin developing their theoretical knowledge and practical experience on patient safety and quality improvement. Excellent feedback from trainees, local and national presentations, and formal incorporation within the Trust's Executive Quality and Safety Committee heightens hopes for sustainability, further spread and improvements in patient safety and medical leadership from the first year of qualification.

Leadership and management development

The final set of activities identified through the literature and commentaries needed to embed sustainable quality improvements are those relating to leadership development. Throughout the last decade, the call for clinical leaders and managers has grown louder (Darzi, 2008; Spurgeon et al, 2011; West et al, 2014), with increasing understanding of what this leadership should comprise and what development is needed. The NHS approach has moved from purely a management focus, to one founded on hero-leaders (King's Fund, 2011), through to consideration of transformational, engaging and shared leadership (Alimo-Metcalfe and Alban-Metcalfe, 2005), and then finally, to the current conceptualisation, that 'collective leadership' is required (West et al, 2014). Although only recently foregrounded in health care, the philosophy and premise of collective leadership lies at the heart of medical professionalism, incorporates a core responsibility to regulatory bodies, and is fundamental to a health-care system founded on meeting universal need (Medical Professionalism Project, 2002; General Medical Council, 2013).

This rhetorical and conceptual shift about what leadership approach is required to improve patient care (which is partly a response to the acknowledgement that neither 'new managerialism' nor transformational leadership have worked) is underpinned by many leadership development activities. Activities include formal award bearing programmes, 'in-house' training and online leadership development. These activities have, until recently, been underpinned by a raft of leadership frameworks which set out the core competencies that all health and social care workers should attain at various stages as they progress through their career.

The NHS Healthcare Leadership Model (NHS Leadership Academy, 2013) (see *Figure 3.3*) takes a different approach from earlier competency frameworks (which have been criticised for being reductionist) and focuses on the leadership behaviours that the NHS must foster to provide the high quality patient care which has been proven to be lacking following the aforementioned reports on NHS failings (Francis, 2013; Keogh, 2013; Andrews and Butler, 2014). These leadership behaviours are defined under nine dimensions which reflect an emphasis on care, compassion and collective responsibility:

1. Inspiring shared purpose
2. Leading with care
3. Evaluating information

4. Connecting our service
5. Sharing the vision
6. Engaging the team
7. Holding to account
8. Developing capability
9. Influencing the results

The way these behaviours are described, for all NHS health professionals, marks an explicit sea-change from an individualist to a collective leadership approach. Doctors will need to move away from a traditional 'command and control' hierarchical leadership style towards a collective leadership style (West et al, 2014). Leadership development and support therefore needs to equip doctors with the knowledge, skills and behaviours to allow them to engage with and facilitate this culture shift (see also Chapter 15 on follower-ship). As well as developing self-insight, leadership skills, and an understanding of systems and organisations, all clinicians should have quality improvement science embedded in their education and training from an early stage. This approach will help enable doctors in training to take responsibility for compassionate and effective patient care, develop quality improvement as 'business as usual' for clinicians and realize Berwick's vision for the NHS to be one of the leading health-care institutions in the world (Berwick, 2013). See also Chapter 7.

Conclusions

Health-care organisations, and the NHS in particular, typically operate as highly complex operational structures. With increasing pressure to meet stake-holder demands and drive innovation within economic constraints, providing high quality patient care has never been more challenging.

Organisations and individuals must move away from systems of quality assurance that measure and promote compliance with rigid standards, and develop a quality improvement culture (Hillman and Roueché, 2011). Quality improvement at its core is 'the combined and unceasing efforts of everyone (health-care professionals, patients and their families, researchers, payers, planners and educators) to make the changes that will lead to better patient outcomes (health), better system performance (care) and better professional development (learning)' (Batalden and Davidoff, 2007). Embedding this approach will provide a better patient experience, and outcomes that do not just depend on health-care provision but on many interlinked social and economic factors.

Integral to this ideological shift is investment and training in patient safety, quality improvement science and leadership development. Mobilising doctors in training as agents for change is essential. They must be afforded the opportunity to actively engage with quality improvement initiatives in local organisations and networks to make practical changes to patient care (The Health Foundation, 2011b; Berwick, 2013). Without organisational and 'shop floor' support and a combination of theoretical and experiential learning to develop quality improvement skills, there is a risk that doctors in training will become frustrated and disengaged. As Bagnall (2012) reminds us, formal incorporation of quality improvement science at all levels of medical education is crucial to harness this large yet under-used part of the medical workforce to deliver meaningful quality improvements and provide high quality, patient-centred care throughout the whole service.

Key points

- Many reports and case studies identify a need for a culture shift from quality assurance towards quality improvement and patient-centred care
- Medical students and doctors in training are central to effecting widespread cultural change but are currently under-used
- Organisational and system change at all levels is needed to fully integrate quality improvement within cultural shifts
- Embedding quality improvement into education and training curricula and supporting doctors to engage in quality improvement initiatives will help clinicians be more effective health-care leaders.

References

Aarvold A, Ardolino A, Boyd R, Kelsall N, McGillion S, Hodkinson S, Goodwin M (2011) Lessons in leadership from an international exchange visit. *International Journal of Clinical Leadership* **17**(2): 87–92

Academy of Medical Royal Colleges (2015) The UK foundation Programme Curriculum. www.foundationprogramme.nhs.uk/download.asp?file=FP_Curriculum_2012_Updated_for_Aug_2015_-_FINAL.pdf (accessed 27 July 2015)

Ackerman L (1997) Development, transition or transformation: the question of change in organisations. In: Van Eynde D, Hoy J, Van Eynde D, eds. *Organisation Development Classics*. Jossey Bass, San Francisco, USA

Agency for Healthcare Research and Quality (2007) *TeamSTEPPS™: Strategies and tools to enhance performance and patient safety.* Agency for Healthcare Research and Quality, Rockville, MD

Agency for Healthcare Research and Quality (2008) TeamSTEPPS™ Fundamentals Course: Module 5. Mutual Support (continued). www.ahrq.gov/professionals/education-tools/curriculum-tools/teamstepps/instructor/fundamentals/module5/igsitmonitor.html (accessed 27 July 2015)

Alban-Metcalfe J, Alimo-Metcalfe B (2013) Reliability and validity of the 'leadership competencies and engaging leadership scale. *International Journal of Public Sector Management* **26**(1): 56–73

Alimo-Metcalfe B (1998) *Effective leadership.* Local Government Management Board, London

Alimo-Metcalfe B, Alban-Metcalfe J (2005) Leadership: Time for a New Direction? *Leadership* **1**: 51–71

Alimo-Metcalfe B, Alban-Metcalfe J (2006) More (good) leaders for the public sector. *Int J Public Sector Man* **19**(4): 293–315

Alimo-Metcalfe B, Alban-Metcalfe J, Bradley M, Mariathasan J, Samele C (2008) The impact of engaging leadership on performance, attitudes to work and wellbeing at work: a longitudinal study. *J Health Organ Manag* **22**(6): 586–98

Alimo-Metcalfe B, Alban-Metcalfe R (2001) The development of a new Transformational Leadership Questionnaire. *J Occup Organ Psychol* **74**(1): 1–27

Alimo-Metcalfe B, Bradley M (2009) 'Darzi and leadership – it's too important to get wrong this time'. *Clin Lead J* **2**(1): 3–11

Alzheimer's Society (2014) *Dementia UK.* 2nd edn. Alzheimer's Society, London

American Psychiatric Association (2013) *Diagnostic and statistical manual of mental disorders.* 5th edn. Washington, DC, USA

Andrews J, Butler M (2014) Trusted to Care: An independent review of the Princess of Wales Hospital and Neath Port Talbot Hospital at Abertawe Bro Morgannwg University Health Board. http://gov.wales/docs/dhss/publications/140512trustedtocareen.pdf (accessed 27 July 2015)

Anning A, Cottrell D, Frost N, Green J (2010) *Developing multiprofessional teamwork for integrated children's services.* Open University Press/McGraw-Hill International, Maidenhead

Arnold L (2002) Assessing professional behavior: Yesterday, today, and tomorrow. *Acad Med* **77**(6): 502–15

Arnold L, Stern DT (2006) What is medical professionalism? In: Stern DT, ed. *Measuring Medical Professionalism.* Oxford University Press, Oxford

Ashforth BE, Humphrey RH (1993) Emotional labor in service roles: the influence of identity. *Acad Manage Rev* **181**: 88–115

Atkinson S, Spurgeon P, Clark J, Armit K (2011) Engaging Doctors: What can we learn from trusts with high levels of medical engagement? www.institute.nhs.uk/images/documents/Leadership/Engaging%20Doctors%20-%20What%20can%20we%20learn%20from%20trusts%20with%20high%20levels%20of%20medical%20engagement.pdf (accessed 8 April 2011)

Atwater L, Roush P, Fischthal A (1995) The influence of upward feedback on self and follower ratings of leadership. *Personnel Psychology* **48**(1): 35–59

Australian Medical Council (2009) Assessment and Accreditation of Medical Schools: Standards and Procedures. www.amc.org.au/images/Medschool/standards.pdf (accessed 16 October 2011)

Avolio BJ, Bass BM (2002) *Developing Potential Across a Full Range of Leadership Cases on Transactional and Transformational Leadership.* Lawrence Erlbaum Associates, Mahwah, NJ, USA

Avolio BJ, Gardner WL, Walumbwa FO, Luthans F, May DR (2004) Unlocking the mask: a look at the process by which authentic leaders impact follower attitudes and behaviors. *Leadersh Q* **15**: 801–23

Aylward M, Phillips C, Howson H (2014a) Simply Prudent Healthcare – achieving better care and value for money in Wales – discussion paper. www.bevancommission.org/sitesplus/documents/1101/Bevan%20Commission%20Simply%20Prudent%20Healthcare%20v1%2004122013.pdf (accessed 23 March 2015)

Aylward M, Howson H, Matthias J (2014b) International examples of prudent approaches to healthcare. www.prudenthealthcare.org.uk/international (accessed 23 March 2015)

Babiak P, Hare RD (2006) *Snakes in suits: When psychopaths go to work.* Harper Collins, New York, USA

Bagnall P (2012) *Facilitators and Barriers to Leadership and Quality Improvement.* The King's Fund Junior Doctor Project. The King's Fund, London

Bak P, Tang C, Wiesenfield K (1987) Self-organized criticality: an explanation of 1/f noise, *Phys Rev Lett* **59**: 381–4

Baker GR, Denis J (2011) Medical leadership in health care systems: from professional authority to organizational leadership. *Public Money & Management* **31**(5): 355–62

Bar-On R (1997) *Bar-On Emotional Quotient Inventory (EQI).* Technical Manual. Multi-Health Systems, Canada

Barr B (2014) The impact of NHS resource allocation policy on health inequalities in England 2001-2011: longitudinal ecological study. *BMJ* **348**: 3231

Barrow M, McKimm J, Gasquoine S (2011) The policy and the practice: early-career doctors and nurses as leaders and followers in the delivery of health care. *Adv Health Sci Educ Theory Prac* **16**(1): 17–29

Barrow M, McKimm J, Gasquoine S, Rowe D (2014) Collaborating in healthcare delivery: exploring conceptual differences at the 'bedside'. *J Interprof Care* **29**(2): 119–24

Bar-Yam Y (2004) *Making things work: Solving complex problems in a complex world.* NECSI-Knowledge Press, Cambridge, MA, USA

Bass BM (2008) *The Bass Handbook of Leadership: Theory, Research, and Managerial Applications.* 4th edn. Free Press, New York, USA

Bass BM, Avolio BJ, Atwater LE (1996) The transformational and transactional leadership of men and women. *Applied Psychology: An International Review* **45**: 5–34

Bass BM, Riggio RE (2005) *Transformational Leadership.* 2nd edn. Psychology Press; New Jersey, USA

Batalden PB, Davidoff F (2007) What is "quality improvement" and how can it transform healthcare? *Qual Saf Healthcare* **16**: 2–3

Battilana J, Casciaro T (2012) Change agents, networks, and institutions: a contingency theory of organizational change. *Academy of Management Journal* **55**(2): 381–96

Battilana J, Casciaro T (2013) The network secrets of great change agents. *Harv Bus Rev* **91**(7-8): 62–8

Baumeister RF, Senders PS, Chesner SC, Tice DM (1988) Who's in charge here? Group leaders do lend help in emergencies. *Pers Soc Psychol Bull* **14**: 17–22

Behavioural Insights Team (2012) *Test, Adapt, Learn: developing public policy with randomised controlled trials.* Cabinet Office, London

Behn R (1980) Leadership in an era of retrenchment. *Public Adm Rev* November/December: 603–4

Belyansky I, Martin TR, Prabhu AS et al (2011) Poor resident-attending intraoperative communication may compromise patient safety. *J Surg Res* **171**(2): 386–94

Berkowitz L (1953) Sharing leadership in small, decision-making groups. *J Abnorm Soc Psychol* **48**: 231–8

Berwick D (2008) The science of improvement. *JAMA* **299**(10): 1182–4

Berwick D (2013) *A promise to learn – a commitment to act: Improving the safety of patients in England.* National Advisory Group Report on the Safety of Patients in England. Department of Health, London

Biller R (1980) Leadership tactics for retrenchment. *Public Adm Rev* November/December: 604–9

Blake RR, Mouton JS (1985) *The Managerial Grid III: The Key to Leadership Excellence.* Gulf Publishing, Houston, USA

Bligh MC, Kohles JC, Meindl JR (2004) Charting the language of leadership: a methodological investigation of President Bush and the crisis of 9/11. *J Appl Psychol* **89**(3): 562–74

Bloom N, Propper C, Seiler S, van Reenen J (2010) The Impact of Competition on Management Quality: Evidence from Public Hospitals. CEP Discussion Paper No 983 May 2010. http://cep.lse.ac.uk/pubs/download/dp0983.pdf (accessed 8 April 2011)

Bohmer R (2010) Leadership with a small 'l'. *BMJ* **340**: c483

Bolden R, Gosling J, Marturano A, Dennison P (2003) A review of leadership theory and competency frameworks. University of Exeter Department of Leadership Studies, University of Exeter, Exeter

Bolman LG, Deal TE (2003) *Reframing Organisations. Artistry, Choice and Leadership.* 3rd edn. Wiley, San Francisco, USA

Boonyasai R, Windish D, Chakraborti R, Feldman L, Rubin H, Bass E (2007) Effectiveness of teaching quality improvement to clinicians: a systematic review. *JAMA* **298**(9): 1023–37

Boyne G (2004) A "3Rs" strategy for public service turnaround: retrenchment, repositioning and reorganization. *Public Money and Management* **24**(2): 97–103

Boyne G (2006) Strategies for public service turnaround: lessons from the private sector? *Adm Soc* **38**: 365–88

Brannick M, Wahi M, Goldin S (2011) Psychometrics of Mayer-Salovey-Caruso Emotional Intelligence Test (MSCEIT) scores. *Psychol Rep* **109**: 327–37

Bromiley M (2009) Would you speak up if the consultant got it wrong? ...and would you listen if someone said you'd got it wrong? *J Perioper Pract* **19**(10): 326–9

Brook R (2010) Medical leadership in an increasingly complex world. *JAMA* **304**: 465–6

Burns JM (1978) *Leadership.* Harper and Row, New York, USA

Burr SA, Leung YL (2013) Towards promoting and assessing clinical compassion. *Br J Hosp Med* **74**(12): 677–81 (doi: 10.12968/hmed.2013.74.12.677)

Campbell D (2013) Mid Staffs hospital scandal: the essential guide. *The Guardian* 6 February (www.theguardian.com/society/2013/feb/06/mid-staffs-hospital-scandal-guide accessed 20 July 2015)

Care Quality Commission (2014) *The state of health care and adult social care in England 2013/14.* Care Quality Commission, London

Cattell RB, Stice GF (1954) Four formulae for selecting leaders on the basis of personality. *Hum Relat* **7**: 493–507

Chadi N (2009) Medical leadership: doctors at the helm of change. *Mcgill J Med* **12**(1): 52–7

Chakraborti C, Boonyasai RT, Wright SM, Kern DE (2008) A systematic review of teamwork training interventions in medical student and resident education. *J Gen Intern Med* **23**: 846–53

Chantler C (1999) The role and education of doctors in the delivery of health care. *Lancet* **353**(9159): 1178–81

Cherry MG, Fletcher I, O'Sullivan H, Shaw N (2012) What impact do structured educational sessions to increase emotional intelligence have on medical students? BEME Guide No. 17. *Med Teach* **34**(1): 11–19

Cherry MG, Fletcher I, O'Sullivan H (2013) Exploring the relationships among attachment, emotional intelligence and communication. *Med Educ* **47**(3): 317–25

Chomsky N (1999) *Profit over People: Neoliberalism and Global Order.* Seven Stories Press, New York, USA

Ciarrochi J, Chan A, Caputi P (2000) A critical evaluation of the emotional intelligence construct. *Pers Individ Dif* **28**: 539–61

Ciarrochi J, Deane D, Anderson S (2002) Emotional intelligence moderates the relationship between stress and mental health. *Pers Individ Dif* **32**: 197–209

Clark J, Armit K (2008) Attainment of competency in management and leadership: no longer an optional extra for doctors. *Clinical Governance: An International Journal* **13**(1): 35–42

Clark J, Armit K (2010) Leadership competency for doctors: a framework. *Leadership in Health Services* **23**(2): 115

Clark J, Nath V (2014) Medical engagement: a journey, not an event. www.kingsfund.org. uk/sites/files/kf/field/field_publication_file/medical-engagement-a-journey-not-an-event-jul14_0.pdf (accessed 27 July 2015)

Cleland J, Dowell J, McLachlan J, Nicholson S, Patterson F (2012) *Identifying Best Practice in the Selection of Medical Students.* General Medical Council, London

Clinical Human Factors Group (2008) Just a Routine Operation teaching video. http://chfg. org/articles-films-guides/films/just-a-routine-operation-teaching-video (accessed 4 February 2015)

Clinical Human Factors Group (2011) Towards a working definition of human factors in healthcare. http://chfg.org/definition/towards-a-working-definition-of-human-factors-in-healthcare (accessed 20 July 2015)

Coats RD, Burd RS (2002) Intraoperative communication of residents with faculty: perception versus reality. *J Surg Res* **104**(1): 40–5

Cockings JG, Cook DA, Iqbal RK (2006) Process monitoring in intensive care with the use of cumulative expected minus observed mortality and risk-adjusted P charts. *Crit Care* **10(1):** R28

Commission on Dignity in Care for Older People (2012) *Delivering Dignity: Securing dignity in care for older people in hospitals and care homes.* A report for consultation. Local Government Association/NHS Confederation/Age UK, London

Cooper GM, McClure JH (2005) Maternal deaths from anaesthesia. An extract from Why Mothers Die 2000–2002, the Confidential Enquiries into Maternal Deaths in the United Kingdom Chapter 9: Anaesthesia. *Br J Anaesth* **94**(4): 417–23 (doi: 10.1093/bja/aei066)

Cosby KS, Croskerry P (2004) Profiles in patient safety: authority gradients in medical error. *Acad Emerg Med* **11**(12): 1341–5

Crawford M (2009) *Getting to the heart of leadership: Emotion and educational leadership.* SAGE, London

Croft C, Currie G, Lockett A (2015) The impact of emotionally important social identities in the construction of a managerial leader identity: A challenge for nurses in the English National Health Service. *Organisation Studies* **36**(1): 113–31

Crolla EL, Bamforth MA (2011) Gender and medicine: the challenges for medical educators. *Med Educ* **45**(6): 544–6

Crosson FJ (2003) Kaiser Permanente: A Propensity for Partnership. *BMJ* **326**(7390): 654

Cruess RL, Cruess SR (2010) Professionalism is a generic term: practicing what we preach. *Med Teach* **32**(9): 713–14

Cruess RL, Cruess SR, Boudreau D, Snell L, Steinert Y (2014) Reframing medical education to support professional identity formation. *Acad Med* **89**(11): 1446–51

Dannhauser Z (2007) The Relationship between Servant Leadership, Follower Trust, Team Commitment and Unit Effectiveness. Doctoral Thesis, Stellenbosch University, South Africa

Darzi AW (2008) *High quality care for all: NHS next stage review final report.* The Stationery Office, London

Dath D, Chan M-K, Anderson G, Burke A, Razack S, Lieff S, Moineau G, Chiu A, Ellison P (2015) Leader. In: Frank JR, Snell L, Sherbino J, eds. *The Draft CanMEDS 2015 Physician Competency Framework: the Leader role – Series IV.* The Royal College of Physicians and Surgeons of Canada, Ottawa, Canada

Davies M, Stankov L (1998) Emotional intelligence: in search of an elusive construct. *J Pers Soc Psychol* **75**: 989–1015

Day DV, Fleenor JW, Atwater LE, Sturm RE, McKee RA (2014) Advances in leader and leadership development: A review of 25 years of research and theory. *Leadersh Q* **25**(1): 63–82

Deming WE (1993) *The New Economics.* MIT Press, Cambridge, USA

Denhardt B, Denhardt V (2006) *The Dance of Leadership: The Art of Leading in Business, Government, and Society.* M.E. Sharpe, Armonk, NY, USA

Department of Health (1989) *Working for Patients.* The Stationery Office, London

Department of Health (2000) *The NHS Plan: A Plan for Investment: A Plan for Reform.* The Stationery Office, London

Department of Health (2001) Learning from Bristol: The Report of the Public Inquiry into Children's Heart Surgery at the Bristol Royal Infirmary 1984–1995. www.gov.uk/government/uploads/system/uploads/attachment_data/file/273320/5363.pdf (accessed 16 March 2015)

Department of Health (2002) *Managing for Excellence in the NHS.* The Stationery Office, London

Department of Health (2009a) *Inspiring Leaders: Leadership for Quality.* Department of Health, London

Department of Health (2009b) *The NHS Constitution: Securing the NHS Today for Generations to Come.* Department of Health, London

Department of Health (2010) *Equity and Excellence: Liberating the NHS.* The Stationery Office, London

Department of Health (2014) *Delivering High Quality, Effective, Compassionate Care: Developing the Right People with the Right Skills and the Right Values.* A mandate from the Government to Health Education England: April 2014 to March 2015. Williams Lea, London

Department of Health (2015) *Prime Minister's Challenge on Dementia 2020.* Department of Health, London

Department of Health and Social Security (1983) *NHS Management Inquiry Report.* Griffiths report. HMSO, London

DeRue DS (2011) Adaptive leadership theory: Leading and following as a complex adaptive process. *Organizational Behavior* **31**: 125–50

Dharamshi T, Hillman T (2011) Going beyond audit. *BMJ Careers* 5 Jul (http://careers.bmj.com/careers/advice/view-article.html?id=20003642 accessed 9 December 2014)

Diaz VA, Carek PJ, Dickerson LM, Steyer TE (2010) Teaching quality improvement in a primary care residency. *Jt Comm J Quality Patient Safety* **36**(10): 454–60

Dickinson H, Ham C (2008) *Engaging Doctors in Leadership: Review of the Literature.* NHS Institute for Innovation and Improvement/ Health Services Management Centre, Coventry

Dickinson H, Ham C, Snelling I, Spurgeon P (2013) *Are We There Yet?* Models of Medical Leadership and their effectiveness: An Exploratory Study. Final report. NIHR Service Delivery and Organisation programme, HMSO, London

Dobson C, Cookson J, Allgar V, McKendree J (2008) Leadership training in the undergraduate medical curriculum. *Educ Prim Care* **19**(5): 526–9

Douglas NJ (2010) Strengthening medical leadership. *Br J Hosp Med* **71**(4): 184–5

Dubois V (2010) *The Bureaucrat and the Poor: encounters in French welfare offices.* Ashgate, Farnham, Surrey

Eckert R, West M, Altman D, Steward K, Pasmore B (2014) *Delivering a Collective Leadership Strategy for Healthcare.* The King's Fund, London

Emslie S, Knox K, Pickstone M (2002) *Improving patient safety: insights from America, Australian and British healthcare.* ECRI Europe and Department of Health. ECRI Europe, Welwyn Garden City

Eva KW, Regehr G (2011) Exploring the Divergence between Self-Assessment and Self-Monitoring. *Adv Health Sci Educ Theory Pract* **16**(3): 311–29

Evans T (2010) *Professional Discretion in Welfare Services: beyond street-level bureaucracy.* Ashgate, Farnham, Surrey

Ezziane Z, Maruthappu M, Gawn L, Thompson EA, Athanasiou T, Warren OJ (2012) Building effective clinical teams in healthcare. *J Health Organ Manag* **26**(4): 428–36

Faculty of Medical Leadership and Management (2014) About Us: Faculty of Medical Leadership and Management. www.fmlm.ac.uk/about-us (accessed 10 February 2015)

Faculty of Medical Leadership and Management (2015) Leadership and management standards for medical professionals. www.fmlm.ac.uk/sites/default/files/content/page/attachments/standards_2_web_ready.pdf (accessed 27 March 2015)

Fineman S (2004) Getting the measure of emotion - and the cautionary tale of emotional intelligence. *Hum Relat* **57**(6): 719–40

Firth-Cozens J (2004) Why communication fails in the operating room. *Qual Saf Health Care* **13**(5): 327

Firth-Cozens J, Redfern N, Moss F (2002) Confronting errors in patient care. Report to University of Birmingham. www.birmingham.ac.uk/Documents/college-mds/haps/projects/cfhep/psrp/finalreports/PS002FinalReportFirthCozens.pdf (accessed 31 March 2015)

Fisher JM (2005) A Time for Change. *Human Resource Development International* **8**(2): 257–64

Fleishman E (1953) The description of supervisory behavior. *J Appl Psychol* **37**: 1–6

Fletcher G, Flin R, McGeorge P, Glavin R, Maran N, Patey R (2003) Anaesthetists' non-technical skills (ANTS): evaluation of a behavioural marker system. *Br J Anaesth* **90**: 580–8

Fletcher I, Leadbetter P, Curran A, O'Sullivan H (2009) A pilot study assessing emotional intelligence training and communication skills with 3rd year medical students. *Patient Educ Couns* **76**(3): 376–9

Fonteyn EM, Kuipers B, Grobe SJ (1993) A Description of Think Aloud Method and Protocol Analysis. *Qual Health Res* **3**(4): 430–41

Forbes T, Hallier J, Calder I (2004) Doctors as managers: investors and reluctants in a dual role. *Health Serv Manage Res* **17**(3): 1–10

Forsyth DR (2013) *Group Dynamics.* 6th edn. Cengage Learning, Independence, Kentucky, USA

Francis R (2013) Report of the Mid Staffordshire NHS Foundation Trust Public Inquiry: executive summary. House Paper 947. www.midstaffspublicinquiry.com (accessed 7 March 2015)

Frank JR, Snell L, Sherbino J, eds (2015) *The Draft CanMEDS 2015 Physician Competency Framework – Series IV.* The Royal College of Physicians and Surgeons of Canada, Ottawa, Canada

Fraser S, Greenhalgh T (2001) Complexity science: Coping with complexity: educating for capability. *BMJ* **323**: 799–803

Fullan M (2003) *Change Forces with Vengeance.* Routledge Falmer, New York, USA

Fullan M (2004) *Leading in a Culture of Change: Personal Action Guide and Workbook.* Jossey Bass, San Francisco, USA

Gallen D, Lynch M, Buckle G (2007) Addressing leadership and management competencies in Foundation Year 2. *Clinician in Management* **15**: 87–93

Gardner JP, Olson DM (2010) The Gift of Empowerment: A New Perspective to Leading Others. *Insights to a Changing World Journal* **4**: 68–75

Gardner WL, Avolio BJ, Luthans F, May DR, Walumba F (2005) Can you see the real me? A self-based model of authentic leader and follower development. *Leadersh Q* **16**(3): 343–72

Garner J, McKendree J, O'Sullivan H, Taylor D (2010) Undergraduate medical student attitudes to the peer assessment of professional behaviours in two medical schools. *Educ Prim Care* **21**(1): 32–7

General Medical Council (2007) *Medical Students: Professional Values and Fitness to Practise.* General Medical Council, London

General Medical Council (2009) *Tomorrow's Doctors: Outcomes and Standards for Undergraduate Medical Education.* General Medical Council, London

General Medical Council (2012a) *Leadership and Management for all Doctors.* General Medical Council, London

General Medical Council (2012b) *Supporting Information for Appraisal and Revalidation.* General Medical Council, London

General Medical Council (2013) *Good Medical Practice.* General Medical Council, London

General Medical Council (2015) Standards and guidance for medical education and training. www.gmc-uk.org/education/26828.asp (accessed 28 July 2015)

George B, Sims P, Gergen D (2007) *True North: Discover your authentic leadership.* Jossey Bass, San Francisco, USA

George JM (2000) Emotions and Leadership: The Role of Emotional Intelligence. *Hum Relat* **53**(8): 1027–55

Giltinane CL (2013) Leadership styles and theories. *Nurs Stand* **27**(41): 35–9

Ginsburg S, Regehr G, Hatala R et al (2000) Context, conflict, and resolution: a new conceptual framework for evaluating professionalism. *Acad Med* **75**(10): S6–S11

Gladwell M (2008) *Outliers: The Story of Success.* Little, Brown and Co., New York, USA

Glassberg A (1978) Organizational responses to municipal budget decreases. *Public Adm Rev* July/August: 325–32

Goldenberg I, Matheson K, Mantler J (2006) The assessment of emotional intelligence: a comparison of performance-based and self-report methodologies. *J Pers Assess* **86**: 33–45

Goleman D (1996) *Emotional Intelligence: Why It Can Matter More Than IQ*. Bantam Doubleday Dell Publishing Group, London

Goleman D (2000) Leadership that gets results. *Harv Bus Rev* **78**(2): 78–90

Goleman D, Boyatzis R, McKee A (2002) *Primal Leadership: Unleashing the power of emotional intelligence*. Harvard Business Review Press, Boston, Massachusetts, USA

Goodrich J, Levenson R (2012) Supporting hospital staff to provide compassionate care: Do Schwartz Centre Rounds work in English hospitals? *J R Soc Med* **105**: 117–22

Gosfield AG, Reinertsen JL (2003) Doing well by doing good: Improving the business case for quality. www.uft-a.com/PDF/uft-a_White_Paper_060103.PDF (accessed 9 December 2014)

Gosling J, Mintzberg H (2003) The five minds of the manager. *Harv Bus Rev* **81**(11): 54–63

Graen GB, Novak MA, Sommerkamp P (1982) The effects of leader-member exchange and job design on productivity and satisfaction: Testing a dual attachment model. *Organ Behav Hum Perform* **30**(1): 109–31

Grant L, Appleby J, Griffin N, Adam A, Gishen P (2012) Facing the future: the effects of the impending financial drought on NHS finances and how UK radiology services can contribute to expected efficiency savings. *Br J Radiol* **85**: 784–91

Greenleaf RK (2002) *Servant Leadership: a journey into the nature of legitimate power and greatness* (25th Anniversary edition). Paulist Press, New York, USA

Greenockle KM (2010) The new face in leadership: emotional intelligence. *Quest* **62**(3): 260–7

Griffin RJ, Ebert RW (2010) *Business Essentials*. 8th edn. Prentice Hall, New Jersey, USA

Grijalva E, Harms PD, Newman D, Gaddis B, Fraley RC (2015) Narcissism and leadership: A meta-analytic review of linear and nonlinear relationships. *Personnel Psychol* **68**(1): 1–47

Grint K, Holt C (2011) *Followership in the NHS*. The King's Fund, London

Hackman JR (2009) Why teams don't work: an interview by Diane Coutu. *Harv Bus Rev* **87**(5): 98–105

Hackman JR, Walton RE (1986) Leading groups in organizations. In Goodman PS et al. eds. *Designing Effective Work Groups*. Jossey-Bass, San Francisco, USA

Hadley L, Penlington C, Black D (2010) A current perspective on a moving target: clinical leadership in postgraduate medical education. *Br J Hosp Med* **71**(4): 220–2

Hafferty FW, Castellani B (2010) The increasing complexities of professionalism. *Acad Med* **85**(2): 288–301

Ham C (2008) Doctors in leadership: learning from international experience. *Int J Clin Lead* **16**(1): 11–16

Ham C, Clark J, Spurgeon P, Dickenson H, Armit K (2010) Medical Chief Executives in the NHS: Facilitators and Barriers to Their Career Progress. www.birmingham.ac.uk/Documents/college-social-sciences/social-policy/HSMC/publications/2010/Medical-Chief-Executives-in-the-NHS.pdf (accessed 27 July 2015)

Ham C, Clark J, Spurgeon P, Dickinson H, Armit K (2011) Doctors who become chief executives in the NHS: from keen amateurs to skilled professionals. *J R Soc Med* **104**(3): 113–19

Hamilton P, Spurgeon P, Clark J, Dent J, Armit K (2008) Engaging Doctors: can doctors influence organisational performance? www.aomrc.org.uk/doc_view/197-engaging-doctors-can-doctors-influence-organisational-performance (accessed 27 July 2015)

Hardman R (2014) The People's Republic of Wales: Soaring NHS waiting lists, plummeting school standards, jobs for the boyos... but still Red Ed hails it as his blueprint for Britain. *Daily Mail* 22 March (www.dailymail.co.uk/debate/article-2586613/The-Peoples-Republic-Wales-Soaring-NHS-waiting-lists-plummeting-school-standards-jobs-boyos-Red-Ed-hails-blueprint-Britain.html accessed 21 July 2015)

Harmer M (2007) Independent Review on the care given to Mrs Elaine Bromiley on 29 March 2005. Clinical Human Factors Group. www.chfg.org/resources/07_qrt04/Anonymous_Report_Verdict_and_Corrected_Timeline_Oct_07.pdf (accessed 4 February 2015)

Hawkes N (2014) East Kent Trust in special measures after being rated inadequate. *BMJ* **349**: g5180

Hay Group (2014) Dr who? Developing medical leadership talent. www.haygroup.com/uk/downloads/index.aspx (accessed 14 October 2014)

Health Service Executive, Ireland (2013) Quality and safety walk-rounds Toolkit. www.hse.ie/eng/about/Who/qualityandpatientsafety/Clinical_Governance/CG_docs/QPSwalkarounds.html (accessed 27 July 2015)

Hegazi I, Wilson I (2013) Maintaining empathy in medical school: It is possible. *Med Teach* **35**: 1002–8

Heifetz RA, Linsky M, Grashow A (2009) *The Practice of Adaptive Leadership: Tools and Tactics for Changing your Organization and the World.* Harvard Business Press, Cambridge, Massachusetts, USA

Held S, McKimm J (2012) Emotional intelligence, emotional labour and affective leadership. In: Preedy M, Bennet N, Wise C, eds. *Educational leadership: Context, Strategy and Collaboration.* Open University Press, Milton Keynes

Heron J (1992) *Feeling and Personhood: Psychology in another Key.* Bloomsbury, London

Hill M, Hupe P (2012) *Implementing Public Policy.* 2nd edn. Sage, London

Hillman T, Roueché A (2011) Quality improvement. *BMJ Careers* 8 Apr (http://careers.bmj.com/careers/advice/view-article.html?id=20002524 accessed 9 December 2014)

Hilton SR, Slotnick HB (2005) Proto-professionalism: how professionalisation occurs across the continuum of medical education. *Med Educ* **39**(1): 58–65

Hjortdahl M, Ringen A, Naess AC, Wisborg T (2009) Leadership is the essential non-technical skill in the trauma team - results of a qualitative study. *Scand J Trauma Resusc Emerg Med* **17**: 48

Ho M-J, Yu K-H, Pan H, Norris JL, Liang Y-S, Li J-N, Hirsh D (2014) A tale of two cities: Understanding the differences in medical professionalism between two Chinese cultural contexts. *Acad Med* **89**: 944–50

Hochschild AR (2012) *The Managed Heart: Commercialization of Human Feeling.* University of California Press, Berkley, USA

Hofstede G, Hofstede GJ, Minkov M (2010) *Cultures and Organizations: Software of the Mind.* 3rd edn. McGraw-Hill, New York, USA

Hogg MA (2001) A social identity theory of leadership. *Pers Soc Psychol Rev* **5**(3): 184–200

Hogwood BW, Gunn LA (1984) *Policy Analysis for the Real World.* Oxford University Press, Oxford

Hollander EP (2012) Inclusive leadership and idiosyncrasy credit in leader-follower relations. In, Rumsey MG, ed. *The Oxford Handbook of Leadership.* Oxford University Press, Oxford

Horsburgh M, Perkins R, Coylke B, Degeling P (2006) The professional subcultures of students entering medicine, nursing and pharmacy programmes. *J Interprof Care* **20**(4): 425–31

House RJ (1996) Path-goal theory of leadership: Lessons, legacy, and a reformulated theory. *Leadersh Q* **7**(3): 323–52

Howe D (2008) *The Emotionally intelligent social worker.* Palgrave MacMillan, Basingstoke

Howell JP (2012) *Snapshots of Great Leadership.* Taylor and Francis, London

Humphrey RH, Pollack JM, Hawver T (2008) Leading with emotional labour. *J Managerial Psychology* **23**(2): 151–68

Hunziker S, Bühlmann C, Tschan F et al (2010) Brief leadership instructions improve cardiopulmonary resuscitation in a high-fidelity simulation: A randomized controlled trial. *Crit Care Med* **38**: 1086–91

Hussey R (2013) Doctors: Leaders of Change. www.1000livesplus.wales.nhs.uk/sitesplus/documents/1011/Doctors%20leaders%20of%20change%2014%20Nov%202013.pdf (accessed 27 July 2015)

Imison C, Giordano RW (2009) Doctors as leaders. *BMJ* **338**: 979–80

Institute for Healthcare Improvement (2015) Science of Improvement: Forming the Team. www.ihi.org/resources/Pages/HowtoImprove/ScienceofImprovementFormingtheTeam.aspx (accessed 22 February 2015)

Institute for Health Policy (2013) Kaiser Permanente Policy Story, V2, No. 2, Foundation of Evidence: Clinical guideline development at Kaiser Permanente. www.kp.org/ihp (accessed 27 July 2015)

Iszatt-White M (2009) Leadership as emotional labour: the effortful accomplishment of valuing practices. *Leadership* **5**(4): 447–67

Jamtvedt G, Young JM, Kristoffersen DT, O'Brien MA, Oxman AD (2006) Audit and feedback: effects on professional practice and healthcare outcomes. *Cochrane Database Syst Rev* (2): CD000259

Jha V, Bekker HL, Duffy SRG, Roberts TE (2006) Perceptions of professionalism in medicine: a qualitative study. *Med Educ* **40**(10): 1027–36

Jones DN, Paulhus DL (2008) Machiavellianism. In: Leary MR, Hoyle RH, eds. *Handbook of Individual Differences in Social Behaviour.* Guilford, New York, USA: 93–108

Kasman D, Fryer-Edwards K, Braddock C (2003) Educating for professionalism: trainees' emotional experiences on IM and pediatrics inpatient wards. *Acad Med* **78**: 730–41

Kellerman B (2004) Thinking about leadership: warts and all. *Harv Bus Rev* **82**(1): 40–5

Kelley RE (1992) *The Power of Followership: How to Create Leaders People want to Follow and Followers who Lead Themselves.* Currency Doubleday, New York, USA

Kelley RE (2008) Rethinking followership. In: Riggio RE, Chaleff I, Lipman-Blumen J, eds. *The Art of Followership: How Great Followers Create Great Leaders and Organizations.* Jossey-Bass, San Francisco, USA

Kenagy J (2009) *Designed to Adapt: Leading Healthcare in Challenging Times.* Second River Healthcare Press, Bozeman, MT, USA

Kennedy I (2001) *Learning from Bristol: the report of the public inquiry into children's heart surgery at the Bristol Royal Infirmary 1984-1995.* Bristol Royal Infirmary Inquiry (Cmnd 5207). The Stationery Office, London

Keogh B (2009) Foreword. In: McCay L, Jonas S, eds. *A junior doctor's guide to the NHS.* BMJ Group, London

Keogh B (2013) *Review into the quality of care and treatment provided by 14 hospital trusts in England: overview report.* NHS Choices, London

Kernick D (2011) Leading in complex environments. In: Swanwick T, McKimm J, eds. *ABC of Clinical Leadership.* Wiley Blackwell, Chichester: 30–3

Khan K, Pattison T, Sherwood M (2011) Simulation in medical education. *Med Teach* **33**: 1–3

Kirkpatrick D (1996) *Evaluating Training Programs: The Four Levels.* 2nd edn. Berrett-Koehler, San Francisco, CA

Kirkpatrick I, Jespersen PK, Dent M, Neogy I (2009) Medicine and management in a comparative perspective: the case of Denmark and England. *Social Health Illn* **31**(5): 642–58

Klaber B, Lee, J (2011) Clinical leadership and management in the NHS – paired learning. *J Roy Soc Med* **104**(11): 436

Klaber B, Lee J, Abraham R, Smith L, Lemer C (2012) Paired Learning: A peer-learning leadership development initiative for managers and clinicians in the NHS. www.imperial.nhs.uk/prdcons/groups/public/@corporate/@communications/documents/doc/id_033648.pdf (accessed 7 April 2015)

Klein R (2006) *The New Politics of the NHS: from creation to reinvention.* 5th edn. Radcliffe, Oxford

Klein R (2007) The New Model NHS: performance, perceptions and expectations. *Br Med Bull* 81–82: 39–50

Klein R (2013) The NHS in the age of anxiety: rhetoric and reality – an essay by Rudolf Klein. *BMJ* **347**: f5104

Kobayashi H, Pian-Smith M, Sato M, Sawa R, Takeshita T, Raemer D (2006) A cross-cultural survey of residents' perceived barriers in questioning/challenging authority. *Qual Saf Health Care* **15**(4): 277–83

Kohn LT, Corrigan J, Donaldson MS (2000) *To Err is Human: Building a Safer Health System.* National Academy Press, Washington, DC, UK

Kotter J (1995) Leading Change: Why transformation efforts fail. *Harv Bus Rev* March-April: 1–20

Kotter JP (2014) *Accelerate.* Harvard Business Review Press, Boston, Massachusetts, USA

Kouzes JM, Posner BZ (2007) *The Leadership Challenge.* 4th edn. Jossey-Bass, San Francisco, USA

Kübler-Ross E (1975) *Death: the Final Stage of growth.* Prentice-Hall, New York, NJ, USA

Laming H (2003) *The Victoria Climbié Inquiry.* The Stationery Office, London

Law K, Wong C, Song L (2004) The construct and criterion validity of emotional intelligence and its potential utility for management studies. *J Appl Psychol* **89**: 483–96

Lea T (2008) *Bureaucrats and Bleeding Hearts: indigenous health in Northern Australia.* University of New South Wales Press, Sydney, Australia

Lee Y, Oh D, Kim M, Lee Y, Shin J (2010) Exploration of a Leadership Competency Model for Medical School Faculties in Korea. *Korean J Med Educ* **22**(4): 313–21

Lee TH (2010) Turning doctors into leaders. *Harv Bus Rev* April: 1–9

Lees P (2011) Establishment of a Faculty of Medical Leadership and Management. http://www.aomrc.org.uk/establishment-of-a-faculty-of-medical-leadership-and-management.html (accessed 27 July 2015)

Leskiw S, Singh P (2007) Leadership development: learning from best practices. *Lead Org Dev Journal* **28**(5): 444–64

Leung YL, Adesara S, Burr SA (2011) Learning to make better clinical decisions. *Br J Hosp Med* **72**(11): 642–5

Levenson R, Atkinson S, Shepherd S (2010) *The 21st Century Doctor: Understanding the doctors of tomorrow.* The King's Fund, London

Levy PF (2001) The Nut Island Effect: When good teams go wrong. *Harv Bus Rev* March: 51–9

Lewin GW (1948) *Resolving Social Conflict.* Harper & Row, London

Lewin K, Lippitt R, White RK (1939) Patterns of aggressive behavior in experimentally created social climates. *J Soc Psychol* **10**: 271–301

Lewis N, Rees C, Hudson N, Bleakley A (2005) Emotional intelligence in medical education: Measuring the unmeasurable? *Adv Health Sci Educ Theory Pract* **10**: 339–55

Leykum LK, Pugh J, Lawrence V, Parchman M, Noel PH, Cornell J, McDaniel RR Jr (2007) Organizational interventions employing principles of complexity science have improved outcomes for patients with Type II diabetes. *Implement Sci* **2**: 28

Light D, Dixon M (2004) Making the NHS more like Kaiser Permanente. *BMJ* **328**(7442): 763–5

Limb M (2014a) Where are the future medical leaders hiding. *BMJ Careers* 30 Sept (http://careers.bmj.com/careers/advice/view-article.html?id=20019422 accessed 17 April 2015)

Limb M (2014b) NHS must invest in engaging doctors in leadership, King's Fund says. *BMJ Careers* 19 July (http://careers.bmj.com/careers/advice/view-article.html?id=20018362 accessed 14 April 2015)

Lingard L, Espin S, Whyte S et al (2004) Communication failures in the operating room: an observational classification of recurrent types and effects. *Qual Saf Health Care* **13**(5): 330–4

Lipsky M (1980) *Street-level Bureaucracy. Dilemmas of the individual in public services.* Russell Sage Foundation, New York, USA

Lobb R, Colditz GA (2013) Implementation science and its application to population health. *Annu Rev Public Health* **34**: 235–51

Lown BA, Manning CF (2010) The Schwartz centre Rounds: Evaluation of an interdisciplinary approach to enhancing patient-centred communication, teamwork and provider support. *Acad Med* **85**(6): 1073–81

Lu WH, Myolona E, Lane S, Wertheim WA, Baldelli P, Williams PC (2014) Faculty development on professionalism and medical ethics: The design, development and implementation of Objective Structured Teaching Exercises (OSTEs). *Med Teach* **36**: 876–82

MacCulloch T (2001) Emotional competence: teaching and assessment issues in health professional education. In: ANZAME Annual Conference 2001: Programme, Papers and Abstracts. Australian and New Zealand Association for the Study of Medical Education, Melbourne

Mahlmeister L (2005) Preventing adverse perinatal outcomes through effective communication. *J Perinat Neonatal Nurs* **19**(4): 295–7

Makary MA, Sexton JB, Freischlag JA et al (2006) Operating room teamwork among physicians and nurses: teamwork in the eye of the beholder. *J Am Coll Surg* **202**(5): 746–52

Mannion H, McKimm J, O'Sullivan H (2015) Followership, clinical leadership and social identity. *Br J Hosp Med* **76**(5): 230–4

Marion R (1999) *The edge of organisations.* Sage, Thousand Oaks, California, USA

Marion R, Bacon J (2000) Organizational extinction and complex systems. *Emergence* **1**(4): 71–96

Martin C (2011) Perspective: to what end communication? Developing a conceptual framework for communication in medical education. *Acad Med* **86**: 1566–70

Mathur N, Skelcher C (2007) Evaluating democratic performance: methodologies for assessing the relationship between network governance and citizens. *Public Adm Rev* **67**(2): 228–37

Mayer J, Salovey P (1997) What is emotional intelligence? In: Salovey P, Sluyter D, eds. *Emotional Development and Emotional Intelligence: Educational Applications.* Basic Books, New York: 3–31

Mayer J, Salovey P, Caruso D, Sitarenios G (2003) Measuring emotional intelligence with the MSCEIT V2.0. *Emotion* **3**: 97–105

Mayer J, Salovey P, Caruso D (2008) Emotional intelligence: new ability or eclectic traits? *Am Psychol* **63**: 503–17

Maynard-Moody S, Musheno M (2000) State Agent or Citizen Agent: two narratives of discretion. *J Public Adm Res Theory* **10**(2): 329–58

McKimm J (2004) *Developing Tomorrow's Leaders in Health and Social Care Education: Case studies in leadership in medical and health care.* The Higher Education Academy, Catherine Cookson Centre for Medical Education, Newcastle

McKimm J (2011a) Leading for collaboration and partnership working. In: Swanwick T, McKimm J, eds. *ABC of Clinical Leadership.* Blackwell Publishing, Oxford: 44–9

McKimm J (2011b) Leadership and management skills. In: McKimm J, Forrest K, eds. *Professional Practice for Foundation Doctors.* Learning Matters, Exeter: 204–20

McKimm J, O'Sullivan H (2011) Medical leadership: from policy to practice. *Br J Hosp Med* **72**(5): 282–6

McKimm J, O'Sullivan H (2012) Developing and assessing medical leadership. *Br J Hosp Med* **73**(9): 484–5

McKimm J, O'Sullivan H (2013) Personality, self-development and the compassionate leader. *Br J Hosp Med* **74**(6): 336–9

McKimm J, O'Sullivan H (2015) Leadership, management and mentoring: applying theory to practice. In Cleland J, Durning S, eds. *Researching medical education.* Wiley Blackwell, Chichester

McKimm J, Petersen S (2010) Developing and testing tools for assessing leadership skills and competencies in emergency medicine trainees. Oral presentation. Ottawa Conference, Miami, 17–21 May

McKimm J, Phillips K (2009) *Leadership and management in integrated services.* Learning Matters Ltd, Exeter

McKimm J, Rankin D, Poole P, Swanwick T, Barrow M (2009) Developing medical leadership: a comparative review of approaches in the UK and New Zealand. International *Journal of Public Services Leadership* **5**(3): 10–26

McKimm J, Spurgeon P, Needham G, O'Sullivan H (2011a) Clinical leadership: the challenge for senior leaders. *Br J Hosp Med* **72**(9): 346–9

McKimm J, Wong J, Wright R, O'Sullivan H (2011b) Developing clinical leadership capacity among UK foundation trainees. *Br J Hosp Med* **72**(7): 406–9

McKimm J, Till A (2015) Clinical leadership effectiveness, change and complexity. *Br J Hosp Med* **76**(4): 166–70

McNaughton N (2013) Discourse(s) of emotion within medical education: the ever-present absence. *Med Educ* **47**: 71–9

Medical Professionalism Project (2002) Medical professionalism in the new millennium: A physicians' charter. *Lancet* **359**(9305): 520–2

Meindl JR, Ehrlich SB, Dukerich JM (1985) The romance of leadership. *Admin Sci Quart* **30**: 78–102

Milgram S (1963) Behavioral study of obedience. *J Abnorm Psychol* **67**: 371–8

Mintzberg H (1973) *The nature of managerial work.* Harper and Row, New York, USA

Mintzberg H (1983) *Power in and around organisations.* Prentice-Hall, Englewood Cliffs, NJ, USA

Moberly T (2014) Why the NHS needs more doctors to become chief executives. *BMJ Careers* 21 July (http://careers.bmj.com/careers/advice/view-article.html?id=20018523 accessed 14 April 2015)

Moneypenny MJ, Guha A, Mercer SJ, O'Sullivan H, McKimm J (2013) Don't follow your leader: challenging erroneous decisions. *Br J Hosp Med* **74**(12): 687–90

Morrison K (2010) Complexity theory, school leadership and management: questions for theory and practice. *Educ Man Admin Lead* **38**(3): 374–93

Morrison T (2007) Emotional intelligence emotion and social work: context, characteristic, complications and contributions. *Br J Soc Work* **37**(2): 245–63

Mosser G, Frisch KK, Skarda PK, Gertner E (2009) Addressing the challenges in teaching quality improvement. *Am J Med* **122**(5): 487–91

National Audit Office (2012) *Healthcare across the UK: a comparison of the NHS in England, Scotland, Wales and Northern Ireland.* The Stationery Office, London

National Leadership Council (2011) Top Leaders. (now 'The Director Programme'). www.leadershipacademy.nhs.uk (accessed 8 September 2015)

National Patient Safety Agency (2005) Medical Error. www.nrls.npsa.nhs.uk/EasySiteWeb/getresource.axd?AssetID=61580&type=full&servicetype=Attachment (accessed 27 July 2015)

Neily J, Mills PD, Young-Xu Y et al (2010) Association between implementation of a medical team training program and surgical mortality. *JAMA* **304**: 1693–700

Nettleton J, Ireland A (2000) Junior doctors' views on clinical audit - has anything changed? *Int J Healthcare Qual Assur* **13**: 245–53

New Economics Foundation (2008) *Five Ways to Wellbeing.* Centre for well-being, New Economics Foundation, London

Newman MA, Guy ME, Mastracci SH (2009) Beyond Cognition: Affective Leadership and Emotional Labour. *Public Adm Rev* **69**: 6–20

NHS Confederation and The Nuffield Trust (1999) *The modern values of leadership and management in the NHS*. NHS Confederation, London

NHS England (2013) Human Factors in Healthcare. A Concordat from the National Quality Board. www.england.nhs.uk/wp-content/uploads/2013/11/nqb-hum-fact-concord.pdf (accessed 27 July 2015)

NHS England (2014) Clinical Audit. www.england.nhs.uk/ourwork/qual-clin-lead/clinaudit (accessed 9 December 2014)

NHS Health Education East Midlands (2014) Action Learning Sets – developing trainees' leadership skills. https://em.hee.nhs.uk/action-learning-sets-developing-trainees-leadership-skills/ (accessed 20 July 2015)

NHS Institute for Innovation and Improvement (2006) *NHS Leadership Qualities Framework*. NHS Institute for Innovation and Improvement, Coventry

NHS Institute for Innovation and Improvement/Academy of Medical Royal Colleges (2008) *Medical Leadership Curriculum*. NHS Institute for Innovation and Improvement, Coventry

NHS Institute for Innovation and Improvement and Academy of Medical Royal Colleges (2010a) *Medical Leadership Competency Framework*. 3rd edn. NHS Institute for Innovation and Improvement, Coventry

NHS Institute for Innovation and Improvement and Academy of Medical Royal Colleges (2010b) *Guidance for Undergraduate Medical Education: Integrating the Medical Leadership Competency Framework*. NHS Institute for Innovation and Improvement, Coventry

NHS Institute for Innovation and Improvement and Academy of Medical Royal Colleges (2011) *Clinical Leadership Competency Framework Project*. NHS Institute for Innovation and Improvement, Coventry

NHS Leadership Academy and NHS Midlands and East (2011) *Releasing Potential: Women doctors and clinical leadership*. NHS Leadership Academy and NHS Midlands and East, London

NHS Leadership Academy (2011) Leadership Framework. www.leadershipacademy.nhs.uk/wp-content/uploads/2012/11/NHSLeadership-Framework-LeadershipFramework-Summary.pdf (accessed 7 April 2015)

NHS Leadership Academy (2013) Healthcare Leadership Model. www.leadershipacademy.nhs.uk/resources/healthcare-leadership-model/ (accessed 10 March 2015)

Nilsen P, Stahl C, Roback K, Cairney P (2013) Never the Twain Shall Meet? A comparison of implementation science and policy implementation research. *Implement Sci* **8**(1): 63–74

Nonaka I, Takeuchi H (2011) The Wise Leader. *Harv Bus Rev* **89**(5): 58–67

Norcini JJ, Anderson B, Bollela V et al (2011) Criteria for good assessment: Consensus statement and recommendations from the Ottawa 2010 Conference. *Med Teach* **33**: 206–14

Obolensky N (2010) *Complex Adaptive Leadership: Embracing Paradox and Uncertainty*. Ashgate Publishing Ltd, Farnham

Oc B, Bashshur MR (2013) Followership, leadership and social influence. *Leadersh Q* **24**: 919–34

O'Connell MT, Pascoe JM (2004) Undergraduate medical education for the 21st century: leadership and teamwork. *Fam Med* **36**(Suppl): S51–S56

Offerman LR (2004) When followers become toxic. *Harv Bus Rev* **82**(1): 54–60

Ogrinc G, Headrick L, Mutha S, Coleman M, O'Donnell J, Miles P (2003) A framework for teaching medical students and residents about practice-based learning and improvement, synthesized from a literature review. *Acad Med* **78**: 748–56

O'Leary MB, Mortensen M, Woolley AW (2011) Multiple team membership: a theoretical model of its effects on productivity and learning for individuals and teams. *Acad Man Rev* **36**(3): 461–78

O'Sullivan H, McKimm J (2011a) Medical leadership and the medical student. *Br J Hosp Med* **72**(6): 346–9

O'Sullivan H, McKimm J (2011b) Doctor as professional and doctor as leader: same attributes, attitudes and values? *Br J Hosp Med* **72**(8): 463–6

O'Sullivan H, McKimm J (2011c) Medical leadership: an international perspective. *Br J Hosp Med* **72**(11): 638–41

O'Sullivan H, McKimm J (2014) The role of emotion in effective clinical leadership. *Br J Hosp Med* **75**(5): 281–6

O'Sullivan H, Moneypenny M, McKimm J (2015) Leading and working in teams. *Br J Hosp Med* **76**(5): 230–5

O'Sullivan H, Van Mook W, Fewtrell R, Wass V (2012) Integrating professionalism into the curriculum. *Med Teach* **34**: 155–7

Øvretveit J (2009) *Does improving quality save money? A review of the evidence of which improvements to quality reduce costs to health service providers.* The Health Foundation, London

Palmer R, Cragg R, Wall D, Wilkie V (2008) Team and leadership styles of junior doctors. *Int J Clin Lead* **16**: 131–5

Papadakis MA, Hodgson CS, Teherani A, Kohatsu ND (2004) Unprofessional behavior in medical school is associated with subsequent disciplinary action by a state medical board. *Acad Med* **79**(3): 244–9

Paskins Z, Peile E (2010) Final year medical students' views on simulation-based teaching: a comparison with the Best Evidence Medical Education Systematic Review. *Med Teach* **32**: 569–77

Paulhus DL, Williams K (2002) The dark triad of personality: Narcissism, Machiavellianism, and psychopathy. *J Res Pers* **36**: 556–68

Persaud R (2004) Faking it: the emotional labour of medicine. *BMJ Careers* 28 August (http://careers.bmj.com/careers/advice/view-article.html?id=394 accessed 30 March 2015)

Petrides KV, Furnham A (2003) Trait emotional intelligence: behavioural validation in two studies of emotion recognition and reactivity to mood induction. *Eur J Pers* **17**: 39–75

Pian-Smith M, Simon R, Minehart RD et al (2009) Teaching residents the two-challenge rule: A simulation-based approach to improve education and patient safety. *Simul Healthc* **4**(2): 84–91

Plsek P, Greenhalgh T (2001) The challenge of complexity in health care. *BMJ* **323**: 625–8

Plsek P, Wilson T (2001) Complexity, leadership, and management in healthcare organisations. *BMJ* **323**: 746–9

Porter-O'Grady T (2010) Leadership for innovation: from knowledge creation to transforming health care. In: Porter-O'Grady T, Malloch K, eds. *Innovation Leadership: Creating the Landscape of Health Care.* Jones and Bartlett, Boston, MA

Powell S, Verma A, Booton P, Bicknell C (2012) How an online questionnaire can explore leadership teaching in an undergraduate curriculum. *JRSM Short Reports* **3**: 62

Power M (1994) *The Audit Explosion.* Demos, London

Prescott D, Rowe M (2015) Leadership in systems, organizations and cultures. *Br J Hosp Med* **76**(2): 101–4 (doi: 10.12968/hmed.2015.76.2.101)

Pressman J, Wildavsky A (1973) Implementation: How Great Expectations in Washington Are Dashed in Oakland; Or, Why It's Amazing that Federal Programs Work at All, This Being a Saga of the Economic Development Administration as told by two sympathetic observers who seek to build morals on a Foundation of ruined hopes. University of California Press, Berkeley, USA

Prochaska JO, Velicer WF (1997) The transtheoretical model of health behavior change. *Am J Health Promot* **12**: 38–48

Reinertsen JL (2003) Zen and the art of physician autonomy maintenance. *Ann Intern Med* **138**(12): 992–5

Reinertsen JL, Gosfield AG, Rupp W, Whittington JW (2007) *Engaging Physicians in a Shared Quality Agenda.* IHI Innovation Series white paper. Institute for Healthcare Improvement, Cambridge, MA, USA

Rogers EM (1962) *Diffusion of innovations.* Free Press, New York, USA

Rowe M (2002) Partnership Working? A tale of two programmes. *J Contemporary Issues Bus Gov* **9**(2): 5–14

Royal Australasian College of Medical Administrators (2011) *RACMA Medical Leadership and Management Curriculum Framework.* Royal Australasian College of Medical Administrators, Victoria, Australia

Royal College of Physicians (2005) *Doctors in Society: Medical Professionalism in a Changing world.* RCP, London

Royal College of Physicians (2010) *Future Physician: Changing doctors in changing times.* Report of a working party. RCP, London

Royal College of Physicians (2011) MSc Medical Leadership Prospectus 2011/12. www.rcplondon.ac.uk/sites/default/files/med-leadership-2011-brochure-1.pdf (accessed 14 August 2011)

Royal College of Physicians and Surgeons of Canada (2005) CanMEDS 2005 Framework. www.royalcollege.ca/portal/page/portal/rc/common/documents/canmeds/resources/publications/framework_full_e.pdf (accessed 27 July 2015)

Royal Liverpool Children's Inquiry (2001) *Summary and recommendations.* The Stationery Office, London

Salovey P, Mayer J (1990) *Emotional Intelligence.* Baywood Publishing, Amityville, NY

Scally G, Donaldson LJ (1998) Looking forward: Clinical governance and the drive for quality improvement in the new NHS in England. *BMJ* **317**: 61–5

Schaeffer LD (2002) The leadership journey. *Harv Bus Rev* **80**(10): 42–7

Schein E (1996) Three cultures of management: the key to organizational learning. *Sloan Manage Rev* **38**(1): 9–20

Schilling L, Chase A, Kehrli S et al (2010) Kaiser Permanente's performance improvement system, Part 1: From benchmarking to executing on strategic priorities. *Jt Comm J Qual Patient Saf* **36**(11): 489–98

Schön D (1983) *The Reflective Practitioner: How Professionals Think in Action.* Basic Books, New York, US

Schyns B, Meindl JR, eds (2005) *Implicit leadership theories: Essays and explorations.* Information Age Publishers, Greenwich, CT, USA

Schyve PM (2005) The changing nature of professional competence. *Jt Comm J Qual Patient Saf* **31**: 185–202

Scottish Executive (2005) Delivery through Leadership. www.gov.scot/Publications/2005/06/28112744/27452 (accessed 7 April 2015)

Scottish Government (2009) Promoting Professionalism and Excellence in Scottish Medicine: A Report from the Scottish Medical and Scientific Advisory Committee. www.gov.scot/Publications/2009/06/12150150/0 (accessed 7 April 2015)

Scottish Government (2010a) Delivering Quality through Leadership. www.gov.scot/Publications/2009/10/29131424/0 (accessed 7 April 2015)

Scottish Government (2010b) *The Healthcare Quality Strategy for NHS Scotland.* Scottish Government: Edinburgh

Scottish Government (2011a) 2020 Vision. www.gov.scot/Topics/Health/Policy/2020-Vision (accessed 7 April 2015)

Scottish Government (2011b) Report on the Future Delivery of Public Services by the Commission chaired by Dr Campbell Christie. www.gov.scot/Publications/2011/06/27154527/0 (accessed 7 April 2015)

Scottish Government (2013a) Everyone Matters: 2020 Workforce Vision. www.gov.scot/Topics/Health/NHS-Workforce/Policy/2020-Vision (accessed 7 April 2015)

Scottish Government (2013b) A Route Map to the 2020 Vision for Health and Social Care. www.gov.scot/Topics/Health/Policy/Quality-Strategy/routemap2020vision (accessed 7 April 2015)

Scottish Government (2014) Professionalism and Excellence in Scottish Medicine - A Progress Report. www.gov.scot/Publications/2014/01/8967 (accessed 7 April 2015)

Seiden S, Galvan C, Lamm R (2006) Role of medical students in preventing patient harm and enhancing patient safety. *Qual Saf Health Care* **15**(4): 272–6

Senge PM (1990) *The Fifth Discipline. The art and practice of the learning organization.* Random House, London

Shah A (2015) Supporting QI at scale in East London. www.fmlm.ac.uk/news-policy-and-opinion/opinion/blogs/supporting-qi-at-scale-in-east-london (accessed 20 July 2015)

Shapiro J (2011) Perspective: Does medical education promote professional alexithymia? A call for attending to the emotions of patients and self in medical training. *Acad Med* **86**: 326–32

Shipman Inquiry reports (2002-2005) http://webarchive.nationalarchives.gov.uk/20090808154959/http:/www.the-shipman-inquiry.org.uk/reports.asp (accessed 16 March 2015)

Shojania KG, Grimshaw JM (2005) Evidence-based Quality Improvement: the state of the science. *Health Affairs* **24**(1): 138–50

Sivasubramaniam N, Kroeck KG, Lowe KB (1997) In the eye of the beholder: folk theories of leadership in an academic institution. *Journal of Leadership Studies* **4**(2): 27–42

Smith KL, Petersen DJ, Soriano R, Friedman E, Bensinger LD (2007) Training tomorrow's teachers today: a national medical student teaching and leadership retreat. *Med Teach* **29**(4): 328–34

Smith SF, Lilienfeld SO (2013) Psychopathy in the workplace: The knowns and unknowns. *Aggress Violent Behav* **18**: 204–18

Snowden DJ, Boone ME (2007) A Leader's Framework for decision making. *Harv Bus Rev* **85**(11): 68–76

Souba W (2011a) The Being of Leadership. *Philos Ethics Humanit Med* **6**(1): 5–15

Souba W (2011b) A new model of leadership performance in health care. *Acad Med* **86**(10): 1241–52

Souba W, Mauger D, Day DV (2007) Does agreement on institutional values and leadership issues between deans and surgery chairs predict their institutions' performance? *Acad Med* **82**(3): 272–80

Spain SM, Harms PD, LeBreton J (2014) The dark side of personality at work. *J Org Beh* **35**: 41–60

Spurgeon P, Clark J, Ham C (2011) *Medical Leadership: From dark side to centre stage.* Radcliffe Publishing, London

Spurgeon P, Klaber R (2011) *Medical Leadership: A practical guide for tutors and trainees.* BPP Learning Media, London

St Pierre M, Scholler A, Strembski D, Breuer G (2012) Do residents and nurses communicate safety relevant concerns? Simulation study on the influence of the authority gradient. *Anaesthesist* **61**: 857–66

Stacey RD (2002) *Strategic Management and Organisational Dynamics: The Challenge of Complexity.* 3rd edn. Prentice Hall, Harlow, USA

Stevenson O (2007) *Neglected Children and their Families: Issues and Dilemmas.* Blackwell, London

Stewart GL, Manz CC (1995) Leadership for self-managing work teams: A typology and integrative model. *Human Relations* **48**: 747–70

Stirling K, Hog G, Ker J, Anderson F, Hanslip J, Byrne D (2012) Using simulation to support doctors in difficulty. *Clin Teach* **9**: 285–9

Studdert DM, Brennan TA, Thomas EJ (2002) What have we learned from the Harvard Medical Practice study? In: Rosenthal MM, Sutcliffe KM, eds. *Medical Error: What Do We know? What Do We Do?* Jossey Bass, San Francisco: 3–33

Sun Tzu (circa 500bc) The Art of War. In: Pockell L, Avila A, eds (2007) *The 100 Greatest Leadership Principles of all Time.* Warner Books, New York, USA

Sutcliffe KM, Lewton E, Rosenthal MM (2004) Communication failures: an insidious contributor to medical mishaps. *Acad Med* **79**(2): 186–94

Swanwick T, McKimm J, eds (2011) *ABC of Clinical Leadership.* Blackwell Publishing, Oxford

Swanwick T, McKimm J (2014) Faculty development for leadership and management. In: Steinert Y, ed. *Faculty development in the health professions: A focus on research and practice.* Springer Science and Business Media, Dordrecht: 53–78

Swick HM (2000) Toward a normative definition of medical professionalism. *Acad Med* **75**(6): 612–16

Sydor D, Bould M, Naik V et al (2013) Challenging authority during a life-threatening crisis: the effect of operating theatre hierarchy. *Br J Anaesth* **110**(3): 463–71

Tee EYJ, Paulsen N, Ashkanasy NM (2013) Revisiting followership through a social identity perspective: The role of collective follower emotion and action. *Leadersh Q* **24**: 902–18

Tepper BJ, Uhl-Bien M, Kohut GF, Rogelberg SG, Lockhart DE, Ensley MD (2006) Subordinates' resistance and managers' evaluations of subordinates' performance. *J Man* **32**(2): 185–209

The Foundation Programme (2012) Team assessment of behaviour (TAB). www.foundationprogramme.nhs.uk/download.asp?file=TAB_F1_and_F2_May_2012.pdf (accessed 20 July 2015)

The Health Foundation (2011a) *Research Scan: Levels of Harm.* The Health Foundation, London

The Health Foundation (2011b) *What's Leadership Got to Do With It? Exploring Links Between Quality Improvement and Leadership in the NHS.* The Health Foundation, London

The King's Fund (2011) *The Future and Leadership Management in the NHS: No more heroes.* The King's Fund, London

The King's Fund (2012) *Leadership and Engagement for Improvement in the NHS: Together we can.* The King's Fund, London

Till A, Pettifer G, O'Sullivan H, McKimm J (2014) Developing and harnessing the leadership potential of doctors in training. *Br J Hosp Med* **75**(9): 523–7

Till A, Bannerjee J, McKimm J (2015) Educating for improvement: Supporting the engagement of doctors in training in health improvement and patient safety. *Br J Hosp Med* **76**(3): 166–9

Timmins N (2012) *Never Again: the story of the Health and Social Care Act 2012 – a study in coalition government and policy making.* Institute of Government, London

Timmins N, Ham C (2013) *The quest for integrated health and social care: A case study in Canterbury, New Zealand.* The Kings Fund, London

Tomlinson J (2013) The Emotional Labour of Care. https://abetternhs.wordpress.com/2013/11/23/burden (accessed 1 April 2015)

Tooke J (2008) *Aspiring to Excellence. Final report of the independent inquiry into modernising medical careers.* Department of Health, London

Tregunno D, Ginsburg L, Clarke B, Norton P (2013) Integrating patient safety into health professionals' curricula: a qualitative study of medical, nursing and pharmacy faculty perspectives. *BMJ Qual Saf* **23**(3): 257–64

Turnbull JK (2011) *Leadership in Context: Lessons from new leadership theory and current leadership development practice.* The King's Fund, London

Uhl-Bien M (2006) Relational leadership theory: exploring the social processes of leadership and organizing. Leadership Institute Faculty Publications, Paper 19. http://digitalcommons.unl.edu/leadershipfacpub/19 (accessed 3 March 2015)

Uhl-Bien M, Riggio RE, Lowe KB, Carsten MK (2014) Followership theory: a review and research agenda. *Leadersh Q* **25**: 83–104

UK Foundation Programme Office (2010) Compendium of academic competencies. www.foundationprogramme.nhs.uk/download.asp?file=Compendium_of_Academic_Competences.pdf (accessed 18 June 2011)

UK Foundation Programme Office (2013) The UK Foundation Programme: Academic Compendium (2e). www.foundationprogramme.nhs.uk/pages/academic-programmes (accessed 1 April 2015)

van Mook WN, de Grave WS, Wass V, O'Sullivan H, Zwaveling JH, Schuwirth LW, van der Vleuten CP (2009a) Professionalism: Evolution of the concept. *Eur J Intern Med* **20**(4): e81–84

van Mook WN, van Luijk SJ, O'Sullivan H, Wass V, Schuwirth LW, van der Vleuten CP (2009b) General considerations regarding assessment of professional behaviour. *Eur J Intern Med* **20**(4): e90–5

van Mook WN, Gorter SL, O'Sullivan H, Wass V, Schuwirth LW, van der Vleuten CP (2009c) Approaches to professional behaviour assessment: Tools in the professionalism toolbox. *Eur J Intern Med* **20**(8): e153–7

Van Wormer KS, Besthorn FH, Keefe T (2007) *Human Behavior and the Social Environment: Macro Level: Groups, Communities, and Organizations.* Oxford University Press, New York, USA

Varkey P, Peloquin J, Reed D, Lindor K, Harris I (2009) Leadership curriculum in undergraduate medical education: A study of student and faculty perspectives. *Med Teach* **31**(3): 244–50

Wachter R (2005) Low on the Totem Pole. webmm.ahrq.gov/case.aspx?caseID=110 (accessed 15 February 2012)

Waddington K (2005) Behind closed doors: The role of gossip in the emotion work of nursing. *Int J Work Org Emotion* **1**: 35–47

Walker AG, Smither JW (1999) A five-year study of upward feedback: What managers do with their results matters. *Personnel Psychol* **52**: 393–423

Walton M (2006) Hierarchies: the Berlin Wall of patient safety. *Qual Saf Health Care* **15**(4): 229–30

Warren OJ, Carnall R (2011) Medical leadership: why it's important, what is required, and how we develop it. *Postgrad Med J* **87**: 27–32

Watkins-Hayes C (2009) *The New Welfare Bureaucrats: entanglements of race, class, and policy reform.* University of Chicago Press, Chicago, USA

Weng H, Hung C, Liu Y (2011) Associations between emotional intelligence and doctor burnout, job satisfaction and patient satisfaction. *Med Educ* **45**: 835–42

West M, Dawson J (2012) *Employee engagement and NHS performance.* The King's Fund, London

West M, Lyubovnikova J (2013) Illusions of Team Working in Health Care. *J Health Org Man* **27**(1): 134–42

West M, Eckert R, Steward K, Pasmore B (2014) *Developing Collective Leadership for Health Care.* The Centre for Creative Leadership and The King's Fund, London

West M, Armit K, Loewenthal L, Eckert R, West T, Lee A (2015) *Leadership and Leadership Development in Healthcare: The Evidence Base.* Faculty of Medical Leadership and Management, London

World Health Organization (2010) *Framework for Action on Interprofessional Education and Collaborative Practice.* World Health Organization, Geneva

World Health Organization (2011) WHO Patient Safety Curriculum Guide. www.who.int/patientsafety/education/curriculum/en/ (accessed 22 February 2015)

Xyrichis A, Ream E (2008) Teamwork: a concept analysis. *J Adv Nurs* **61**: 232–41

Yukl G (2002) *Leadership in Organizations.* 5th edn. Prentice Hall, Upper Saddle River, NJ

Zaccaro SJ (2007) Trait-based perspectives of leadership. *Am Psychologist* **62**(1): 6–16

Index